Object Databases
in Practice

ISBN 0-13-899725-X

9 780138 997250

90000

Hewlett-Packard Professional Books

Atchison	Object-Oriented Test & Measurement Software Development in C++
Blinn	Portable Shell Programming: An Extensive Collection of Bourne Shell Examples
Blommers	Practical Planning for Network Growth
Caruso	Power Programming in HP OpenView: Developing CMIS Applications
Chaudhri, Loomis	Object Databases in Practice
Cook	Building Enterprise Information Architectures
Costa	Planning and Designing High Speed Networks Using 100VG-AnyLAN, Second Edition
Crane	A Simplified Approach to Image Processing: Classical and Modern Techniques
Day	The Color Scanning Handbook: Your Guide to Hewlett-Packard ScanJet Color Scanners
Eisenmann and Eisenmann	Machinery Malfunction Diagnosis and Correction: Vibration Analysis and Troubleshooting for the Process Industries
Fernandez	Configuring the Common Desktop Environment
Fristrup	USENET: Netnews for Everyone
Fristrup	The Essential Web Surfer Survival Guide
Grady	Practical Software Metrics for Project Management and Process Improvement
Grosvenor, Ichiro, O'Brien	Mainframe Downsizing to Upsize Your Business: IT-Preneuring
Gunn	A Guide to NetWare for UNIX®
Helsel	Graphical Programming: A Tutorial for HP VEE
Helsel	Visual Programming with HP VEE, Second Edition
Holman, Lund	Instant JavaScript
Kane	PA-RISC 2.0 Architecture
Knouse	Practical DCE Programming
Lee	The ISDN Consultant: A Stress-Free Guide to High-Speed Communications
Lewis	The Art & Science of Smalltalk
Lund	Integrating UNIX® and PC Network Operating Systems
Madell	Disk and File Management Tasks on HP-UX
Mahoney	High-Mix Low-Volume Manufacturing
Malan, Letsinger, Coleman	Object-Oriented Development at Work: Fusion in the Real World
McFarland	X Windows on the World: Developing Internationalized Software with X.Motif®, and CDE
McMinds/Whitty	Writing Your Own OSF/Motif Widgets
Mikkelssen/Pherigo	Practical Software Configuration Management
Norton/DiPasquale	Thread Time: The Multithreaded Programming Guide
Orzessek, Sommer	Digital Video: An Introduction to Digital Video Services in Broadband Networks
Phaal	LAN Traffic Management
Pipkin	Halting the Hacker: A Practical Guide to Computer Security
Poniatowski	The HP-UX System Administrator's "How To" Book
Poniatowski	HP-UX 10.x System Administration "How To" Book
Poniatowski	Learning the HP-UX Operating System
Poniatowski	The Windows NT and HP-UX System Administrator's How-To Book
Ryan	Distributed Object Technology: Concepts and Applications
Thomas	Cable Television Proof-of-Performance: A Practice Guide to Cable TV Compliance Measurements Using a Spectrum Analyzer
Weygant	Clusters for High Availability: A Primer of HP-UX Solutions
Witte	Electronic Test Instruments

Object Databases in Practice

Mary E. S. Loomis
Hewlett-Packard Company

Akmal B. Chaudhri
The City University, London

To Join a Prentice Hall PTR Internet mailing list, point to:
http://www.prenhall.com/mail_lists/

Prentice Hall PTR
Upper Saddle River, New Jersey 07458

Library of Congress Cataloging-in-Publication Data

Chaudhri, Akmal.
 Object databases in practice / Akmal Chaudhri, Mary Loomis.
  p.   cm.
 Includes index.
 ISBN 0-13-899725-X
 1. Object-oriented databases. I. Loomis, Mary E. S. II. Title.
QA76.9.D3C427 1998
05.75'7--dc21   97-40480
                                                    CIP

Acquisitions editor: John Anderson
Cover designer: Design Source
Cover design director: Jerry Votta
Manufacturing manager: Alexis R. Heydt
Marketing manager: Miles Williams
Compositor/Production services: Pine Tree Composition, Inc.
Manager, Hewlet-Packard Press: Patricia Pekary

       Published by Prentice Hall PTR
       Prentice-Hall, Inc.
       A Simon & Schuster Company
       Upper Saddle River, New Jersey 07458

Prentice Hall books are widely used by corporations and
government agencies for training, marketing, and resale.

The publisher offers discounts on this book when ordered in
bulk quantities. For more information contact:

 Corporate Sales Department
 Phone: 800-382-3419
 Fax: 201-236-7141
 E-mail: corpsales@prenhall.com

 Or write:

 Prentice Hall PTR
 Corp. Sales Dept.
 One Lake Street
 Upper Saddle River, New Jersey 07458

Printed in the United States of America
10 9 8 7 6 5 4 3 2 1

ISBN: 0-13-899725-X

Prentice-Hall International (UK) Limited, *London*
Prentice-Hall of Australia Pty. Limited, *Sydney*
Prentice-Hall Canada Inc., *Toronto*
Prentice-Hall Hispanoamericana, S.A., *Mexico*
Prentice-Hall of India Private Limited, *New Delhi*
Prentice-Hall of Japan, Inc., *Tokyo*
Simon & Schuster Asia Pte. Ltd., *Singapore*
Editora Prentice-Hall do Brasil, Ltda., *Rio de Janeiro*

Contents

**4   Building a Push-Based Information System Using an Active
     Database   47**

II APPLICATIONS AND DESIGN   75

**5   Flight-Simulator Database: Object-Oriented Design
     and Implementation   79**

6   An Object-Oriented Image Database For Biomedical Research   95

Preface

INTRODUCTION

Today, the rate of technological change is rapidly accelerating. Organizations are faced with increasingly difficult decisions about their choices for hardware and Software platforms. Furthermore, increasing deregulation in many countries has forced companies into more aggressive deadlines and timescales to compete and survive. At present, object-oriented technology is viewed as being able to deliver more reliable and better quality software, because it enables the building of more modular software by using well-defined interfaces and hiding implementation details. This can be seen in Table P–1, which shows the results of a survey of visitors to Object World UK in 1995.

According to Leach [Lea95], the top reason shown in Table P–1 was also number one in 1993 and 1994.

The total worldwide sales of object-oriented development tools by US companies in 1995 were valued at US$1.3 Billion [OOS96]. A breakdown of the figures shows that object-oriented languages were the largest (US$440 Million), followed by application development environments (US$380 Million) and then object-oriented databases (US$218 Million).

Object-oriented languages are quite mature; Simula (the precursor to languages such as C++) has been in existence since the late 1960s. Other languages, such as Smalltalk, have also been used for several decades. On the analysis and design side, efforts are well underway through the Object Management Group (OMG) to develop a standard modeling language to communicate object-oriented designs. The need for a standard modeling language is analogous to Electrical Engineering's

Table P–1   Main Reasons for Moving to Object Technology [Lea95]

Flexibility to change	40%
Reduced time to market	24%
Distributed application requirements	23%
Programmer productivity	19%
Application complexity	18%
Ease of use	9%
Financial savings	7%
Don't know	5%
Other	17%

need for a standard notation to communicate electrical circuit designs. A standard notation will be understood by engineers wherever they were in the world.

Object databases, however, are still relatively rarely used in production [LC96]. The reason for this has been that a database is often at the core of many business processes within a company. Changing it can be difficult and expensive, as there may be many application dependencies. In contrast, applications can often be re-written in another language without affecting existing applications. An organization can also switch modeling languages and notions without affecting existing systems or application designs.

THE GROWTH OF OBJECT DATABASE USAGE

Most of the major commercial object database products were developed towards the end of the 1980s and early 1990s. Many of them were built around object-oriented programming languages and had as their primary objective providing persistence for programming language objects. The computer-aided design vendors were early adopters of this technology. Previously, their approach was typically to store design objects in a relational database or to use some proprietary or flat file system. This approach often resulted in unsatisfactory performance. To retrieve design objects, for example, many database objects may have to be read and reassembled together in memory. For storage, the design objects would need to be flattened or decomposed to be manageable in conventional record or tuple structures. Some examples to illustrate these problems have been described by Loomis [Loo95]. Over the years, object database technology has become increasingly popular within other industry sectors as well. Evidence of this shift towards non-engineering applications has been reported in [Lea95] and shown in Table P–2.

Additional evidence showing the shift to increasing mainstream commercial usage of object databases has been reported by Barry [Bar97], based on a study of

Table P–2   Use of Object Databases

Commercial applications	17%
Other applications	14%
Multimedia applications	12%
Document management	9%
Workflow and financial modeling	9%
Mapping and GIS	8%
CASE	7%
Network management	5%
Scientific applications	5%
Manufacturing	4%
CAD	1%
Transportation	1%
No applications will run on ODBMS	28%

twenty-four organizations. Results of another survey of 700 Information Technology (IT) professionals in [DBW97] showed that nearly 50 percent of respondents indicated that object-oriented databases were a technology area that their companies may use, with the Leisure, Transport, Retail, Healthcare, and Utility industries leading the interest.

The market for this technology has grown steadily over the last decade, although it still accounts for only a few percent of total sales of database products [LC96]. Part of the reason for this relatively slow market penetration is that the relational vendors have not totally ignored developments in object technology, and have begun to incorporate object features in their products. This is in stark contrast to the way that the hierarchical and network vendors ignored developments in relational technology several decades ago. Relational database usage grew fairly rapidly, because there was no apparent alternative for the capabilities offered by these products.

Many companies are hesitant to move to a new data management technology [Hod89] partly because there is only a limited experience base to leverage. It is the aim of this book to document examples that demonstrate the use of object database products to solve real-world problems.

This book brings together, for the first time, a large collection of papers that describe first-hand experiences with object database technology. Eighteen papers are presented in four categories:

1. Systems Architecture
2. Applications and Design
3. Object Database Selection and Migration
4. Performance

The papers include experiences with five of the major object database products: O2, GemStone, Objectivity/DB, ObjectStore, and VERSANT. The example applications are from a wide-range of domains, such as financial and scientific applications. We expect that this book will appeal to a wide audience, ranging from people who are just starting to look at object database technology to experience object database professionals.

REFERENCES

[Bar97] D. K. Barry: *Just the facts, please.* Distributed Object Computing. 1 (1): 56–57, 59, 1997 .

[DBW97] DBWorld: *Report and directory 1997/8.* London: Interactive Information Services Ltd., 1997.

[Hod89] P. Hodges: A relational successor? *Datamation.* 35 (21): 47–50, 1989.

[LC96] M. E. S. Loomis and A. B. Chaudhri: *The a to z guide to object data management (Tutorial).* ACM International Conference on Object-Oriented Programming Systems, Languages, and Applications (OOPSLA'96), San Jose, California, October 1996.

[Lea95] E. Leach: *Object Technology in the UK.* Introduction to COBRA. London, UK, September 1995.

[Loo95] M. E. S. Loomis: *Object Databases: The Essentials.* Reading, Massachusetts: Addison-Wesley, 1995.

[OOS96] OOS: *The object-oriented software development tools market.* Object-Oriented Strategies, May 1996.

I

Systems Architecture

INTRODUCTION

One of the major problems facing many organizations today is running multiple generations of database technology in parallel. For example, many banks and airlines are still using network and hierarchical database systems for performance reasons. As relational database technology has matured and optimizers have improved over the last decade, so relational systems have become more widely used. Object databases provide another data management alternative, although there are still few examples of large-scale commercial applications. An obvious issue is that organizations no longer wish to see just islands of information, but want to view all data, no matter what the underlying storage technology, in useful and meaningful ways to support business processes. One solution to this problem is described in Chapter 1 by Keller, Mitterbauer, and Wagner. They describe a framework that integrates multiple, heterogeneous data sources at a large German bank. Their experiences show that such a framework can provide considerable benefits in terms of performance.

A special case of an integration framework is an access layer that encapsulates object databases. At first, this may seem somewhat redundant, given the efforts of the Object Database Management Group (ODMG) to provide standard language interfaces. However, as other experience papers in this book testify, the ODMG effort is far from complete and suffers from a number of deficiencies.

Chapter 2 by Coldewey describes an effort to build an access layer that encapsulates database-specific code, defines tuning controls and hides query considerations. These factors are significant, since object database applications are rarely designed without considering product-specific features, and the use of clustering and other physical accelerators can provide significant performance improvements. The experiences reported by Coldewey show that all these factors can be adequately addressed and an access layer can be beneficial, although the effort involved in developing the access layer can be considerable.

When building three-tier architectures, it is sometimes not known in advance what database technology (e.g., relational or object) will be used in the middle-tier. Ideally, there should be sufficient flexibility in the overall design to allow one database system to be replaced by another as requirements change. Chapter 3 by Cockburn tackles this issue through the use of the EndGame pattern to help localize design issues to a team or single person. The chapter shows how several well-defined steps can be taken to manage the design process. The workstation part can be designed with little or no knowledge of the middle-tier. Another benefit of this approach is that conflict between design teams is reduced, leading to smoother system development.

Chapter 4 by Talbot also describes a three-tier system, called HOODINI. ObjectStore is the ODBMS that is used to provide the front-end, so that financial traders can get instant updates to trading information held in a Sybase relational database. Part of the motivation behind HOODINI is that Sybase is unable to handle current access patterns, which involve considerable navigation. The problem that HOODINI attempts to solve is providing financial traders with accurate and up-to-date information based on the idea of a Predicate Maintained Collection (PMC). According to Talbot, a PMC is a self-maintaining collection and is used as a generic mechanism for building: (i) an active query facility and (ii) an active collection facility. PMCs are needed, he argues, since information currency is vital to decision making for financial traders and PMCs can be used to increase this currency. In the case of HOODINI, they also solve the problems of existing financial systems, which are usually divided into front, middle and back office (with the consequent duplication and mapping problems that may occur between these systems). The approach provides common objects that can be subscribed-to by applications in any of these systems.

1

Object-Oriented Data Integration:

Running Several Generations
of Database Technology in Parallel

Wolfgang Keller, sd&m GmbH
Christian Mitterbauer, HYPO-Bank
Klaus Wagner, sd&m GmbH

ABSTRACT

Large IS shops often work with three or more generations of database technology. It is very common to find some pilot projects using object technology while the mass of software is still being produced using 3GL technologies and relational databases. Parallel to this application portfolio, older applications have to be maintained. These applications often use hierarchical or even older database technology. In most cases, hierarchical databases still manage the main workload of commercial data processing. It is therefore important to be able to federate all the above generations of database technology.

Object-oriented application development has to be able to reach data provided by other software generations. This may not result in changes to older applications. Object-oriented databases as a technology are not sufficient to provide this kind of parallel data integration. This chapter introduces an integration framework for several generations of database technology. The framework can be filled with multiple categories of database, middleware, and other products. These are introduced and discussed in a separate section.

This work has been partially sponsored by the German Ministry of Research and Technology under contract 01 IS 508 A 0. We would like to express our thanks. Special thanks to Dr. Thomas Becker for proofreading.

As an example, we will discuss a solution to the data integration problem for a large German financial institution, using an object-oriented access layer for heterogeneous databases. The focus here was on integration of all existing data sources. Object-oriented client/server applications have to coexist with classical host environments. This chapter features special conditions and requirements that can be found in a large IS shop. These requirements and the characteristic software environments that can be found there still rule out most commercially available integration products such as access layer products or object-oriented databases with relational gateways.

INTRODUCTION

Many large IS organizations, like banks, are facing an introduction decision for object technology. Some or most have collected first experiences with object technology and have started pilot projects. This results in a coexistence problem of old and new technology generations. Big bang replacement strategies are seldom used and are not advisable for large IS shops [BS95]. Most likely, migration will take ten or more years to complete. Several generations of software technology will have to coexist during such a time span. Old data resources will probably live on even longer than that.

Host applications will have to coexist with object-oriented client/server applications. Decoupling the two branches of development is essential. It is not realistic to expect that that there will be a clean separation of data resources for different generations of software development technology. Enterprise data models have been invented to provide tight integration of information systems over an organization and not to provide separate islands of data. They are still an enormous source of benefit for IS organizations. Nobody believes that this integration will be thrown away just because some new technology emerges. Technological renovation has to go along with solid business advantages.

The above factors result in larger IS shops being confronted with three to four[1] generations of database technology that have to be tightly coupled.

- We will use the term first generation for hierarchical database systems like IMS-DB. Hierarchical databases often still manage the main workload of commercial data processing.
- The second generation are relational databases like DB2. Most larger IS shops use at least generations one and two. The second generation is often still in the process of replacing the first one.

---

[1]Most large IS shops also use VSAM or similar file systems instead of database systems to a significant extent. This could be called the zero generation of database systems—resulting in four generations of database technology that have to be integrated.

- Object-oriented database management systems (OODBMS) [Cat96, Kim95, Cat94] can be seen as generation three. Products that can be found here are at the brink of use for mission critical applications. Some have well passed that border.

The developer, regardless of whether the language is C++, Smalltalk, COBOL or PL/I, should be confronted with only that image of the enterprise data that conforms to his or her technology generation. Advantages of enterprise data models should not be thrown away. The same data resources must be usable by conventional host applications and object-oriented applications at a time. The data resources must be readable and writable by all other technology generations. "Writable" especially is the prime killer criterion for many integration products. Solutions are highly nontrivial.

The market for object-oriented database technologies is still small and unstable compared to the market for relational databases. Six months can be seen as a normal innovation cycle. This explains why many experts have given up writing books on the topic—they tend to be outdated the day they appear in a bookstore. IS managers can be sure that their solution is technically outdated the very day it is implemented.

That is why we plead for a clean separation of concerns in any solution for an object data integration problem. This will allow projects to react to market movements by installing cheaper or better components than the ones selected for a first solution at project startup time.

There is no such thing as only *one* solution for the object-oriented integration of database technologies. But it is nevertheless possible to provide an integration model that is valid for many solutions in many different software environments and for many different constellations of specific requirements. Such a frame is then filled up with available components from the market that are integrated with self-written glue. The final choice of components for a specific project is dependent on the chosen project and the enterprise's own installed software environment consisting of database systems, programming languages, transaction monitors, and middleware components. A limit for possible project costs and investments will usually be set by potential positive financial impacts the project is expected to have on business. The choice of products will also depend upon the actual object-oriented databases and integration software on the market at project start time.

The next section will introduce a proven integration model for data resources of various ages. Product surveys are outdated the day they are written, so the following section will list product categories instead of actual products. We will show how these categories can be integrated in our solution framework. The final section contains an application case study. The architectural framework has been used to create persistent client objects in a typical financial institution's software environment. The model has been extracted from project experience and not the other way round. This chapter summarizes some five years of experience gained in various data integration projects in our various companies.

INTEGRATION FRAME

The object data integration model describes a software architecture that provides persistence[2] for objects. This also allows us to provide persistence for object-oriented applications on top of legacy data resources. The architecture can best be compared with an architecture for a very simple[3] object-oriented database system. The salient feature is the ability to store data in arbitrary legacy data stores, such as relational or hierarchical database systems. This provides an object-oriented integration mechanism for several generations of database technology. An integration of distributed data can also be supported.

One of the very useful features of object-oriented database systems is to give a programmer the impression of having to deal with objects only. Database details are hidden as much as possible. An object-oriented database system will first provide a persistent programming language together with typical database features, such as independence of data from a programming language, transactions, locking, and more.

We will therefore first show a programmer's view of our integration model. After that we will discuss the internal structure of the integration framework.

Programmer's View

The programmer's view is illustrated by an example of a typical interface for persistent objects in C++. This interface is as similar as possible to the object-oriented database standard [Cat96]. By far, the example does not contain all possible constructs of the ODMG specification. A relatively small subset has proven sufficient for real-world projects. Expensive constructs,[4] such as OQL [Cat96] have not been implemented. Our example is in no way complete. The user code example is there to present the basic ideas of a persistent programming language.

The following actions are presented in Figure 1–1:

- Getting an `oldCustomer` by name from the database
- Dereferencing the customers `confirmedOrders`
- Creation of a new `Customer` instance by assigning the freshly created object to a smart pointer

---

[2]Persistence is the property of objects to survive termination of a process and to be alive in the next process started, if required to do so [Atk+83, Sou94].

[3]The degree of reduction of functionality compared to an OODBMS depends on the possible investment in an object layer. In the case of an OODBMS with a relational gateway that fits into the given environment, the functional properties are not worse than those of any OODBMS except maybe performance. In the case of a custom solution, it would be too expensive to implement advanced features such as OQL, schema evolution, nested transactions, language mappings, and such that should be part of an OODBMS.

[4] Expensive features to implement are OQL, schema evolution, nested transactions, and language mappings, for example.

```
void example ( String CustomerName ) {
try                         // database errors are handled by C++ exceptions

        Transaction trans;                // create a transaction and
        trans.begin()                     // start it
                // Declaration of some variables for our example
                Ref<Customer> oldCustomer;    // Ref is a smart pointer to a persistent
                              // object
                Set<Ref<Order>> orders;       // Set<Ref<Order>> represents a set of
                              // persistent objects

                // Fetch a Customer
                oldCustomer = Customer::getByName(CustomerName);    // This will only load
                              // and check an ObjectId and assign a smart pointer. It's
                              // a database method.

                // Dereferencing a set of orders
                Orders = oldCustomer->confirmedOrders;       // The Orders variable
                              // is assigned a whole set of confirmedOrders.

                // Create a new customer
                Ref<Customer> newCustomer = new(Customer);

                newCustomer->Name = someValue         // the newCustomer object is changed
                              // by assignment of a value to an instance variable.

                // Assignment of whole set of orders
                newCustomer->confirmedOrders = oldCustomer-> confirmedOrders;
                newCustomer->markModified();          // marking object dirty
                              // results in object to be written to the database
                              // at time of next commit

                // Delete oldCustomer
                oldCustomer->requestDelete();

                // Finish transaction and commit it
        trans.commit()
}

catch ... // Error handling has to take place - but is not shown here
};
```

Figure 1–1   Sample user code.

- Assigning a whole set of orders at a time
- Deleting a `Customer` object by requesting its deletion

One thing is invisible here—relational database code or actions. The application programmer's view of persistent objects is very similar to his or her view of volatile objects. The visible difference is methods like `getByName`, `markModified` or `requestDelete` and smart pointers (`Ref<SomeType>`). The methods are acquired by protocol inheritance from an abstract base class `PersistentObject`. This interface is not the ideal vision of a persistent object's interface where persistent objects cannot be discriminated from volatile objects. For a further discussion of the above interface see [Cat96].

Layered Model

The apparatus necessary for implementing the above interface is comparable to an object-oriented database system with heavily reduced functionality. The term *object layer* will be used for a system providing an interface like the above.

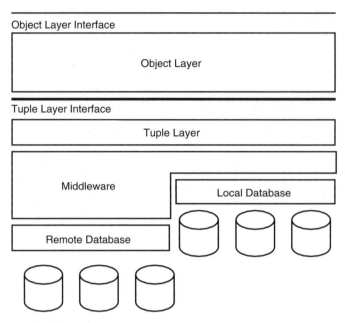

Figure 1–2   Persistent objects integration model.

Data are not stored in an OODBMSs data management system but in legacy database systems like RDBMS or hierarchical database systems. Therefore, we need an interface that presents data from more than one database in relational tuple form secured by transactions. This will be called the *Tuple Layer*.

The corresponding layered architecture is shown in Figure 1–2. The object layer's services are described in more detail below. Another section, entitled "Tuple Interface," lists requirements that have to be fulfilled by a tuple layer. The above model serves as an integration frame or architecture for a custom solution as well as for product solutions. The above frame can be filled with prefabricated or self-written components. The next section describes product categories for prefabricated components. These components span very different parts of the integration framework.

Object Layer

The object layer could be implemented using an OODBMS, a prefabricated framework, or a custom solution. Each possible solution should be close to the ODMG standard. The functional units are always similar. Figure 1–3 provides an overview of the important functional units in an object-oriented access layer.

Functional Units

If legacy data sources are to be integrated, an object layer has to use some kind of tuple layer as its storage medium. This is why an integration architecture

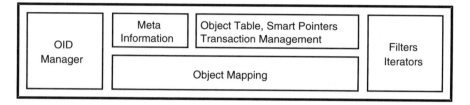

Figure 1–3 Functional units in an object-oriented access layer.

differs in its architecture from OODBMS products. The tuple layer offers an interface to relational tuples over primitive data types. Abstractions like complex data
types, inheritance, and relations are unknown at this level. They have to be implemented by the object layer. Thus, the object layer has to provide the following services to map full-fledged objects to a tuple layer:

- Complex data types and objects must be assembled from primitive data types.
  This involves casting raw data types into application data types as part of the
  object mapping.
- Mapping tuple fields to object attributes must happen with respect to inheritance and interobject relations. This is also done by the *object mapping* with
  the help of *meta information*.
- Object identities have to be constructed from key fields at the tuple layer's
  level. The *OID manager* takes care of this part.
- Associations at object level are built using foreign key fields and relation tables at the tuple layer level. This is done by the *object mapping* in collaboration with the *OID manager*.

A description of all internal details of an object layer is beyond the scope of this
chapter. Several of the references at the end of the chapter[5] deal with special aspects
of building an access layer in more detail.

  Besides the services described above, further services have to be provided by
an object-oriented access layer:

- There should be objects for *transaction management*.
- The identity of objects in volatile memory must be guaranteed by an *object
  table* [Hah+95].
- A *smart pointer* [Str91] mechanism is needed to prevent large chunks of objects from being loaded into volatile memory if a first object is touched that
  has transitive associations with a great number of other objects [Kel95b].

---

  [5] The different building blocks are described in more detail in an array of papers by different authors. See [CK95, Hah+95, Kel95a, Kel95b, KS95, Lip95] if you are interested in more details.

- There should be efficient support for list boxes. List boxes are typically filled with a selection of a few attributes from a very large set of objects. With respect to low bandwidth of today's client/server communications lines in wide area networks, it does not make sense to load complete objects for presentation in list boxes. Instead, only the portion needed out of all possible attributes should be loaded. Blocked read operations should deliver only as many records as can be seen in a list box at a single time. *Filters* are used as surrogates for OQL queries. Smart and lazy *iterators* are used to browse the result sets of those queries.

Discussion

Object-oriented database products are sufficient in a pure object-oriented target environment. Such products may be evaluated using the object-oriented database standard as a reference model.

If relational or hierarchical data sources have to be used and if data resources must be used in parallel with existing legacy applications, shrink-wrapped products can hardly be found. Detailed knowledge of interfaces between an object layer and storage management facilities is needed to evaluate products in this category. The separation between object layer and storage mechanisms might run right through a product. If a storage manager is to be substituted or written in such a situation, deeper knowledge of object-oriented versus relational storage concepts is needed. Different product categories and their role in our integration architecture are discussed in the next section.

Tuple Interface

A Tuple Layer [CK95] is able to deliver a unified relational view upon relational and hierarchical data sources. Some user transaction construct is also provided. The task is comparable to a subset of a federated database system [Kim95]. A tuple layer should be able to cope with the following requirements:

- At least read, insert, update, delete, and read multiple operations should be supported for each tuple presented by the tuple layer. These operations are identical to a simple relational access layer that is used in many non-object-oriented projects.
- The physical source of data is hidden by the tuple layer. The tuple layer provides a view of a single integrated database.
- The tuple layer is able to map hierarchical data resources to relational tuples.
- The tuple layer is able to provide transparent user transactions over multiple database systems. This is not a trivial task if data sources from more than one server are involved. In general, a 2-phase-commit would be needed for this task. It is also not a trivial task if transaction servers like CICS or IMS-TM hosts are being used.

There are several options for implementing a tuple layer. The choices include federated database systems [Kim95], DRDA products [OH94] and remote-SQL-interfaces for less challenging requirements. The term "Middleware" in Figure 1–2 is used to sum up these choices. Depending on the power of products, more or less attention for this middleware block is needed. Available product categories are also discussed below.

Some Performance Considerations

Performance in object/relational access layers needs very special attention. Some points crucial to performance are:

- *Smart-Pointer Concept*: You need a smart-pointer mechanism that allows loading only those objects that are needed for the actual use-case. The concept analogous to C++ Smart-Pointers in Smalltalk is called "Surrogate Objects." A lack of such concepts may result in loading all objects that have any relation to the object first touched in a use case, resulting in poor performance.

- *Caching*: A concept of object identity will not only guarantee integrity but will also prevent objects from being loaded twice from the database in a single transaction.

- *Vary Lazy Object Relations*: Changes to other objects that are involved in a use-case via interobject relations should be evaluated lazily to prevent too many objects from being loaded from the underlying database (for a problem statement see [Kel95b]).

- *Design of Physical Database Tables and Mapping*: The design of the physical database model and the mapping used to connect it to objects will heavily influence performance of an object/relational access layer. In the presence of inheritance and polymorphism on the object level, there are table layouts that favor read access. Others mapping schemes favor write access and updates while yet others represent a compromise. Be sure you know your requirements concerning read versus write/update frequency before you start designing the database tables. If you have a legacy database scheme, you do not have any options. You have to live with the table design present.

- *Mass Updates*: It does not make sense to use the above integration model for mass updates.[6] Executing mass updates at an object layer level could mean replacing efficient mechanisms of the underlying database system by inefficient treatment of single records at object layer level.

- *Batch Design*: If an access layer is to be used for any kind of batch processing, thorough analysis is needed. If the analysis shows that an access layer will be too inefficient for such a task, one should consider bypassing the ac-

---

[6]SQL statements of the kind `update` . . . `where` are denominated as Mass Updates. One statement is able to manipulate large sets of records.

cess layer and coding embedded SQL statements straight into object methods. This requires special attention with regard to object identity and transaction integrity. Access layers are best suited for single record dialog processing. The typical work sequence here is selecting an object from a listbox, manipulating it, and committing changes to the database. So, in most cases, only one or a few objects are written.

- *No Batches on a Client*: Batch processes should be executed as close as possible to their databases. This means executing them on the database server and not on a remote client. In case batches are suitable for processing with an access layer (no mass updates or only mass updates that can be coded into isolated object methods), a second instance of the access layer stack has to be compiled and installed on a central database host [CK95].

In addition to the above performance considerations, you should obey the general good practices of access to relational databases [KC96].

Further Reading

It is not surprising that there is no such thing as a monograph dealing with the subject of this chapter. Partial aspects are treated in numerous articles. Some authors discuss the situations when it is best to use relational and when it is best to use object-oriented databases [Bur94, Kim95]. Persistence mechanisms can be classified by their storage mechanisms and preferred use of objects (complex versus simple)—see [Kim95, Sou94]. The problem of how to integrate relational and object-oriented database technology is being discussed in many articles, such as [Bur94, Kim95, Gra95], to quote a few. Mapping objects to relational databases has also been discussed extensively. Sample sources here are [Hah+95, Kel95b, PB94]. Architectures for access layers have been published in [Hah+95, KS95, Lip95, NeXT].

PRODUCT CATEGORIES

There are numerous products on the market that can be used to implement parts of the integration framework described above. This section will facilitate the search for products by giving an overview of existing product categories. Some components that are needed for an individual legacy data integration project might already be implemented in your enterprise. They must be identified and can then be reused for object-oriented data integration. We are not able to give a complete list of products here. The market for integration and middleware products is moving too fast. This is why we concentrate on product categories and give some prominent product examples. But we do not claim to be able to enumerate even a significant portion of all possible products.

Remote Database Access Products

RDA (Remote Data Access) products [OH94] enable access to a remote relational database over a network. They allow a client to execute SQL-statements on a remote server. RDA products can be used to implement parts of a tuple layer. RDA products will seldom offer access to more than one vendor's database at a time or in parallel. They are rarely suited for distributed transactions or even access to hierarchical databases.

Objectified Relational Databases

Objectified relational database products will offer an object-oriented view[7] of a relational database system. Most of these frameworks need an additional RDA product using dynamic SQL to provide their services. These products are also suited to implement parts of a tuple layer. Typical products that fall into this category are Rogue Wave's DBtools.h++ [http://www.roguewave.com] or a similar data access framework by Taligent [Cot95].

Federated Databases

Federated database systems will provide a unified view of several physically independent databases [Kim95]. They offer the user an illusion of using only one database system while using multiple databases in parallel. IBM's DRDA architecture [OH94] implements aspects of a federated database system. Federated databases might have to unify different SQL dialects while offering their own SQL interfaces. Some systems also allow integration of hierarchical data (DRDA). Federated systems can again be used to implement parts of a tuple layer. Examples include IBM's DataJoiner   (http://www.software.ibm.com/data/dbtools/data-join.html), UniSQL/M (http://www.unisql.com) or IBM's DRDA architecture in general [OH94].

Object-Oriented Databases with Relational Gateways

A few object-oriented database systems offer relational gateways to their products. A gateway is usually implemented by installing a special storage manager that replaces the normal storage manager for certain objects of the database. Many vendors offer adapted storage managers as tailored project solutions in addition to their OODBMSs. It should be straightforward to tailor such a storage manager for an arbitrary tuple layer, as long as it has been possible to implement it for any reasonable tuple interface.

An OODBMS plus relational gateway could be a turnkey solution for our integration problem. This should not lead to euphoria because problem points like integration of hierarchical database systems, reengineering of existing data resources, problems of object identity, and the coupling with host transaction systems have to be checked thoroughly. Classical host environments can seldom be supported.

---

[7]Typical objects that are presented to the libraries users are Table, Row, Query, etc.

Product examples that fall in this category are ONTOS (`http://www.ontos.com`) or Hewlett Packard's Odapter for their OpenODB product.

Object-Oriented Access Layers

There is also a category of products that offers the programmer an interface similar to that of an OODBMS but exclusively uses external database systems (or better data sources) as storage mechanisms. These systems do not have their own low-level storage management component. The critical points to look at are again support for host databases (like IMS and DB2) and the question of collaboration with transaction systems like IMS or CICS.

Some typical products that can be named here are Persistence (`http://www.persistence.com`) or NeXT's Enterprise Objects Framework (`http://www.next.com`).

Object-Relational Databases

Besides OODBMS there is yet another family of database systems that claims to provide object-oriented data management—object-relational databases [Kim95]. These databases expand relational databases by providing user-defined data types, inheritance, stored procedures, and further constructs. The differences, advantages, and disadvantages with respect to object-oriented databases are discussed by Kim [Kim95]. Object-relational databases have their own emerging standard—SQL3. Object relational database systems might be used with an access layer to implement the integration model's object layer. Some products like UniSQL (`http://www.unisql.com`) also offer database federation at the level of the tuple interface. This can also be used to implement services of the integration model. Informix (`http://www.informix.com`) is another object-relational product.

CASE STUDY: PERSISTENT OBJECTS IN A LARGE BANK

As an application example, we will discuss the specific solution for the legacy data integration problem that has been implemented in a large German bank. First we will list the requirements relevant to the solution and the software environment that could be found. The use of turnkey solutions was made impossible by an array of factors that is also disussed here. This resulted in a solution that will be presented.

Situation, Requirements, and Software Environment

The project has been part of a larger effort to introduce object technology in a large IS shop. It is one task to provide persistence for C++ objects.

The data resources created cannot only be isolated in new databases. As in most large organizations, existing data resources from hierarchical or relational databases have to be used. The integration solution has to provide good decoupling of conventional software development from object-oriented pilot projects while both development tracks are using the same integrated data resources. The access to legacy data must not lead to any changes in existing applications. Even recompilation would be too expensive.

The software and hardware environment is typical of a large IS shop. A client/server concept incorporates a central MVS-host that will play the role of an enterprise server. The programming environment for this host is IMS-TM, PL/I, DB2, and IMS-DB. Clients run OS/2 and have been programmed in C before and will now be programmed in C++. Clients are clustered in LANs. Each LAN has its own array of LAN servers that concentrate traffic with the enterprise server. The client/host connection is implemented using APPC. A client programmer needs an integrated view of the enterprise's data resources. The situation can be summarized as a multilayer client/server model.

9600 baud telephone lines between branch offices place serious restrictions on the degree of carelessness one can afford concerning communication bandwidth. This resulted in the use of compression schemes, blocked data transfers, and maximum lazy access schemes. The pilot solution for persistent objects will be promoted to an enterprise standard after some successful pilot projects.

The project's task was to create a programming interface for persistent objects in a new software development environment. This interface had to be as close as possible to the object-oriented database standard specification to allow migration to off-the-shelf products later. As usual with persistent languages, the programmer must not be annoyed with database details. What he or she sees are persistent objects.

Why Products Failed in 1995

It has always been our goal to avoid a custom solution. We would have preferred off-the-shelf products as system software development is seldom the core business of a financial institution. This is why quite a lot of products were evaluated. This evaluation phase ran in parallel to the specification of a custom solution to use time gains by simultaneous engineering. However, the evaluation phase in 1995 did not produce any products that were suitable for use in the given software and hardware environment. The reasons which provide a good basic checklist for similar evaluation efforts are:

- Most solutions did not support DB2 [OH94]. If the OS/2 variant DB2/2 is supported, the solutions will use dynamic SQL in most cases. The use of dynamic SQL for central host databases is still forbidden by convention and for reasons of security in many DB2-MVS shops. This is motivated by internal control procedures, authorization schemes, and control of transaction load— many of which are based on the use of static SQL.
- No product on the level of the object layer was able to read or even write IMS-DB from our client platform OS/2.

- Most object layer products that offered a relational gateway were able to work with arbitrary legacy table schemes for object storage, inheritance, and storing relations. Many products were designed for forward engineering and not for reengineering badly structured legacy data sources.
- The notion of object identity [Cat94] plays an important role in OODBMS. If products need to insert a new object identity into existing tables, they cannot be used in parallel to existing applications. Legacy applications don't know how to treat an additional field. They would have to be changed to update the new OID field. This is too expensive when thousands of legacy programs are involved.
- In 1995 we did not find a single product that was able to deal with data sources that run under a host transaction monitor (like CICS or IMS-TM). The special challenge that results from using such transaction systems is the different length of transactions on client and host. Each call to a host running a transaction system in transactional mode results in committing all open transactions on return of the call. This has to be mapped to long user transactions by using dirty reads and deferred updates and some further measures.
- None of the products was able to deal with multi-server client/server architectures (LAN servers plus MVS enterprise servers) and 2-phase-commit. This is a necessary long-term requirement in the environment we found.

The above problems prevented us from using off-the-shelf products. Today, in 1997, the situation has become slightly better due to better modularization of some products.

Our Architecture

With no shrink-wrapped solutions in sight, a custom solution had to be developed from products at hand. Figure 1–4 gives an impression of the solution's architecture. This solution follows the architecture already described. We will only discuss those aspects here that had to be tailored with respect to existing software components or special requirements. We will describe the architecture following the layered model from the bottom up.

Data access on DB2/MVS is done using conventional access layer modules. These are programmed in PL/I and generated from description files. The access modules offer the usual functionality of a relational access layer (read, insert, update, delete, multiple-read). The modules can also be used by non-object-oriented host applications. This alone has been an improvement compared to the old host architecture that did not incorporate a separate access layer.

Host access modules are called from the client sites via a transaction monitor (IMS/TM). No extra remote database access product for DB2 has to be installed. The price of this is some extra communication software. Coming from the client side, write operations have to be bundled in packages and are executed no earlier than at the client transaction's commit time. The bundling results in several update operations to

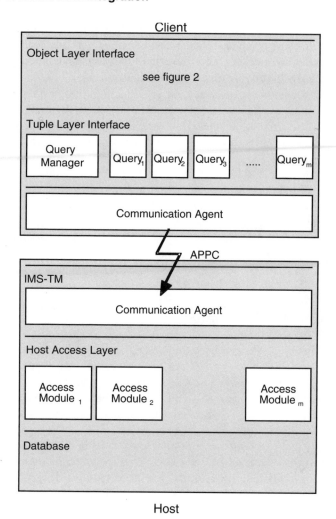

Figure 1–4 Project example for an object data integration problem.

be executed in a single IMS transaction. This can best be compared to on-the-fly generation of a batch program. Buffering is provided by communications agents. APPC is used instead of DRDA [OH94] products, like DDCS/2. This may look strange at a first glance. But if *license costs + installation costs – programming effort – maintenance effort* are taken into account, this solution can be cheaper than shrink-wrapped products. This will not hold for each and every IS organization and any number of licenses, but it should be recalculated for each business case or project.

A set of query objects on the client forms a tuple layer. Query objects are objectified access layer modules. In a manner of speaking, they are proxies for access layer modules on the remote server. Arbitrary queries are made possible by using a query-server concept. Possible hard-coded dependencies between higher layers and queries are cut off by this server concept, which can be compared to a broker architecture. Special precautions are necessary with respect to slow communication links connecting clients and server. Multiple reads can be executed using blocked transfers.

The object layer is constructed using the principles outlined above. As before, no product could be used since most products are based on dynamic SQL as the interface paradigm for the tuple layer. Having to use an MVS enterprise server with expensive existing security and administration structures meant that it was not an option for a pilot project to restructure central IS procedures. Anyway, a customized storage manager project solution offered by OODBMS vendors would not have been any cheaper than the solution chosen.

A technical note at the end: Similar projects and the requirement to use static SQL have suggested the use of code generation also for C++. This is tempting at first, but it comes back as a maintenance and flexibility boomerang after some time. Runtime repositories and templates are to be preferred to code generation. This can be confirmed by a look at other architectures [KS95, Lip95, NeXT, WN95].

EXPERIENCES AND SUMMARY

The above architecture has produced good results in a first pilot project and in two more projects that followed from 1995 to 1997. Average time to process one of our database transactions on the MVS host is below 0.5 seconds and about 90 percent of all transactions take less than one second to complete. Performance can be rated better than the performance of other comparable client/server systems that do not use an access layer but hand-coded database access.

It is a pity that we could not find suitable products in the first half of 1995 that fit a typical software environment for a large IS shop. As far as we know, the situation has slightly improved now with the advent of modular object-relational database access frameworks that allow for better customization. There should be a considerable market for integration technologies, especially in large shops with a predominantly blue software environment.

Considering the very short innovation cycles in object-oriented database technology, the modularization of a solution cannot be overstressed. Clear interfaces close to standards allow the exchange of custom-made parts or glue with commercially available software as soon as better solutions appear on the market.

Integration products should be checked rigorously before use. The above architecture, product categories, performance hints, and project experiences should be helpful for an evaluation.

Factors that look marginal at first glance can turn out to be expensive cost drivers. Such factors are add-ons that have nothing to do with direct database functionality, such as integration of an access layer into a security system. Classical transaction systems offer a wide range of control mechanisms that may have to be reimplemented at a horrendous price in access layers.

A conventional database access layer for PL/I applications has been an important windfall profit of the project. A generator system for conventional database access modules alone can justify the rest of the costs of an integration solution.

REFERENCES

[Atk+83] M. P. Atkinson, P. J. Bailey, K. J. Chisholm, W. P. Cockshott, R. Morrison: *An Approach to Persistent Programming*. The Computer Journal, 26 (4), 1983.

[BS95] M. L. Brodie, M. Stonebreaker: *Migrating Legacy Systems, Gateways, Interfaces & The Incremental Approach*. Morgan-Kaufmann Publishers, 1995.

[Bur94] D. K. Burleson: *Practical Application of Object-Oriented Techniques to Relational Databases*. John Wiley & Sons, 1994.

[Cat94] R. G. G. Cattell: *Object Data Management*. Addison-Wesley, 1994.

[Cat96] R. G. G. Cattell (ed.) et al.: *Object Database Standard: ODMG-93 - Release 1.2*. Morgan-Kaufmann Publishers, 1996.

[CK95] J. Coldewey, W. Keller: *Objektorientierte Datenzugriffe auf dem VAA Datenmanager*. GDV Bonn, 1995. See
http://www.sdm.de/g/arcus/publicat/pubindex.phtml.

[Cot95] P. Cotter: *Inside Taligent Technology*. Addison-Wesley, 1995.

[Gra95] I. Graham: *Migrating to Object Technology*. Addison-Wesley, 1995.

[Hah+95] W. Hahn, F. Toennissen, A. Wittkowski: *Eine objektorientierte Zugriffsschicht zu relationalen Datenbanken*. Informatik Spektrum 18 (Heft 3/1995), 143-151, Springer Verlag, 1995. See also
http://www.sdm.de/e/www/fachartikel/#oozugriffsschicht.

[Kel95a] W. Keller: *Problems Reengineering RDBMS to Object-Oriented Databases,* see
http://www.sdm.de/g/arcus/publicat/pubindex.phtml.

[Kel95b] W. Keller: *Associations in Object-Oriented Access Layers,* see
http://www.sdm.de/g/arcus/publicat/pubindex.phtml.

[KS95] M. Keller, T. Stalzer: *Ein Erfahrungsbericht über den Einsatz von VisualAge und Vaser*. OBJEKTspektrum, 2 (4), July/August, 1995.

[KC96] W. Keller, J. Coldewey: *Relational Database Access Layers: A Pattern Language*, in *Collected Papers from the PLOP '96 and EuroPLoP '96 Conferences*. Washington University, Department of Computer Science, Technical Report WUCS-97-07, February, 1997. See
http://www.cs.wustl.edu/~schmidt/PLoP-96/.

[Kim95] W. Kim (ed.): *Modern Database Systems*. ACM Press, 1995.

[Lip95] P. Lipps: *Enterprise Objects Framework—Fachspezifische Objekte in Open Step*. OBJEKTspektrum, 2 (5), September/October, 1995.

[NeXT] NeXT Inc.: Several product descriptions on NeXT Enterprise Objects Framework can be found in WWW entering from
http://www.next.com.

[OH94] R. Orfali, D. Harkey: *Client/Server Survival Guide.* Van Nostrand Reinhold, 1994.

[PB94] W. Premerlani, M. R. Blaha: *An Approach for Reverse Engineering of Relational Databases.* Communications of the ACM, 42 (9), 1994.

[Sou94] J. Soukup: *Taming C++ - Pattern Classes and Persistence for Large Projects.* Addison-Wesley, 1994.

[Str91] B. Stroustroup: *The C++ Programming Language (2nd. Edition).* Addison-Wesley, 1991.

[WN95] K. Walden, J. M. Nerson: *Seamless Object-Oriented Software Architecture.* Prentice Hall, 1995.

[www.xxx.com] marks references to World Wide Web sites that contain product information on products quoted in this article.

2

An Access Layer for Object Databases:

Experience Report

Jens Coldewey, sd&m GmbH

ABSTRACT

Is it a good idea to employ a database access layer for object databases? This article describes a database access layer that has been successfully implemented for a single-user CAD system. It outlines the forces and sketches the design.

A DATABASE ACCESS LAYER FOR ODBMS?

Does it make sense to employ a database access layer for ODBMS (Figure 2–1)? Encapsulating database specific code in a separate layer has become good practice when using relational databases [KC97]. However, ODBMSs are much more integrated into the programming language. The following project story reflects our experiences encapsulating an object database.

Starting in 1993 we had to design a configurator for large fire alarm systems protecting chemistry plants, airports, or nuclear power stations. These systems usually consist of up to 100 independent control units, linked with a special network—

Jürgen Hohndel and Andreas Wittkowski helped to design and review the access layer. I would also like to thank Akmal Chaudhri, David Jenkins, Chad Smith, Wolfgang Keller, and Klaus Renzel for reviewing this paper and giving me many helpful hints.

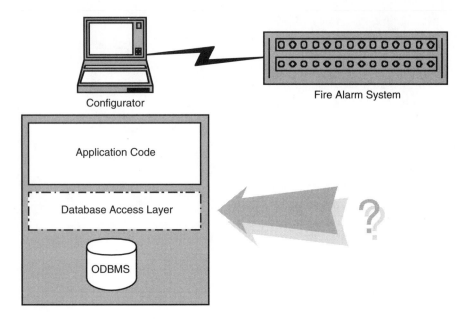

Figure 2–1   Does it make sense to employ a database access layer for ODBMS?

either locally within a site or over a distance of several miles using public telephone dialing systems. Each control unit monitors up to 10,000 sensors, organized in groups and areas. Moreover, a fire alarm system in a large factory usually does more than just ring the fire bell. Production has to stop in endangered zones, transport of flammable material into the zone has to stop, and special ventilation systems have to start to prevent further damage. Fire protection doors have to lock, emergency exits have to be opened, and so on. Designing these systems is a complex task that is nearly impossible to accomplish without the aid of a computer.

When we started the technical design of the system, we already knew that a simple, flat file data storage would not do, even though we designed a single user system. Handling up to a million objects was far beyond the scope of this cheap solution. Consequently, we had to look for a suitable database system. We had plenty of experience with connecting relational databases to object-oriented systems by building complex database access layers [BW96, CK96a]. With comparably simple object models of 30 to 40 classes this technique resulted in acceptable performance. However, we had found 60 classes during domain analysis, which surely would lead us to the edge of a hybrid design. After some evaluation, we finally decided to use our first ODBMS.

While developing the architecture for the system, we had to decide whether to build an access layer for the database. In our practice we had used database access layers for more than ten years with considerable success [Den91], so, it was hard to decide whether to quit this habit. To get a sound decision, we compared the goals of traditional access layers with the problems we expected to have with our ODBMS:

- *Encapsulation of the Technical Database Structure*: Usually it is not a good idea to organize the tables of a relational database in exactly the same structure as the domain application needs them. To achieve acceptable performance, database layout tuning is necessary, which would result in changes to the complete system. With small applications, this may be fine. Larger systems need a facility that allows the database design to change, one of the major tasks of an access layer, without having any impact on the domain code. With ODBMS, this objective becomes obsolete. The class structure has only very little impact on the performance. Special precautions are not necessary any more. However, that is only half of the truth, which leads to the next issue.

- *Database Tuning*: Tuning a relational database means denormalizing the database structure, creating suitable indices, and choosing the proper SQL statements. Most ODBMSs also use indexes to speed up access, but the most powerful "screw" a designer has with ODBMS is clustering. By telling the database to position arbitrary objects close to each other, the designer is able to directly control the physical data layout. As an example, consider a sensor attached to a certain line. If the clustering of the database represents this attachment, there is a good chance that a single page access reads all sensors of this line. Clustering is a database-specific task, although it is most effective when it also considers domain knowledge. Hence, it is preferable to have the clustering code in a separate location where it is easy to find.

- *Education:* Database programming still requires a considerable amount of training and experience, regardless of the database technology. Naive approaches will result in unacceptable performance. We lacked any ODBMS experience in our team, so we had to pay for external consultants to help us. It was reasonable to minimize the corresponding costs by encapsulating all database-specific code. The expert would be able to concentrate on that small part of the code without having to understand the complete system. On the other hand, encapsulation would also give the expert the chance to train a database team in the most efficient way.

- *Different Transaction Models:* In large database applications you usually define a logical transaction model, determined by the business processes of the client. This model may comprise long-running transactions or nested transactions, to mention just two examples. It is frequently necessary to map this model to the technical transactions of the DBMS. Because our system was a single-user application, we could ignore issues of concurrency control and could concentrate on the recover capabilities of the transactions. Still, we were unhappy with the technical model of the DBMS. A database connection lasted only as long as the enclosing transaction. Thus every commit resulted in a loss of the database connection—not an appealing thought. Consequently, we had to translate the transaction model. This also gave us the opportunity to use a nested transaction concept in the application. We were prepared for future multi-user extensions.

- *Error Management*: Our ODBMS supported a UNIX-style signaling technique to indicate errors during execution. We had decided to use C++ Exceptions for our internal error management, so we needed some kind of transformation. We wanted this transformation encapsulated at a single place and not cluttering the code.
- *Market Situation*: The market for ODBMS was, and is still, comparably small. Estimates of market volume are about $200 million. The top ten vendors had revenues of less than 10 percent of the large RDBMS companies. The market history of the 1980s teaches that even large manufacturers of RDBMSs vanished from the market, ruining millions of dollars of investments. Though there are ODBMSs with 100,000 installations worldwide, our vendor's fate was a major risk to our product. Designing the system to make the ODBMSs interchangeable was therefore a matter of risk management.

With all these problems in mind, we decided to introduce a database access layer. We knew we were entering virgin territory; we had searched for people, who had built access layers for ODBMSs before, and they all reported severe performance penalties. As a consequence, we spent a considerable amount of time and two technical prototypes to design the encapsulation.

THE ARCHITECTURE

Figure 2–2 shows the basic architecture of the access layer. It consists of two major parts. The administration part contains a database class, transaction processing, and error management. The query part contains filters and iterators.

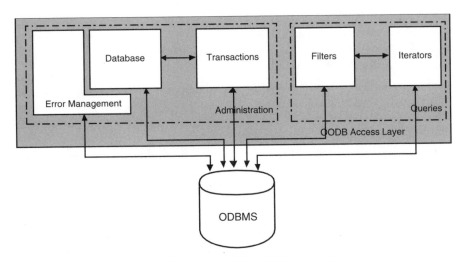

Figure 2–2   Clusters of the OODB access layer.

Database

We decided to organize our database in several different database files. There was one file containing configuration information and another file for each user project. This enabled the user to copy and archive projects with a minimum effort. The application kernel only worked with the logical project names that the user had assigned. The database subsystem mapped these logical names to physical file names using the configuration database.

Because the user was able to open more than one database file at the same time, all queries were only in the scope of a single fire alarm project. Thus, we introduced the notion of an "active database" as the default scope for creating new and searching existing objects. The database subsystem managed the active database transparently.

Finally, the database subsystem encapsulated all ODBMS calls for database maintenance. This implied creation and deletion of databases as well as up- and downloading for archiving and backup purposes.

Transactions

Dealing with transactions was by far more elaborate than a simple wrapper. Basically, we had to translate a logical transaction concept into a technical one. Figure 2–3 shows the difference between the logical transactions on the left side and the technical on the right.

Let's start with the logical transactions. The user displays some data with dirty reads, thinks about changes, and does manipulations at the GUI. Eventually she presses the OK button of a dialog or drops an object (Figure 2–3, ❶). At this moment a logical transaction starts, and the GUI triggers all the appropriate changes of domain objects. When all the updates have been successful, the system logically commits and waits for the next user action.

However, this simple transaction concept was hard to implement with our database for two reasons. At first, the ODBMS needed an open transaction *before* opening a particular database. Second, every technical commit caused the ODBMS to clear its object cache. Therefore, the user would have suffered a considerable delay every time she presses the OK button. This behavior is unacceptable.

Using nested transactions would have been the most elegant solution, but the ODBMS offered only single-level transactions. On the other hand, most of the restrictions resulted from the concurrency control of the ODBMS. Because we had a single-user system and we only used the transactions as recovery mechanisms, we could afford a translation by brute force. During the system startup we opened a technical transaction (Figure 2–3, ❷) and set a checkpoint every time a logical transaction committed (Figure 2–3, ❸). During shutdown we did the final commit (Figure 2–3, ❹). In the case of a system crash, the ODBMS would recover to the latest checkpoint, which was exactly what we wanted to achieve.

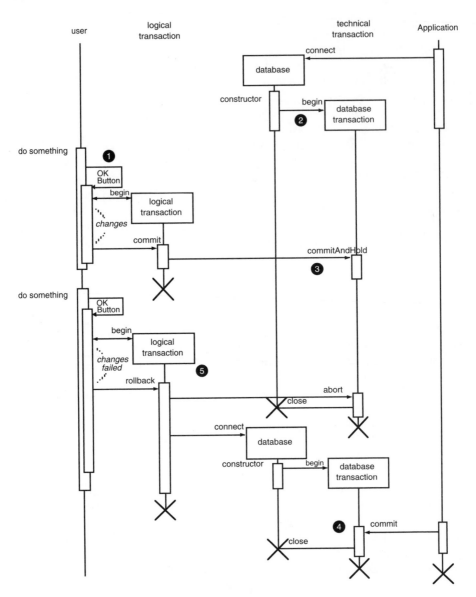

Figure 2–3 Logical transactions (left side) and technical transactions (right side). The numbers indicate references in the text.

The transaction subsystem encapsulated this mapping. It presented the logical transaction model to the domain objects and controlled the corresponding activities of the access layer. Occasionally, the transaction subsystem performed a complete commit to enable cleanups of the database.

Still, one problem remained. During a rollback, the ODBMS terminated the transaction and closed the database (Figure 2–3, ❺). The transaction subsystem automatically reopened the next transaction and therefore provided complete transparency to the application kernel.

Although this solution worked fairly well with our single-user system, its locking behavior would have been disastrous in a multiuser environment. Complete encapsulation in a single subsystem provided the possibility of coping with this problem in future releases of the ODBMS using nested transactions.

Error Management

Another problem we had to attack was the management of database errors. The ODBMS used a UNIX-style error management. Errors raised a special signal, causing the invocation of an error handler module. Global variables contained additional information on the type and the context of the error. Depending on the error classification and the return value of the error handler, the database either resumed operation or terminated the application.

Because our application used C++ exceptions, we disliked the idea of a second error handling mechanism. However, a transformation from the signaling mechanism to exceptions was a hard task. The error handler was called from deep inside the database code. Just throwing an exception would have resulted in internal corruption of the ODBMS—a worst-case scenario.

The only safe place to throw an exception was outside the error handler. This was an easy task for the wrapper classes, such as database or transaction. The error handler just sets a flag and returns a resume value. The wrapper classes check this value at the end of each ODBMS call and throw an exception when they find the error flag set. However, there are other ways to call the ODBMS besides explicit calls. Simply following a smart pointer may trigger a complete database access with hundreds of possibilities for a failure. To encapsulate smart pointers would have been rather expensive in relation to the benefit, especially after the ODBMS vendor promised to incorporate "true" exception handling into a later version. On the other hand, following smart pointers is unlikely to result in errors on a single-user system.

We finally chose a pragmatic approach and decided not to catch database errors after each call to the ODBMS but only at the end of each method. So we included a special call `dbErrorHandler.throwExceptionOnError` into the post-method frame. This call checked the current error status and threw an appropriate exception when the flag was set. We accepted the risk of deferred detection of database errors.

Interface to the Application Kernel

Separating the application kernel from the database access layer was by far the most difficult design issue we had to solve. Relational DBMSs present data structures such as tables and rows at their APIs. These structures usually map to `structs` or similar constructs of the programming language. Hence, it is easy to present these constructs at the interface of the access layer, while still encapsulating the complete database (for detailed information see [KC97]).

ODBMS are more closely integrated into the programming language. They *extend* the type system of the language with persistent types, rather than using existing types. This kind of integration is one of the most important features of the ODBMS, because it offers nearly transparent usage of the database. It is one of the main reasons for the high speed of ODBMSs. To encapsulate this extension means to copy parts of the runtime system of the database—a very unpleasant idea.

After some experiments, we decided to use a design that we had implemented several times before when building access layers for relational databases. We separated the layers on a method level instead of putting them into different classes. Each method was uniquely assigned either to the application kernel or to the access layer. A naming convention expressed the assignment (see [CK96b]). This trick solved several problems at once:

- *The ODBMS cared for the allocation management of persistent objects.* Alternatively we could have split the objects into a persistent part—managed by the ODBMS—and a transient part—allocated manually. This would have required a synchronization of both parts, causing several problems.
- *We paid no performance penalty.* Because the database stored "true" application objects, we introduced no additional level of indirection. Separation at class level would have required an additional level of objects, and it would have blurred the fetch characteristics of the application.
- *Database issues were concentrated.* The database access methods contained all the database specific code of the class:
  — *Creation and Deletion of Persistent Objects*: When creating new objects, the ODBMS needs to know the database file that holds the object. Consequently, we assigned the constructor to the database access layer. The application kernel only presented (static) class methods that called the constructor. For reasons of symmetry we also assigned the destructor to the database access layer.
  — *Manipulation of Associations*: The ODBMS offered a broad range of opinions to manage associations. Assuring referential integrity and delete propagation were the two most important ones. Because there were a number of special calls to control these features, we encapsulated them in simple inline methods such as `Line::attachSensor`. If we had to change the ODBMS, we only had to touch these methods.
  — *Clustering*: Two methods for each class dealt with clustering. A regular member function `d_Locate` analyzed the attributes of the object and determined a closely related object that should be located near by. All meth-

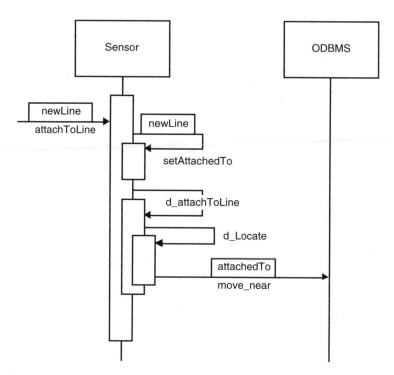

Figure 2–4   The complete scenario of determining the new location of a sensor.

ods that changed associations implicitly called the d_Locate member function. For example, a sensor should be located near its line (Figure 2–4). Consequently the d_Locate method tells the ODBMS to move the sensor near the line object designated by the attachedTo member variable. The d_attachToLine member function calls d_Locate to adjust the object to its new location.

A second static member function did the same job but got all information through its parameters. The constructors used this class method during object creation to determine the default location. Because these two methods were the only codes in each class for clustering, we had introduced a well-defined set of "screws" for tuning.

Despite our initial concerns about this rather unusual separation of layers, we found it to be a pragmatic solution that sufficiently fitted our needs.

Filters and Iterators

Though the ODBMS offered filter objects and iterators, they were insufficient for our needs. The iterators allowed only forward iteration, which resulted in significant effort to support scrolling. Additionally, there were several ways to instantiate an iterator depending on the physical database design; iterating all objects of a class needed a different instantiation than iterating objects using an index.

Thus, we introduced database iterators with interfaces conforming to the iterators of our container library. The iterators allowed bidirectional scrolling and filtering. During instantiation, the client could attach a filter object that was able to generate a database query according to the physical database layout.

At first glance, this may sound like a very complex design that needs fairly intricate classes. In fact, a single filter class was rather simple. The iterators retrieved their corresponding database queries from the filters, according to the strategy design pattern [Gamt95]. General filters encapsulated dynamic queries; specialized filters generated highly tuned queries. Because the application kernel needed to know only the name and the parameters of a filter, the access layer completely hid the query compilation.

Referencing Transient Objects

Sometimes persistent objects temporarily referenced transient objects. These references needed special handling. Because the database stores pointers as binary images, the application was not able to tell whether the reference was still valid. A special smart pointer template class solved this problem. In addition to the memory address, it also stored a transaction id. The pointer was considered valid, as long as it was set in the same transaction. This simple solution satisfied our needs, so we spent no more effort to find a more elaborate one.

SOFTWARE PRODUCTION ENVIRONMENT

While the architecture helped us to hide the object *manipulation*, we still had to deal with object *definition*. The ODBMS used a proprietary object definition language (ODL), similar to C++ header files. This ODL augmented C++ syntax with constructs to define unidirectional and bidirectional associations, propagation specification, and other constraints. Our goal was also to encapsulate this ODL to facilitate a future change of the ODBMS.

We decided to generate the ODL from a class specification using keywords. According to our methodology, we had class definitions that specified attributes and methods of every class with a keyword syntax. Because we already had a tool to turn these specifications into C++ header files and code frames [Kel95], we extended this generator with constructs to generate the ODL and default implementations for the database methods.

EXPERIENCES AND SUMMARY

After several months of development, we were confronted with a rather unexpected obstacle. "When I started this project, I hoped to learn about the ODBMS, but I can't see anything of it," an application developer complained. Hence our efforts to encapsulate the database were successful. When we had to change the mapping of transactions, it took us only two days of regression tests instead of a complete re-design. Tuning was as easy as we expected. We have adapted these ideas success-fully into other projects still running.

Performance also met our expectations. We never did formal benchmarks be-cause we only had the standard performance constraints of a dialog system. How-ever, the additional level of indirection used with filters and iterators had no signifi-cant effect on the reaction time. Moreover, the ease of tuning the cluster definition facilitated database tuning. Finally, the gain in terms of disk accesses was worth much more than the loss in terms of processor cycles.

Nevertheless, we encountered an unexpected problem. The generation of the ODL was by far more complicated than we had estimated. Finally, we had invested an effort of half a man year into the generator until we could work with it. The gen-erator's input was nearly as complex as the ODL itself, so no real benefit resulted from this approach. Directly writing ODL would have been the better way.

Today the ODBMS vendor has solved some of the sketched problems. Refer-encing transient objects is easier now and many ODBMSs also offer backward iter-ation and nested transactions in recent versions. However, other forces for the ac-cess layer still persist. Encapsulating database specific code, defining "screws" for tuning, and hiding query considerations are topics even the best ODBMS cannot generally solve. Therefore, building an access layer for ODBMS is still a good idea.

REFERENCES

[BW96] K. Brown, B. G. Whitenack: *Crossing Chasms, A Pattern Language for Object-RDBMS Integration;* in *Pattern Languages of Program Design 2,* J. Vlissides, J. Coplien, N. Kerth (eds.). Addison-Wesley, 1996

[CK96a] J. Coldewey, W. Keller: *Objektorientierte Datenintegration—ein Migra-tionsweg zur Objekttechnologie;* OBJEKTSpektrum 4/96, 1996.

[CK96b] J. Coldewey, W. Keller: *Multilayer Class,* in *Collected Papers from the PLoP'96 and EuroPLoP'96 Conferences;* Washington University, Depart-ment of Computer Science, Technical Report WUCS-97-07, February 1997. Available at
http://www.cs.wustl.edu/~schmidt/PLoP-96/.

[Den91] E. Denert: *Software Engineering—Methodische Projektabwicklung,* Springer Verlag, 1991

[Gam+95] E. Gamma, R. Helm, R. Johnson, J. Vlissides: *Design Patterns—Elements of Reusable Object-Oriented Software.* Addison-Wesley, 1995.

[KC97] W. Keller, J. Coldewey: *Relational Database Access Layer—A Pattern Language;* in *Pattern Languages of Program Design 3,* R. C. Martin (ed.). Addison-Wesley, 1997 (to appear)

[Kel95] W. Keller: *Seliger denn tippen;* in *Mulituser-Multitasking-Magazin,* ix, 1/95, Verlag Heinz Heise GmbH & Co. KG.

3

A Use of the EndGame Design Strategy

Alistair Cockburn, Humans and Technology

ABSTRACT

The EndGame design strategy secures ever-larger areas of the design space, reducing the area of indecision. This produces decisions and interfaces that allow an increasing number of people to work in peace. It prevents requirements perturbations from leaking out of a controlled area. This "control of the trajectory of change" is a major goal in software system design.

EndGame proved useful while designing a client-server system when we were not sure whether the server would stay relational or be converted to an object-oriented database. This chapter describes EndGame, how we used it to produce a safe design for the client-side objects, and how we used the design template to train the OO novices on the team.

INTRODUCTION

It was fairly typical for today's object-oriented design projects: added to the goal of delivering a software system was that of training OO novices. The few experts among the dozen novices each had his or her own design philosophy. On any particular design problem, their design techniques, rationales, and solutions looked different. Their professional evaluations of the end design also differed. By the end of the project, I distinguished four approaches to design that could be taught, plus other intuitive approaches the experts used that couldn't be taught.

And still, we had to get the newcomers to design a usable and resilient system.

We found the EndGame technique when time was running out, tempers were getting short, and opinions were divided. It gave us designs for which the process was compelling. Briefly, the process is to create a series of design decisions that shrink the area of contention down to a local design matter, assigned to a single person or team.

EndGame is not always applicable. It appears to work in what feels like one-dimensional design situations—there is a simple, linear quality to the design decisions that makes it possible to work in a straight line from the front of the problem to the back. It works nicely when it is applicable, and it fits well within the history of software design.

Our experience carries four lessons. Moving from specific and concrete to general and abstract, they are:

- The specific design for our specific problem
- The specific steps used to create that design
- The technique and when it is applicable
- How the technique fits in with other design techniques

This chapter is broken into six main parts to bring out those lessons:

1. Teaching Our Newcomers a Design Style
2. Design a Persistent Account Class
3. The EndGame Design Technique ("Squeegee")
4. Application of the EndGame Strategy
5. How would One Decide It Is Time to Try EndGame?
6. Comparison of EndGame with Other Design Strategies

TEACHING OUR NEWCOMERS A DESIGN STYLE

It was a three-tier system: a client workstation running an OO application, connected to a UNIX server with database, and a mainframe with a relational database. However, we could not decide what sort of database would be used on the Unix server: object or relational. The initial guess was relational.

As experts, our assignment was to get the OO novices to produce fairly decent designs fairly consistently. Their tendency was to produce persistent objects that looked mostly like relational tables. Their discussions were full of references to the tables. This was natural, given the presence of the relational database on the server and the need to normalize the database. It made the experts nervous and for two reasons: our sense as purists, and our fear that the server database might suddenly be switched to objects. We realized that the former reason sounds weak, but when design experts uniformly feel uncomfortable, there is likely to be a real danger, even if the people cannot articulate it.

So we sought a pattern of thinking we could give the newcomers so that the relational tables would not enter into their discussions, and they would produce designs based on other reasoning.

The situation came to a crisis with the design of a particularly complicated business class—the Account Class. It was complex, and it needed to be stored on the server and use caching of intermediate results. It had been redesigned several times, and the team leads were losing their ability to work through the design carefully and impartially. Time was short, as were tempers. We needed to come up with a way to talk through the problem that:

- would get agreement at every intermediate stage, so that the different experts would not simply disagree with the end result.
- would produce a legitimate design not based on relational table structure, so that we could cut over to an object database without trauma.
- could be passed on to the newcomer designers, so they could use it and also so that the different experts could agree with their line of reasoning.

DESIGN A PERSISTENT ACCOUNT CLASS

The problem has two levels of difficulty. Assume in what follows that there are two design teams, the workstation design team and the server design team.

The Simple Problem

Let there be a common checking account, an Account class, as might be. Each Account object keeps track of its balance and its transaction history. Some balance information and all the transactions are stored on a server. The server uses either a relational or an object database, but we don't know which. The workstation is connected to the server over a 9600 baud phone line.

The Harder Problem

For performance reasons, let the server produce various summaries of each account: by month, by geographic area, and by type by month. It is considered a local matter, local to the server designers, whether the summaries are stored or computed on the fly. That matter will be resolved according to their performance goals. Also for speed reasons, the workstation should cache any summary that has been sent by the server for the current account. This prevents the user from growing impatient with screen refreshes.

I have not cluttered up the design problem with the relational tables then in use, nor have I introduced the design personalities of the various team leaders. Those two factors made the problems considerably more complicated than as just outlined.

It is the cached values that concern us here, the balance and the summaries. The obvious solutions are:

- Create a balance instance variable, because we need it quickly, and it is cached in the database anyway.
- Create summary classes, for the same reasons.

Although these are "obvious," we found our arguments contained phrases that were not convincing, phrases such as, "because it is on the database anyway," "because it is (or is not) object-oriented," "because it violates encapsulation," and so on. We wanted to get away from these sorts of personality-sensitive reasons. So we developed the EndGame technique.

THE ENDGAME DESIGN TECHNIQUE ("SQUEEGEE")

The intent this technique is to narrow design decisions so that earlier decisions do not have to be revisited. The strategy is named after the chess endgame, where the purpose is to secure increasing areas of the board and reduce the opponent's region of movement. This is akin to squeezing water to one side with a squeegee, hence the nickname. In design, it means securing ever-larger areas of the design space, reducing the area of indecision

The forces affecting the choice of a strategy are revealed by looking at strategies that may not work. Here are some weaker strategies.

1. *Wait until the requirements settle down and the decision can be made rationally.*

There are times when the requirements simply will not settle down. Often work must be done now, knowing that the requirements will not be stable for some time or that they will certainly change a year from now.

2. *Make the workstation design mirror the database.*

The design of the workstation object loses the resiliency offered by OO design. Every change in the server causes a change in the object, which causes a change in its client. This is an undesirably large trajectory of change.

3. *Split the design space and negotiate the interface. In this strategy, the workstation team, separated from the server database team, negotiate on their interface.*

The interface negotiation becomes a tug-of-war. Perhaps the loudest speaker wins; perhaps the line of reasoning gets "polluted" by knowing there is a relational database, and the workstation object starts to mirror the database structure; perhaps the workstation team is worried into indecisiveness by not knowing what the final decision will be on the selection of server database technology.

Summarizing the forces:

- Need to make progress making decisions.
- Need to control the area of change.
- Need to control the emotional content of the design.

The EndGame strategy is given in a series of moves, each move securing a new design area while protecting previous areas. Each move results in a decision that is not reversible. Figure 3–1 shows in a schematic way how each move produces a decision that secures a new area, so that previous decisions are safe.

The EndGame strategy is difficult to apply when there are a number of closely interacting design issues. It relies on being able to isolate the topics.

APPLICATION OF THE ENDGAME STRATEGY

Here is how we devised a series of moves for designing classes in case we changed from a relational to an OO database. I illustrate it with the Account problem mentioned above.

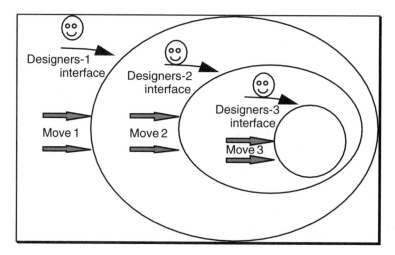

Figure 3–1   EndGame consists of a series of moves that lock down the design space.

Move 0: Problem Setup—Identify the Possible Area of Containment

We decided that the area of highest risk was the server design, and that this would be the last move (corresponding to the inside circle in Figure 3–1). The objects on the workstation, ideally, should not care what server technology is used. Even more importantly, whatever the persistent business object (the Account) knows about the server, its clients absolutely should not know. We created these four zones of design (see Figure 3–2):

1. The end-client's interface. During Move 1, we concentrate on the dialog between the workstation class (the Account) and its clients, ensuring they have an appropriate interface and a dialog absolutely independent of the server technology. After Move 1, the workstation object's clients no longer care about the details of distribution or the nature or the implementation of the server database. The design of that interface is sound and stable, subject only to necessary changes that come from the bare fact of distributing computation.

2. The workstation object's internal design, as though processing were all local. During Move 2, we pretend there is no database to clutter up the discussion, and derive a clean and sound local design—even though we know this is not a true assumption and some parts of the design will have to change. After Move 2, the object has a sound OO design and is *relatively* stable. It is untouched by questions of the server database or by the current relational tables.

3. Distribution. During Move 3, we add the facts of distribution, accounting for performance loss through delays and multiple concurrent users. After Move 3, the design of the workstation object is stable and sound with respect to perfor-

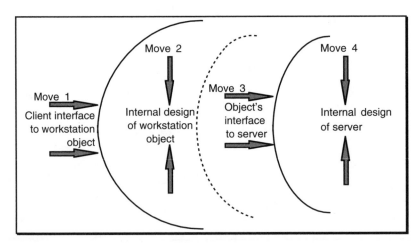

Figure 3–2   Client-server design in four moves.

mance delays and distribution. The workstation object no longer cares about the implementation of the server. This is the end of the story from the workstation team's perspective.

4. **The server's internal design.** During Move 4, the server team designs the server portion of the object, taking into account their own special requirements. After Move 4, the design of the server is complete. Note that the implementation technology on the server may be changed without damaging the workstation object or its clients.

Here are the details of the moves for the Account class.

Move 1: Secure the End-Client's Interface

The Account class must support a known set of questions about balance and transaction history since the beginning of the year, sorted and summarized by month, by area, and by type by month. It supports:

- `balance` -> returning a monetary value.
- `summariesByArea` -> returning an alphabetically ordered collection of summaries. Each summary can provide the sum of all deposits and withdrawals since the beginning of the year, and can produce the date-ordered collection of transactions.
- `summariesByMonth` -> returning a date-ordered collection of month summaries. Each month's summary answers the sum of all deposits and withdrawals across all areas during that month. It can produce a collection of summaries by month and type, which sum the deposits and withdrawals by the type of the deposit or withdrawal and can produce the date-ordered collection of transactions.

There was really no room for negotiation about these services the Account class would offer, since they were needed by the application (see Figure 3–3).

Move 2: Secure the Workstation Object's Internal Design

Even assuming a fast, local processor and large amounts of local memory, it makes sense to create summary objects rather than recompute the summaries every time the user opens a window. Assuming the software would work entirely from local memory, we decided the design would consist of the classes named: `Account`, `Transaction`, `SummaryByArea`, `SummaryByMonth`, `SummaryByType-ByMonth`.

Therefore, `Account` has a local storage variable for the current balance and knows of two collections, its `summariesByAreas` and its `summariesBy-Months`. It does not need to know all of its `Transactions`, nor does it know the `SummaryByTypeByMonth`. Each `SummaryByMonth` knows those, which com-

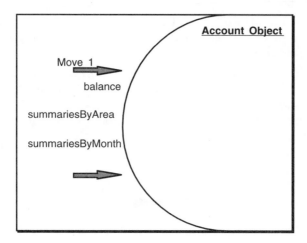

Figure 3–3   Move 1 secures the workstation object's client interface.

prise its breakdown into types of transaction. Only `SummaryByTypeByMonth` and `SummaryByArea` know of Transactions directly (see Figures 3–4 and 3–5).

Move 3: Secure the Distribution Service

In distributing the services, we could choose to have the server deliver all the transactions and let the workstation do the adding to build the summaries, or we could choose to have the server build the summaries. In a situation where transmission speed was not a problem, as on a local area network, we might have chosen to let the workstation do the addition, in order to offload the server. However, we had

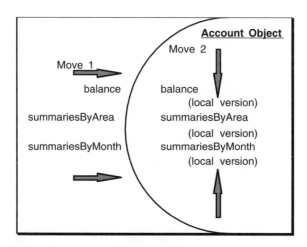

Figure 3–4   Move 2 secures the workstation object's interal design.

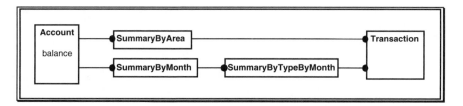

Figure 3–5   The OMT-style class diagram of the workstation classes.

slow telephone lines to contend with, so minimizing the transmission traffic was paramount.

Therefore, we decided that the server should support the exact services the workstation needed, namely `balance`, `summariesByArea`, `summariesBy-Month`, and so on (see Figure 3–6).

Is everything exactly the same—has anything at all changed with the distribution? There is a subtle but significant difference. Recall that many people are working on different workstations at the same time. When any one user requests the balance or a summary, the server guarantees the freshness of the answer. That answer soon becomes out-of-date as this user and the other users add transactions. The balance and summaries on each workstation reflect the changes made on that workstation, but not the changes the other users made. Although "balance" on the workstation and "balance" as a service from the server sound the same, they have different meanings and will carry different values.

It was difficult for us to get used to the idea that the balance variable on the workstation and the balance from the server are actually different. What we have established at this point is that the workstation stores such a variable rather than re-

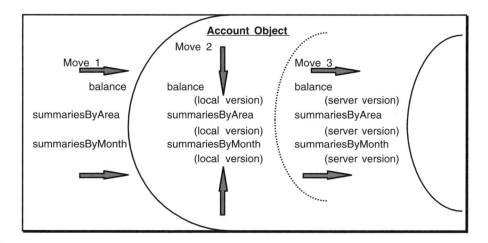

Figure 3–6   Move 3 secures the server's service interface.

computing it every time, but we have not yet established whether such a storage exists on the server (nor do we care).

To deal with the staleness of the data on the workstation in the presence of multiple users, we changed the client interface to add one more function, "refresh." When the user presses the "refresh" button, the workstation objects go out to the server to get up-to-date values.

If the server guarantees to provide the workstation with the promised data, the workstation programmers do not care whether the server uses a relational or object database, or whether data are stored or recomputed. The workstation team is now finished.

Move 4: Secure the Server's Internal Design

We started with a relational database. On the relational database, it was soon decided that the balance and the summaries would be computed on the fly. That kept the database clean and guaranteed fresh data on every request. For about half a year, we were left uncertain whether the server would be changed to an object database. The design produced here gave us a tidy design and left us in the best possible shape for the conversion (see Figure 3–7).

Results of Applying the EndGame Technique.

We invented the four-move sequence just for the Account class, but it applied to every business class. The experienced designers understood the line of reasoning and applied it almost unconsciously. The novice designers usually copied working designs, so they got the results by copying. Therefore, once we detailed the technique, we did not have to revisit it and work through it carefully very often. We ran through the four-move sequence when a design was looking shaky and there was growing disagreement in the discussion.

The result was that the expert designers gained a confidence that the novices were producing adequate designs, ones that would not jeopardize the project in case the database were switched. The novices gained an appreciation for OO design, even when their lives were otherwise full of screen layouts and relational tables.

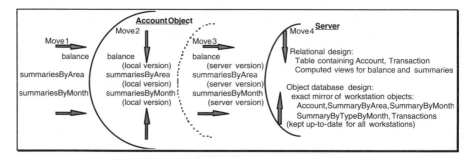

Figure 3–7   Move 4 settles the server's implementation.

HOW WOULD ONE DECIDE IT IS TIME TO TRY ENDGAME?

I said that EndGame has a sort of one-dimensional quality to it. You work the problem from front to back, creating sound, irreversible decisions. Ideally, the problem separates so that no single design issue affected several moves.

In the example problem, and in our application of EndGame on the project, there was generally no question about the object's client interface (Move 1). If there was no server, the internal design was typically straightforward (Move 2). There was some discussion about the distribution service, but that became fairly obvious given the client interface and internal design (Move 3). After that, it was a local matter to the server team (Move 4), and there was no need for others to discuss it.

Use EndGame when you need to reach these intermediate agreement points. They give the novices and individual teams a stable interface and help the experts reach consensus on the designs.

I applied EndGame to the overall architecture of the workstation architecture, which is not a one-dimensional problem [Coc96]. The EndGame process produced a prioritized set of design principles, which allowed us to address ever-smaller design topics using previously set decisions. The design principles did not all follow from one base principle, but from a small set of basic principles. When someone questioned a design decision, we could back up the chain of decisions to find where they disagreed with a principle or its priority. This proved useful in defending the design and evolving it.

Therefore, although I said that EndGame addresses one-dimensional problems, it can be used on more complicated problems if the different lines of reasoning can be fairly well isolated.

COMPARISON OF ENDGAME WITH OTHER DESIGN STRATEGIES

The previous section concludes the discussion of the practical aspects of the techniques. From the scholastic perspective, there is more to say about the nature of the technique and how it fits in with other techniques.

Polya addresses general mathematical problem solving with his book *How to Solve It* [Pol45]. This book gives an overall framework for addressing mathematical problems, with a compendium of heuristic techniques and questions [Pol45]. I had hoped that Polya would have documented the EndGame strategy in his list of heuristics, however, the questions faced by software designers fall between his general question-asking framework and his specific heuristics. In particular, he distinguishes what he calls "practical problems," which "are usually far from being perfectly stated." Our problem fell into that category. Therefore, his list of problem-solving heuristics was not helpful to us.

Polya's question-asking framework sheds some light on what is going on in EndGame, even if without offering the tangible advice software designers need. Culling through his book, I find the the following advice, scattered across sections:

1. Ask, what is the unknown, what are the data, what is the condition
2. Keep only part of the condition
3. Imagine a more accessible problem
4. Apply a "unilateral reduction" to the problem

This the EndGame approach. Polya's list of suggestions is a bit vague, so here is how EndGame fixes them:

- For suggestion 2, what part of the condition should we keep? In EndGame, we keep the part of the condition corresponding to the outer circle of design (the client interface in our sample problem).
- For suggestion 3, what should the more accessible problem do for us? The answer in EndGame is, create a stable interface. Being more accessible means that it has fewer design constraints and is easier to agree upon.
- For suggestion 4, what is the nature of the unilateral reduction and what should it lead to? The EndGame answer is, a unilateral reduction in the number of considerations affecting the design with each successive step. It leads to an irreversible decision on part of the condition, with a smaller area of potential area of change for the rest.

Thus, with each step, we keep part of the condition, make the problem more accessible and reduce the problem. The number of moves needed in EndGame corresponds to the number of times we split the problem to reduce it and make it more accessible.

Gries, in *The Science of Computer Programming* [Gri86], also follows that general approach. There is a consistent theme in his design of algorithms, of continually reducing the area of intellectual risk, of gradually pushing the problem into a corner, as it were. I accept that I am taking some great liberty in summarizing so briefly two decades of work, and yet that similarity of approach is striking, and in contrast to the more common OO design techniques.

I mentioned earlier four teachable design approaches I saw in use on the project. They are:

1. *Responsibility-Driven Design.* Adequately described by Beck and Cunningham [BC87] and Wirfs-Brock [Wir+90], RDD is good for evaluating the quality of the subsystem partitioning. Used with CRC cards [BC87], it is good for quickly generating and evaluating numerous alternative ideas.

2. *EndGame Design*. As described in this chapter, it is good for one-dimensional problems and is suitable whenever you need to secure stepwise agreement to the solution.

3. *Client-Side Design*. Discussed informally among OO designers, this consists of describing the use of a component by its clients. It is good for working on the quality of the component's interface. At the outermost system level, it leads to use case design.

4. *Theory-Building*. Peter Naur describes software design as building a theory of operation of the domain and of the solution [Nau92]. We found it not only to be a description of the design process in general, but also an effective technique for fixing someone else's bugs: The new designer takes the time to create a theory of operation for the system and makes changes in harmony with that theory. The quality of the fix is related to the accuracy of the theory and the degree of harmony between the fix and the theory.

The four approaches differ in their overall angle of attack on a design problem. Only EndGame maps to Polya's term "unilateral reduction." There are other considerations affecting selection of design strategy. For example, we used *Design in a Goldfish Bowl* as an alternative to EndGame, when the design had to satisfy the skeptical scrutiny of varied people. In *Design in a Goldfish Bowl*, the designers worked in front of the skeptical audience, using a variety of techniques, principally RDD and scenario analysis. The purpose of *Design in a Goldfish Bowl* is to let the audience see that design constraints and alternatives have been examined. Presence of stakeholders and visibility of the discussion is key. The constraints leading to selection of *Design in a Goldfish Bowl* appear somewhat similar to those for EndGame, and yet the technique itself is different (i.e., the design approach itself is unconstrained).

I wonder what the typology might look like for problem-solving approaches to software design, to include not just algorithm and data structure design, but specifically also system partitioning, subsystem structures, and interface design?

SUMMARY

Using the EndGame approach, we were able to produce a design for a complicated workstation class, that:

- made the design insensitive to changes in server database technology.
- got divergent expert designers to accept the design.
- got the object newcomers to stop thinking about the then-relational database.
- was simple enough to teach.
- allowed the divergent expert designers to arbitrate other designs.

The EndGame approach secures ever-larger areas of the design space, reducing the area of indecision. It consists of a series of moves, each move closing out certain design topics, narrowing down the area of greatest contention, until it is in a simple form. The simple form can then be debated, or ideally, given to one person as a local matter.

The advantages to EndGame are that it permits control of the trajectory of change and creates agreements that allow an increasing number of people to work independently. It may be limited to areas of the design where the decisions can be linearized (see Cockburn [Coc96] for an attempt to linearize a larger design space).

EndGame is one of four teachable design strategies we identified on the project, the others being Responsibility-Driven Design, Client-Side Design, and Theory Building. These four strategies have slightly different characteristics and purposes leading them to be applied in different situations.

REFERENCES

[BC87] K. Beck, W. Cunningham: *A Laboratory for Teaching Object-Oriented Thinking*. Proceedings of the OOPSLA Conference, ACM Sigplan, October, 1987, pp.1–7.

[Coc96] A. Cockburn: *The interaction of Social Issues and Software Architecture*. Communications of the ACM, October 1996, pp. 40–46.

[Gri86] D. Gries: *The Science of Computer Programming*. Springer Verlag, 1986.

[Nau92] P. Naur: *Computing as a Human Activity*. ACM Press, 1992.

[Pol45] G. Polya: *How to Solve It*. Princeton University Press, 1945, 1985.

[Wir+90] R. Wirfs-Brock, B. Wilkerson, L. Wiener: *Designing Object-Oriented Software*. Prentice-Hall, 1990.

4

Building a Push-Based Information System Using an Active Database

Stephen Ross-Talbot, ObjX By Design Ltd.

ABSTRACT

HOODINI (Highly Object-Oriented Development in Nomura International) is one of the largest Object-Oriented developments being undertaken in the global financial services community. The whole ethos behind HOODINI is to build a true three-tier client/server architecture to allow the distribution of processing in an effective manner. The three tiers, presentation, business logic, and resource are bound together using various "new" technologies including TIBCO's Transaction Express, Rendezvous and Iona's Orbix for communication, Sybase and Object Design's ObjectStore for storage resources, and a dynamic Model View Controller (MVC) based toolkit for presentation.

One of the many problems that HOODINI seeks to address is active dissemination (pushing) of semi-static data as objects to a trader's workstation. ObjectStore and Rendezvous are the base technologies that address this requirement. ObjectStore is used as a persistent front-end cache with Sybase offering secure longer-term storage and Rendezvous is the scalable broadcast medium used for notification. This chapter explores the ways in which ObjectStore and Rendezvous have

---

We would like to thank Nomura and Object Design for allowing us to publish this work, in particular Nick Caine and Martin White for their help and criticism and the RDM/OStore team.

been used to address this requirement. In particular, the concept design and implementation of what we call "Predicate Maintained Collection" (PMC) is described.

A PMC is a query that is always kept up to date. Objects that are created, updated, or deleted may result in potential changes to one or more PMCs. A PMC in this context is a predicated broadcast notification based on set membership.

INTRODUCTION

HOODINI (Highly Object-Oriented Development in Nomura International) is one of the largest object-oriented developments being undertaken in the global financial services community. The whole ethos behind Hoodini is to build a true three-tier client/server architecture to allow the distribution of processing in an effective manner. Central to this is the active pushing of objects throughout the system.

The focus of this paper is to describe how an object database management system [Obj96] and a reliable broadcast transport mechanism [Tib96] can be used to build both active database models and push-based information systems through the use of Predicate Maintained Collections (PMCs). A PMC, in HOODINI, is a collection that maintains itself in the face of change. It is used as a generic mechanism for building both an active query facility and an active collection facility.

In the world of finance, information currency and speed of thought are essential. Information currency fuels the decision-making processes. We will show how PMCs can be used to increase currency. Indeed, this is the main driving force in the development behind PMCs.

Financial systems are divided between front, middle, and back office. The front office is responsible for making the trades, the middle for supporting the trader and maintaining reference information, and the back for accounting, settlements, corporate risk management, and regulatory reporting. The way that many systems have been built has led to two major problems. Firstly, duplication of what should be common functionality and common data across all areas of the business and, secondly, serialization of back and middle office systems that should be more independent. This first problem, which may include the way in which positions and profit and loss (derived data), as well as basic common data, has a knock-on effect throughout the system. Because the front, middle, and back offices do their own calculations in their own way and because they maintain their own common data, they are often out of sync with each other. This leads to many trades being rejected, having failed their validation in the back or middle office as the various back or middle office systems try to reconcile both base and derived data against their own view of common data and functionality. The second problem, that of serialization of back and middle office systems, is a direct consequence of a failure to model the flows of objects in the system as a whole. During validation in any one of the middle or back office systems, the object being validated (e.g., a trade) cannot proceed to any other system until that validation is complete, regardless of the semantic coupling between the systems. This serial approach greatly decreases the overall throughput of the system and this in turn limits the speed and accuracy of decisions.

HOODINI does it differently. It solves the problem of duplication by having common objects to which front, middle, and back office applications can subscribe. Furthermore, the back office functions can be performed independently where necessary by adopting a workflow approach. In this way they can perform the validation that is appropriate to them rather than waiting for validation to proceed serially. This approach reduces the number of exceptions that occur by making each back, middle, and front office process responsible for itself. If a trade is rejected by the settlement system, it doesn't necessarily follow that it will be rejected by any other system, contrary to the serial flows of the system described above. Exceptions are managed as some form of compensating transaction, which is more akin to the workflow approach.

Active distribution of common data is a key factor in reducing the likelihood of exceptions occuring. Furthermore, it increases the bandwidth of trades on a global basis. For example, the traders, the risk management component, and all other subscribers to common data can be sure that they are up-to-date or at least provide a consistent picture. Thus, the bank as a whole can increase the bandwidth for trading to the limit.

Reducing this window, making it as small as possible, and providing greater currency of information by the active pushing of objects is what PMCs have been designed to achieve.

All applications that require data currency in this way can express their working set intentionally as a number of predicates that can be applied to collections of objects. The role of a PMC is to inform the viewer of any changes to its underlying collection of results. Thus, a trader who trades with particular counterparties or particular instruments can attach to one or more PMCs that express, intentionally as predicates, the counterparty and instrument objects that the trader wants to see. Any subsequent changes to those objects are then broadcast to that trader and other subscribers.

RELATED WORK

The term "active" when applied to databases can mean different things. Some systems use the term to describe simple event notification mechanisms [Poe96, Ver96, Obj96, Gem95]. Others use the term to describe trigger and constraint mechanisms most of which follow an Event-Condition-Action (ECA) paradigm [MD89, Geh+92, Dia+91]. PMCs are more akin to the former but also have some flavor of the latter. The intention behind PMCs is twofold. The first reason is to provide a public mechanism for predicate-based notification. In this it is comparable in intent to the approach taken by Poet, VERSANT, GemStone, and ObjectStore. Second, it provides a modeling facility, called an active collection (a PMC with a predicate that is always true), that can be used to construct active models. It is comparable to the ECA approaches inasmuch as a PMC can be considered as a "canned" ECA. The events that PMCs deal with are "item added," "item updated," and "item removed" from an underlying collection. The condition in a PMC is the predicate that defines the members of the underlying collection and the action to add, remove, or update the object in the results set and notify any viewers. In this sense, the PMC system forms a partial foundation upon which a richer, more dynamic ECA system could be built.

Event notification systems, such as those espoused by Poet, GemStone, and ObjectStore and the monitoring facilities provided by Sentinel, all suffer from the same problem of efficiency. Poet, GemStone, and ObjectStore provide object-based notification. All objects that are of interest must be explicitly registered before any notification of change can begin. The problem with this approach is entirely one of granularity. It is preferable for an application to be able to write one or more predicates that express their working set rather than to write an exhaustive list of objects. A predicate-based system allows the application to use the same basic mechanism to express a working set that includes existing objects and objects yet to be created, and thereby intentionally—as opposed to extensionally—defines a working set. Sentinel uses rules and reactive and notifiable objects to allow predicates (the condition part of an ECA triple) to be defined that can apply to object instances not yet created. What Sentinel doesn't do, however, is to maintain a collection of those objects that meet that predicate so that they are immediately accessible, although it is easy to see how one could do this with a particular ECA triple. All of these systems use point-to-point communication between the notifier (database) and the notified (interested clients). This is inherently nonscalable as more and more clients are connected to the system. The ability to define the objects of interest by means of a predicate and maintain the collection coupled with a reliable broadcast protocol [Tib96] offers a more scalable solution. It cuts down network contention and provides materialized pools of objects that are immediately available to clients. Furthermore, the use of a predicate to scope objects of interest allows a more flexible and richer system to be more easily constructed.

The VERSANT ODBMS notification system provides the client with the ability to register interest on a range of database events and to attach a predicate to that event. Thus, they go some way towards providing a PMC-like mechanism. Furthermore, they do not mandate any particular delivery mechanism—rather, they require the application to register an event delivery service per database. The event service is responsible for the delivery of events to interested parties. This means that the event service could be implemented using a broadcast or multicast protocol if needed.

In ODE, implemented in C++, constraints are used to maintain object consistency and triggers monitor database conditions—both of which allow the user to build an active database model. In ADAM, a PROLOG, implementation, the focus is on uniformity of rules and provision of events for database modeling. Because ADAM is implemented in PROLOG, it is more dynamic than ODE. Sentinel [Cha+93] is built upon the work of ADAM and ODE and implemented on top of

Zeitgeist [Bla+90]. Sentinel adds the concept of monitoring client objects, and, more importantly, the ability for rules to be triggered from instances that may not be in the same class. By allowing an ECA to be defined in such a way that the condition may examine events on more than one type of object makes it perhaps the closest in terms of its overall intention to PMCs. PMCs could easily be built on top of VERSANT ODBMS, but the heavyweight server approach is not scalable in a large network of clients. PMCs, on the other hand, can be centrally and locally maintained which more effectively distributes the processing around the network.

The monitors are similar in intention to the PMCs predicate-based notification, and the use of Sentinel rules in its new wider context are akin to using PMCs as a modeling facility for relationships where the "many" part of a relationship is implemented as an instance of a PMC. It is important to bear in mind that PMCs were never conceived to address the wider ranging remits of Ode, ADAM, or Sentinel. Rather, they are a practical and efficient attempt to meet the objectives of monitoring (based on predicates as opposed to individual objects), active modeling (using PMCs as active collections), and the pushing of objects in the system. Furthermore, the approach taken by both Sentinel and PMC in allowing predicates or rules to be expressed across classes is a key feature of both systems. In particular, it is often the case that applications really want to register interest in the relationships between two objects rather than the objects themselves. This is what navigable predicates do.

DESIGN RATIONALE

The design of PMCs was driven by a number of objectives: the provision of a cached predicated notification system, the provision of an active collection facility for modeling, scalability in a network environment, and ease of use. In addition to these objectives were a number of constraints: TIBCO's Rendezvous (RV) mechanism was to be used as the reliable broadcast system for notification and Object-Store was to be used as the object database management system. This meant that all notification messages would have to be synchronized through some process (a single point of notification), since RV does not guarantee synchrony across multiple broadcast sources.

A number of possible solutions arise from these constraints. First, we could get ObjectStore to broadcast the changes along with the cache-replaced pages using an RV broadcast for efficiency across many clients, instead of the point-to-point rpc calls it uses at present (see Figure 4–1a). Second, we could use ObjectStore's own notification system (ONS) to inform a notifier process of the updates and have that process broadcast the changes on RV (see Figure 4–1b). Third, we could use a single real updater that could send out notifications through RV, having committed the data to the database, and have pseudo updaters read direct from ObjectStore but send their updates to the update process (see Figure 4–1c).

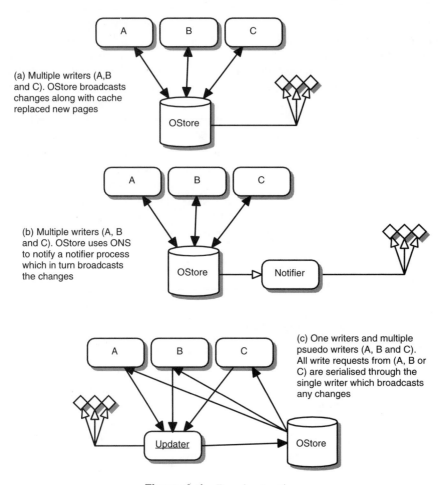

(a) Multiple writers (A,B and C). OStore broadcasts changes along with cache replaced new pages

(b) Multiple writers (A, B and C). OStore uses ONS to notify a notifier process which in turn broadcasts the changes

(c) One writers and multiple psuedo writers (A, B and C). All write requests from (A, B or C) are serialised through the single writer which broadcasts any changes

Figure 4–1   Broadcast options.

The first approach required changes to ObjectStore and was, therefore, outside of our direct control. Given the time constraints on the project it was ruled out in the short term.

The second approach relied on the ObjectStore Notification System (ONS) and required the ability to monitor collections. Given that the ONS works by registering interest in addresses or address ranges rather than an object per se, there is no convenient way of registering interest in a collection object in such a way as to get back what had changed in the collection and so this was ruled out, too.

This left the third approach, which required a restriction on the number of real updaters and introduced a level of indirection. This was deemed acceptable for a number of reasons. First, HOODINI adheres to a three-tier model and so the single updater is no more than the object manager for that component, and the whole PMC system would be under our control. Second, as long as the PMC system was clean and had few interfaces with the rest of HOODINI, we could deliver it to the vendors or use it with a different set of components.

In the next sections we discuss, in detail, the design of PMCs, the notification subsystem, and the techniques employed to make it easy to use.

Predicate Maintained Collections

The Predicate Maintained Collection (PMC) system is divided into two parts. The first part is the collection maintenance subsystem, which is responsible for keeping the custodial result collections up to date in the face of change and recording the changes that have been made. The changes are stored in a structure that we call a "russian doll." The second part is the notification subsystem, which is responsible for taking a russian doll and broadcasting it to interested parties as well as receiving the russian doll and passing it to interested parties. The two subsystems are loosely coupled by a blower/sucker protocol. Access to the collection maintenance subsystem classes by users is strictly through a proxy interface layer. Figure 4–2 below shows the architectural breakdown of the PMC system as a whole.

The Collection Maintenance Subsystem

A PMC is a predicate-based, intentionally defined collection. It consists of a predicate, the intention, used to test objects for membership, and a collection of current members. When an object is created, it may be added to the PMCs collection of current members. The PMC tests the incoming object against its predicate. If the predicate evaluates to true, then the object is added to the collection of current members. If an attempt is made to remove an object from a PMC, it tests that object for membership against the predicate. If the predicate evaluates to true and the ob-

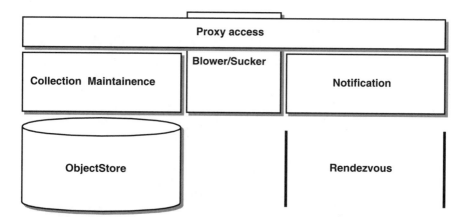

Figure 4–2 PMC architectural.

ject is already contained in the current collection of members, it is removed. Finally, if an object is updated, the PMC is informed. The object is tested for membership. If the predicate evaluates to true and the object is already contained in the collection of members, it notes the update. If the object was not in the collection of members and the predicate evaluated to true, then the object is added to the collection of members. If the predicate evaluates to false and the object was already in the collection of members, it is removed. This technique allows us to incrementally maintain a PMCs collection of current members.

In the PMC system, a predicate is an instrance of the abstract predicate class and can be either a query predicate object (the equivalent of an ObjectStore query) or a function predicate object (the equivalent of a C++ function that returns true or false), both of which derive from the abstract predicate class. All abstract predicates must implement two methods, one to evaluate an object against a query or function and one to evaluate all the members of a target to yield an initial collection of results. The function predicate currently implemented allows runtime type information to be queried, which is used to determine membership against a target class. If the incoming object is of class C and the function predicate looks for class A and its subclasses, then it evaluates to true if C is a subclass of A. Figure 4–3 shows the abstract query and function predicate classes in the context of a partial class lattice.

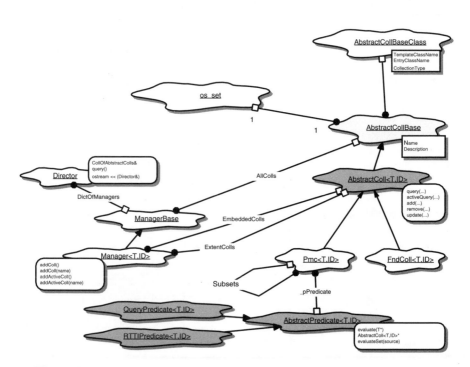

Figure 4–3   Partial class lattice for abstract query and function predicate classes.

In the ObjectStore database, PMCs form a strict hierarchy based on their targets. Those PMCs with an explicit predicate are run against some target PMC. That target may be a PMC that was defined with an explicit predicate or a PMC with an implicit predicate (a logical class extent). Implicit predicates always evaluate to true. A PMC system for a given application is thus a Directed Acyclic Graph (DAG) of PMCs rooted at a logical class extent.

The process of evaluation starts at the top of the DAG performing a depth-first evaluation. If any node in the DAG finds it has nothing more to do, then the evaluation proceeds no further, and so on.

The rationale for "caching" the current collection of members is to shift the burden of maintenance away from the clients and onto the "effective" server—the update process—because of the limited resources available on a trader's workstation. In this way we are able to centrally maintain common PMCs on the update server. At the same time, it is possible to run a query (active or passive) locally against a PMC to which a trader is connected. Active queries are maintained locally because their PMC instance is wholly transient in contrast to the centrally maintained PMCs, which are persistent. Locally maintained PMCs are maintained in much the same way as the centrally maintained PMCs. This provides us with a mechanism to shift the burden of processing from the server to the clients and vice versa so that we can effectively load balance across the network. The incremental behavior of locally maintained PMCs allows the clients to use RAM and CPU more efficiently than they could otherwise.

All PMCs have names. The naming scheme allows applications to easily connect to persistent PMCs. A manager class maintains a persistent collection of PMCs, and this is used when a client application connects to a named PMC by means of a read or write proxy. The only stipulation is that the names must be unique within a class.

Three classes have been implemented that model collections in some form—the abstract collection, foundation collection, and predicate maintained collection. The abstract collection class publishes an interface to which the other two adhere. The foundation collection is little more than a lightweight wrapper around Object-Store's own collection, whereas the PMC provides a record of change (the russian doll). Application designers can use the abstract collection to model the "many" part of uni- or bidirectional relationships. By using the abstract collections in the application model it is possible to use a PMC or a foundation collection as the basis for those embedded collections that participate in a relationship. Furthermore, by providing a change representation method, it is possible to mutate the underlying collection from a foundation to a predicate maintained collection and back, which allows a relationship to change from passive to active or active to passive during the life of the database.

PMCs are separated into three distinct categories. Those that have a predicate that is always true are used as root PMCs for that class; the logical extents and embedded PMCs fall into this category. Those PMCs that have a predicate that has no navigation form the second category—the nodes of a DAG of PMCs, although in practice we may have multiple DAGs, one or more being rooted to the former category of PMCs (a forest rather than a single tree). The third category consists of those that include some navigational expression. These are handled in a completely different way than the other two categories requiring incremental connection between write proxies in an application. Any request to members of this category to evaluate their predicate results in the whole query being run again regardless of the incoming object. This is necessary because the requests for re-evaluation may not have occurred as a result of a change (insert, update, or remove) to objects of the type for which the PMC is defined, but may have occurred due to a change in an object of any of the types that form a component in the navigational expression.

The structure of the collection classes and their associated managers are shown in Figure 4–3. All of the classes in Figure 4–3 may be persistent. They represent the notional object schema for any PMC system in ObjectStore.

The Notification Subsystem

Access to an abstract collection is managed by proxy. Readers and writers attach to a read or a write proxy respectively, naming the abstract collection of interest. If the abstract collection is a PMC, then all of the notification behavior becomes available on demand. The write proxy is the interface between the PMC and the notification subsystem. When an insert, update, or remove is requested, the write proxy delegates the operation to the abstract collection to which it refers. If it is a PMC rather that a foundation collection, it parcels up russian doll, which is a list of lists of DAG nodes that changed, and sends it out over RV as a broadcast. Read proxies listen for broadcast russian dolls of interest to them. These are the same list of lists sent out by the write proxies. The reading application has, in its process space, a portion of the DAG representing the ancestors of the requested PMC. Notification is passed from parent read proxies down to the children read proxies in an analogous fashion to the update server, except that the layers of the notification message are stripped away, and the processing of each layer is analogous to the opening of a russian doll. Any application that explicitly takes a view on a read proxy is then informed of the change. A partial class lattice for the proxies is shown in Figure 4–4.

Figure 4–4 illustrates the proxy access to the PMC system classes. The proxies delegate to the underlying objects to which they are attached. Those objects may be persistent, as in the case of a centrally maintained PMC, or transient, as in the case of a locally maintained PMC.

The efficiency of the notification transport is fundamental to the scalability of PMCs. Point-to-point notification, although more efficient for small systems, does not scale very well for larger systems. The more applications are added to the network, the slower the notification becomes since each client must be visited in turn by the notification process. The notifier has to establish contact and send a notification message to each application that needs to be notified. In a broadcast-based sys-

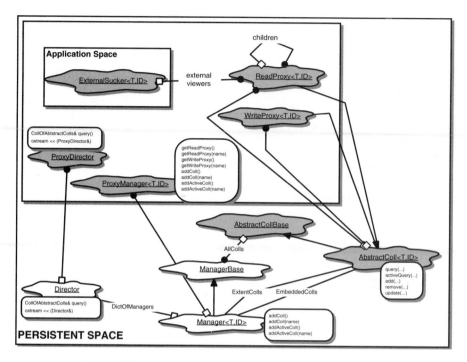

Figure 4–4 Partial class lattice for proxies.

tem, this has to be done exactly once. All notifiable applications register interest by subject and only perform actions if the notification message was broadcast on their subject by the notifier.

In our design we have opted for the single updater that writes to ObjectStore and notifies through RV. One of the reasons behind this is the lack of virtual synchrony in RV. Virtual synchrony would enable us to have multiple sources of notification—and therefore updaters—without having to worry about the order in which notification messages arrive. All broadcast mechanisms suffer from this problem unless they explicitly address the issue of synchronicity [Mul92].

The notification part of PMCs is based around two classes, blowers and suckers. A blower class is a broadcaster that blows to its suckers. Suckers are receivers of information and suck information from their blower. This design pattern is often called "subject and observer" or "publish and subscribe" [Gam+95] and is a common technique in OO design. Two forms of the sucker and blower exist. A blower and sucker receive and send russian dolls internally. This describes the extent of changes to a DAG of PMCs. The more basic form of sucker and blower takes an element of the russian doll: a transaction id, object id, object key, the name of the PMC that changed, and the operation that was used to make the change. The blowers and suckers are implemented as virtual classes. They need to be derived and fully implemented by an application. In this case PMCs are themselves an application that use the blowers and suckers and they present a basic sucker blower protocol for users of the PMC system. To understand more fully the protocol consider the following code fragment:

```
class Blower_t
{
    Blower_t()
    virtual void enrole(Sucker_t& sucker)
    virtual void Changed(Object_t& Myobj)
    {
        for each enroled Sucker_t sucker
                sucker.SuckOn(Myobj)
    }
}
class Sucker_t
{
    Sucker_t(Blower_t& b)
        { b.enrole(this); }
    virtual void SuckOn(Object_t obj)= 0;
}
class Application_t: public Sucker_t
{
    virtual void SuckOn(Object_t& Myobj)
    {
        do something with the changed object
    }
}
```

The SuckOn method is implemented by the application-derived classes so that the application can take appropriate action. In the case above, what is required is that the application refreshes something on screen. The sucker blower protocol used within PMCs is not much different to that described above. The protocol that is presented to the user of PMCs is a little more complex because it needs to differentiate based on the type of change (i.e., an object was added, removed, or updated). The simpler protocol is used between the PMCs, the write proxy, and the notification subsystem to build and to transport a notification message (the russian doll—see Figure 4–5) out onto RV and then between the notification subsystem and the partial DAG of the read proxies to route the change to the appropriate application viewer.

Once the message is processed by a read proxy, the read proxy uses a basic blower-sucker protocol to communicate with the application. Thus, the equivalent of the SuckOn method above decodes the russian doll and calls any one of the virtual methods EltChanged, EltAdded, or EltRemoved that the application implements. Only those read proxies with enrolled application suckers need to do anything in response to this. The static and dynamic behavior of the blowers and suckers is shown in Figures 4–6 and 4–7.

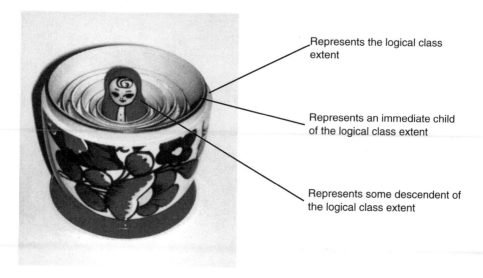

Represents the logical class extent

Represents an immediate child of the logical class extent

Represents some descendent of the logical class extent

Figure 4–5 The Russian Doll.

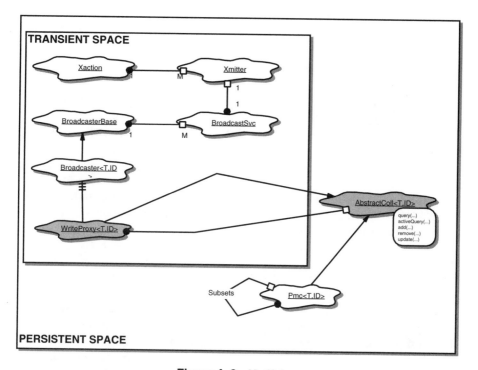

Figure 4–6 Notifying.

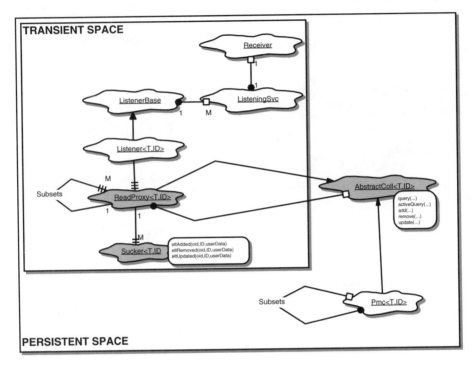

Figure 4–7   Notified.

Complex Predicates

Complex predicates require special processing since a change in one class may affect the membership of objects in a PMC of a different class. To do this, we parse the query string and extract the path expressions and their component path elements. We use the ObjectStore Meta Object Protocol (MOP) library to enable us to correctly identify the types of path elements. Once the path elements have been identified and their types recorded, we connect the custodial PMCs for those types to the PMC requesting the complex query by means of a notification objects blower-sucker protocol. This is shown in Figure 4–8.

The notification object identifies the class that changed and, optionally, the attributes that changed. When any changes occur to any member of any class on a path, the sucker receives notification objects from the top level PMC for the class that changed. If the notification object has not included any attributes marked for change, the custodial results collection is reevaluated. If attributes are included, the custodial collection is only reevaluated if the change might affect its results set. The addition of the attributes allows active navigational queries to be reasonably efficient. Without the attributes, the reevaluation process is very expensive, since reevaluation will take place regardless of the change in the object.

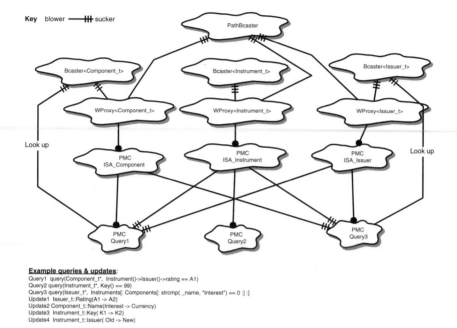

Example queries & updates:
Query1 query(Component_t*, Instrument()->Issuer()->rating == A1)
Query2 query(Instrument_t*, Key() == 99)
Query3 query(Issuer_t*, Instruments[: Components[: strcmp(_name, "Interest") == 0 :] :]
Update1 Issuer_t::Rating(A1 -> A2)
Update2 Component_t::Name(Interest -> Currency)
Update3 Instrument_t::Key(K1 -> K2)
Update4 Instrument_t::Issuer(Old -> New)

Figure 4–8   Updater at run time.

Since the PMCs are loosely coupled to the notification subsystem, those PMCs with a navigation expression must send a russian doll out and onto RV by looking up the appropriate singleton broadcast object and blowing their russian doll to this object.

Ease of Use

Making things easy to use is difficult. For PMCs this has been no exception. Making PMCs easy to use gave rise to a number of requirements as to how to build the system as a whole:

1. Notification (the ability to send or receive) should be parameterized. When a user of PMC requires notification, the whole notification subsystem should be created as a result of that request (see Figure 4–3), and therefore the user should have no knowledge of the underlying network protocol that PMCs use. This is why the read and write proxies have a single parameter to notify or not to notify.
2. PMCs should be templated to allow maximum reuse, and more importantly, to allow them to be used unchanged with any application model.
3. The burden of contractual obligations should be minimal.
4. The system should be safe to use.

Notification—in Detail

The ability to provide notification as a result of the value of a parameter necessitates that the read and write proxies create a number of suckers and blowers that work together to move the notification message from the notifier to RV and from RV to the application. Figures 4–6 and 4–7 show what is constructed in response to this parameter being set to NotifyOn for both a read and write proxy.

Templates

Clearly, PMCs need to be templated on the application object class T. They also require a further template argument so that the "find" method will search on the correct type ID. The ID is the effective primary key for objects of type T.

Contractual Requirements

The interface imposes certain contractual obligations on the user. First, all application classes with instances that are stored in the predicate maintained collections must provide methods to access their type name, used by the ObjectStore query facility, and ID. The type name is in fact represented by an ObjectStore schema generated method called get_os_typespec used for persistent allocation [Obj96] The ID used in the find method, requires the class to include at least a hash function so that ObjectStore can compare objects of type ID.

Safety

Friendship   Friendship has been used to promote rather than break encapsulation. This is particularly evident in the friendship exhibited between blowers and suckers that results in a protected protocol that is not public beyond the classes that derive from it. Thus, the read proxy implements the virtual methods as protected methods, leaving the public interface of the abstract collection unchanged. The same is true of the write proxy class. The class lattice for the protocol is shown in Figure 4–9.

Constness.   The abstract interface presents a number of methods that are overloaded as const and non-const. An example of this is the find method. The philosophy behind this is that a read-only interface (i.e., that provided by the read proxies) implements the const methods and makes the non-const methods protected.

USING PREDICATE MAINTAINED COLLECTIONS

An Example

Consider the application model defined in Figure 4–10 below. All instruments are issued by an issuer, which may issue more than one instrument. An instrument may

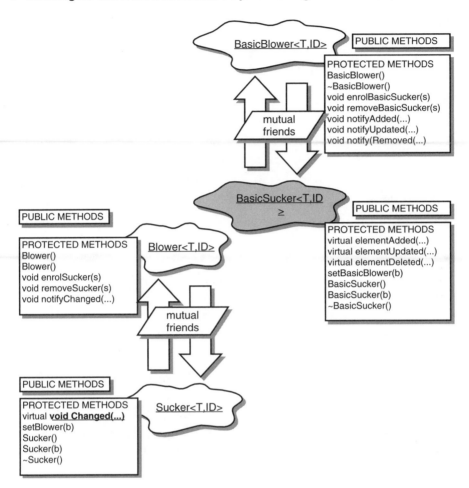

Figure 4–9   Safe blowers and suckers

be any one of three derived class instances, namely Bond (Bond_t), Interest Yielding Bond (IBond), or Currency (Currency_t). All instrument instances are composed of one or more components (Component_t). In this particular model, all classes derive from a single base class (Base_t).

In order to construct an active model, we can either model the "many" part of the relationships as active collections and use embedded PMCs, or we could "attach" the PMCs to ordinary ObjectStore collections. The former is the direct way of active modeling, and the latter is the way in which activeness can be added to a previously passive model. In either case, the update processes for the application model are contractually obliged to manage the notification.

This model is partially defined in C++ as follows:

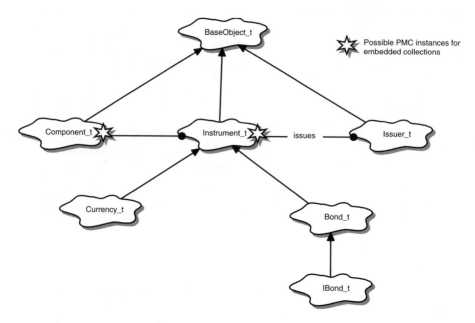

Figure 4–10   An object model.

```
class Base_t {
public:
        Base_t(const Id_t);
        virtual   Base_t();
        Id_t                      id() const;
        static os_typespec*       get_os_typespec();
protected:
        Base_t(const Id_t, ExtentMgmt_t = off);
        Id_t                      _id;
};

class Issuer_t : public Base_t {
public:
        Issuer_t(const Id_t);
        Issuer_t(const Id_t, const char*, const char*);
        virtual   Issuer_t();
            ........
        os_Ref<AbstractColl<Instrument_t,Id_t> Instruments();
        static os_typespec*               get_os_typespec();
protected:
      Issuer_t(const Id_t, ExtentMgmt_t = off);
      Issuer_t(const Id_t, const char*, const char*, ExtentMgmt_t = off);
              ........
      Id_t                                _key;
      ShortName_t                         _name;
      char                                _rating[3];
      os_Ref<AbstractColl<Instrument_t,Id_t>   _rInstruments;
private:
};
```

```
class Instrument_t : public Base_t {
public:
        Instrument_t(Issuer_t&, const Id_t);
        Instrument_t(Issuer_t&, const Id_t, const char*);
        virtual   Instrument_t();
                ........
        os_Ref<AbstractColl<Component_t,Id_t>        Components();
        static os_typespec*                          get_os_typespec();
protected:
        Instrument_t(Issuer_t&, const Id_t, ExtentMgmt_t=off);
        Instrument_t(Issuer_t&, const Id_t, const char*, ExtentMgmt_t=off);
                ........
        Id_t                 _key;
        ShortName_t          _name;
        os_Ref<Issuer_t>     _rIssuer;
        os_Ref<AbstractColl<Component_t,Id_t>        _rComponents;

private:
};


class Component_t : public Base_t {
public:
        Component_t(Instrument_t&, const Id_t);
        Component_t(Instrument_t&, const Id_t, const char*);
        virtual   Component_t();
                ........
        static os_typespec* get_os_typespec();
protected:
        Component_t(Instrument_t&, const Id_t, ExtentMgmt_t=off);
        Component_t(Instrument_t&, const Id_t, const char*, ExtentMgmt_t=off);
                ........
        Id_t                      _key;
        ShortName_t               _name;
        os_Ref<Instrument_t>      _rInstrument;

private:
};
class Bond_t : public Instrument_t {
public:
      Bond_t(Issuer_t&, const Id_t);
      Bond_t(Issuer_t&, const Id_t, const char*);
      virtual   Bond_t();
      static os_typespec* get_os_typespec();
protected:
      Bond_t(Issuer_t&, const Id_t, ExtentMgmt_t=off);
      Bond_t(Issuer_t&, const Id_t, const char*, ExtentMgmt_t=off);
private:
};


class Currency_t : public Instrument_t {
public:
      Currency_t(Issuer_t&, const Id_t);
```

```
        Currency_t(Issuer_t&, const Id_t, const char*);
        virtual   Currency_t();
        static os_typespec* get_os_typespec();
protected:
        Currency_t(Issuer_t, const Id_t, ExtentMgmt_t=off);
        Currency_t(Issuer_t, const Id_t, const char*, ExtentMgmt_t=off);
private:
};


class IBond_t : public Bond_t {
public:
        IBond_t(Issuer_t, const Id_t);
        IBond_t(Issuer_t, const Id_t, const char*);
        virtual   IBond_t();
        static os_typespec* get_os_typespec();
protected:
        IBond_t(Issuer_t, const Id_t, ExtentMgmt_t=off);
        IBond_t(Issuer_t, const Id_t, const char*, ExtentMgmt_t=off);
private:
};
```

The relationship between Instrument_t and Issuer_t is implemented as an Object-Store reference to an abstract collection of instruments and an ObjectStore reference to an issuer. Likewise, the same relationship exists between an Instrument_t and a Component_t.

In building an active model, it is necessary to implement some active semantics that manage the notification of changes to the model's instances; whereas, the addition of active queries does not require the model to be imbued with any extra semantics at all. In the PMC system, all that is required is that the extents are active and managed accordingly. The only extra code required is to manage updates to objects already in an extent.

The following code fragment shows how instruments, bonds, and issuers set up their class extents—the other classes are analogous. Note the use of the protected constructor, called from Bond_t. This is to ensure that the extent management happens once and at the correct point in the construction of the object, otherwise an object could be added to an extent once for each superclass from which it is derived and without the benefit of being fully constructed. An alternative approach to this would be to implement a factory or manager class that would perform all allocation, updating, and deletion of objects of a given type and perform all extent maintenance. Although we have not taken that approach here, it is one that we have adhered to in HOODINI and one that we consider to be the better of the two.

Note the use of the manager proxy class to construct write proxies for the class extents, and also note the use of the write proxy constructor to attach a proxy directly to an embedded collection.

```
//
// Adding a new instrument to the database
//
Instrument_t::Instrument_t(Issuer_t& i, const Id_t id, const char* s)
:Basebject_t(id, off),
 _key(id)
{
        _name = s;
        _Issuer(i);
        //
        // Extent Mgmt
        //
        ManagerProxy<Instrument_t,Id_t>& mgr = ManagerProxy
                                        <Instrument_t,Id_t>::singleton();
        WriteProxy<Instrument_t,Id_t> *wp mgr.readProxy(NotifyOn);
        wp->add(this);
}


// Protected constructor
Instrument_t::Instrument_t(Issuer_t&amp; i, const Id_t id, const char* s,
                        ExtentMgmt em=off)
:Basebject_t(id, off),
_key(id)
{
        _name = s;
        _Issuer(i);
        if (em == on)
        {
                // Extent Mgmt
                ManagerProxy<Instrument_t,Id_t>& mgr = ManagerProxy
                                        <Instrument_t,Id_t>::singleton();
                WriteProxy<Instrument_t,Id_t> *wp = mgr.writeProxy(NotifyOn);
                wp->add(this);
        }
}
//
// Managing the relationship between Instruments and Issuers
//
Instrument_t::_Issuer(Issuer_t I)
{
        _rIssuer = I;
        i._addInstrument(*this);
}
Issuer_t::_addInstrument(Instrument_t& I)
{
        //
        // Attach write proxy directly to the embedded collection and
        // add instrument to issuers embedded PMC and notify of addition
        //
        WriteProxy<Instrument_t,Id_t> wpForInstr(_rInstrument,NotifyOn);
        wpForInstr.add(&amp;i);
```

```
        //
        // Notify that this issuer has been changed
        //
        ManagerProxy<Issuer_t,Id_t>& mgr = ManagerProxy
                                    <Issuer_t,Id_t>::singleton();
        WriteProxy<Issuer_t,Id_t> *wp = mgr.writeProxy(NotifyOn);
        wp->update(this);
}
//
// Adding a new bond to the database
//
Bond_t::Bond_t(Issuer_t&amp; i, const Id_t id, const char* s)
:Instrument_t(id, off),
 _key(id)
{
        _name = s;
        _Issuer(i);
        //
        // Extent Mgmt
        //
        ManagerProxy<Instrument_t,Id_t>& mgr = ManagerProxy
                                    <Instrument_t,Id_t>::singleton();
        WriteProxy<Instrument_t,Id_t> *wp = mgr.writeProxy(NotifyOn);
        wp->add(this);
}
```

Changes or updates to either end of the relationship between an Instrument_t and an Issuer_t are handled as follows:

```
// changing an instruments issuer should result in the old issuer
// sending notification that it's embedded collection of instruments
// changed, that it's class extent changed, that the new issuer's
// embedded collection changed and the class extent for the issuer
// changed and that the instrument's class extent changed.
void Instrument_t::Issuer(Issuer_t&amp; I)
{
        _rIssuer->_removeInstrument(this);
        _rIssuer = I;
        _rIssuer->_addInstrument(this);
        ManagerProxy<Instrument_t,Id_t>& mgr = ManagerProxy
                                    <Instrument_t,Id_t>::singleton();
        WriteProxy<Instrument_t,Id_t> *wp = mgr.writeProxy(NotifyOn);
        wp->update(this);
}
```

Consider the following database with instances of those classes described in the model above. With respect to the PMCs, we might have something akin to that shown in Figure 4–11 below.

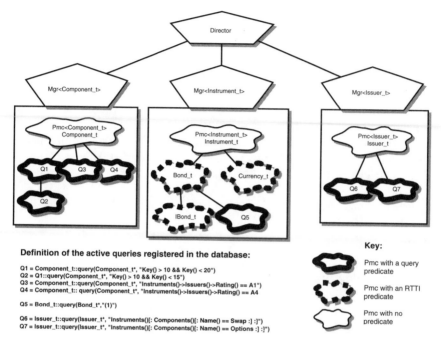

Definition of the active queries registered in the database:

Q1 = Component_t::query(Component_t*, "Key() > 10 && Key() < 20")
Q2 = Q1::query(Component_t*, "Key() > 10 && Key() < 15")
Q3 = Component_t::query(Component_t*, "Instruments()->Issuers()->Rating() == A1")
Q4 = Component_t:: query(Component_t*, "Instruments()->Issuers()->Rating() == A4

Q5 = Bond_t::query(Bond_t*,"(1)")

Q6 = Issuer_t::query(Issuer_t*, "Instruments()[: Components()[: Name() == Swap :] :]")
Q7 = Issuer_t::query(Issuer_t*, "Instruments()[: Components()[: Name() == Options :] :]")

Key:

Pmc with a query predicate

Pmc with an RTTI predicate

Pmc with no predicate

Figure 4–11 An example database showing the DAG of PMCs

A reader attaches to PMCs by naming them through the ManagerProxy for that template elaboration. Thus, for the queries Q2, Q3, and Q6, we would have to write something akin to:

```
ManagerProxy<Component_t,Id_t>& componentMgr = ManagerProxy
                                    <Component_t,Id_t>::singleton();
ReadProxy<Component_t,Id_t> *pQ2, *pQ3;

ManagerProxy<Issuer_t,Id_t>& issuerMgr = ManagerProxy
                                    <Issuer_t,Id_t>::singleton();
ReadProxy<Issuer_t,Id_t> *pQ6;

pQ2 = componentMgr.readProxyFor("Q1",NotifyOn);
pQ3 = componentMgr.readProxyFor("Q3",NotifyOn);
pQ6 = issuerMgr.readProxyFor("Q6",NotifyOn);
```

If we wished to create active queries on the fly, we would need to query against some target and thereby create a locally maintained active query. Suppose we wished to do this for the query Q7. We would do the following:

```
ReadProxy<Issuer_t,Id_t> *issuers, *pLQ7;

// Get extents
issuers = issuerMgr.readProxy();
pLQ7 = issuers->query("Issuer_t*","Instruments()[:Components()[: name =
    "Swap":]:]");
```

The applications "view" their read proxies by attaching a PmcBasicSucker to the proxies on creation. Thus the application that wants to receive notifications for the queries above (both centrally and locally maintained) would derive from PmcBasic-Sucker some "viewing class" (which we call "class Viewer") for each template elaboration and attach as follows:

```
new componentViewer(pQ2);
new componentViewer(pQ3);
new issuerViewer(pQ6);
new issuerViewer(pLQ7);
```

The viewers for the two reader processes (Reader A and Reader B) are denoted by matchstick men icons, in Figure 4–12. The attachment of the viewers to their proxies is the same kind of attachment as that between the source of the locally maintained active query LQ7 and its results write proxy. The returned read proxy for this locally maintained active query is informed of change from the associated write proxy in the same process space.

    In the simple case when an object that is a member of the any of the centrally maintained PMCs (e.g., Q1 through to Q7) changes, a russian doll message is generated on the updater and broadcast. Any listener that is interested does the following:

```
FOREACH sucker (rp) // The Listener is a blower of russian dolls
    BLOW russian doll
```

Each of the receiving suckers, which are all read proxies for class extents (Instrument_t, Component_t, and Issuer_t), does the following:

```
IF outer layer is for me THEN
    BLOW basic change // either notifyUpdates, notifyAdded or notifyRemoved
    BLOW inner layer of the russian doll
```

In this way the russian doll is opened, processed, and discarded, and the inner doll is passed down the DAG. Each read proxy that has something to process blows a basic change to the application viewers attached to it.

    In the complex case, the application may have a complex predicate being maintained locally (e.g., LQ7). In this case, any changes to instances of the owning type (Issuer_t) are handed on to a write proxy for the local (transient) PMC. This write proxy acts as a specialized issuer viewer. In response to an EltAdded, EltUpdated, or EltRemoved, an appropriate call is made through the write proxy and delegated to the local PMC. Any russian dolls generated as a result are passed through

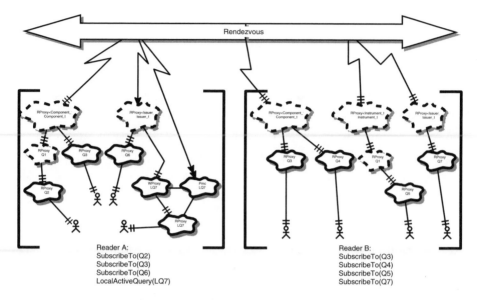

Figure 4–12   Client proxies showing two processes and their partial DAGs.

the normal russian doll blower-sucker connection to the read proxy and then to the real application viewer for the local active query. For changes to related object instances, the local PMC listens to the path change, channel (denoted by the double headed arrow), which informs the local PMC of changes to other class instances. In response to such a change, the PMC may re-evaluate itself and look up its read proxy so that it can send a russian doll that describes the changes that may have taken place. The rest is analogous to the simple case.

EXPERIENCES AND SUMMARY

Problems

A number of problems arise from the approach we have taken.

1. The need to enforce an update method that is only required to inform the system about a change. It would be much better if this could be done automatically by using some ObjectStore notification and an appropriate action to direct the update internally. This would have the effect of making the interface to the abstract collection and its derivatives much cleaner and more akin to normal collection behavior, which only knows about insertions and deletions.
2. The current compiler does not scale well for large template elaborations and PMCs are heavily templated. A solution to this is to provide an in-line template interface with the internals, as far as possible, being non-templated.

Future Work

CGI/Java Interface for Active Queries

A more immediate future development is to use predicate maintained collections across the world wide web. This work requires us to build a CGI or Java interface that pushes data out based on notifications received. A simple interface could be constructed such that the read proxies for a PMC would sit on an ObjectStore client and the viewers that attach to the proxies would provide a CGI or Java interface to the requesting WWW client. Our initial investigations suggest that this will work well with Netscape's Navigator and would provide us with the ability to attach Netscape to predicate maintained collections and for that session to be continually updated asynchronously.

Performance Evaluation

A real data model is being constructed using PMCs. Extensive performance evaluation will take place to establish the costs and the benefits of this approach as compared to continually re-evaluating queries on demand. We expect to see a marked improvement over the latter, particularly with respect to large scale networks of clients.

REFERENCES

[Bla+90] J. A. Blakeley, C. W. Thompson, A. M. Alashqur: *Zeitgest query language (zql)*. Technical Report TR-90-03-01, Texas Instruments, USA.

[Cha+93] S. Chakravarthy, E. Anar, L. Maugis. *Design and Implementation of Active Capability for an Object-Oriented Database*. Technical Report UF-CIS-TR-93-001.
   (http://www.cise.ufl.edu/~sharma/publication/tr93.list.html).

[Dia+91] O. Diaz, N. Paton, P. Gray: *Rule Management in OODBMS: A Unified Approach*. Proceedings 17th Intl Conf on VLDB, Barcelona, Spain, September 1991.

[Gam+95] E. Gamma, R. Helm, R. Johnson, J. Vlissides: *Design Patterns—Elements of Reusable Object-Oriented Software*. Addison-Wesley, 1995.

[Geh+92] N. H. Gehani, H. V. Jagadish, O. Shmueli, *Event Specification in an Active Oriented-Database*. Proceedings ACM SIGMOD Intl Conf on Management of Data, San Diego CA, June 1992, pp. 81–90.

[Gem95] *GemStone Programming Guide*. Chapter 12, section 34.
   (http://www.gemstone.com).

[MD89] D. R. McCarthy, U. Dayal: *The Architecture of an Active Database Management System*. Proceedings ACM SIGMOD Intl Conf on Management of Data, Portland, OR, May-June 1989.

[Mul92] S. Mullender (ed.), *Distributed Systems*, Chapter 15. Addison-Wesley, 1992.

[Obj96] *ObjectStore C++ API Reference Release 4.*
(http://www.odi.com).

[Poe96] *Poet 3.0 Technical Overview.*
(http://www.poet.com).

[Tib96] *Rendezvous API Reference Manual.*
(http://www.tibco.com).

[Ver96] *Versant Reference Manual C++ API*, Chapters 12 and 13.
(http://www.versant.com).

II

Applications and Design

INTRODUCTION

We are not aware of any previously published work that describes the use of object databases for flight-simulation, so Chapter 5 by Alagic is particulalry interesting and unique. It shows how OO techniques in general, such as inheritance, polymorphism, etc. can be used to model the complex control systems of an aircraft. The chapter also presents code examples for use on the O_2 object database system, illustrating application of some of these OO modeling concepts. The chapter also includes a useful critique of the O_2 data model and the ODMG model, highlighting the limitations of each for supporting flight simulations. Such product critiques can be quite valuable, particularly because vendors can claim to support a standard, but there is no certification process to test such claims.

A typical situation in many organizations is that considerable data are held in file systems, perhaps using some kind of hierarchical structure and naming scheme to identify a particular datum. Genome and biomedical data are commonly managed this way. Individual scientists will typically keep data local to them, giving themselves both flexibility and control. However, inevitably, a result is that data sharing between scientists can be very poor. Chapter 6 by Stacy, Augustine and Robb describes a compromise solution to these competing demands. They describe a system, called the Biomedical Object Storage System (BOSS), that provides image visualization and analysis of biomedical data. Several applications are built using VERSANT to view and manipulate images held in the file system.

In Chapter 7, Fäustle describes an integration framework for a scheduling system using Rational Rose and Objectivity/DB. He reports the features of both products that were found to be useful, and offers insights about some of these products' limitations. He also emphasizes the importance of understanding access paths in improving performance. According to Fäustle, 50–60 percent performance improvements were achieved by using clustering alone. Tuning using other product-specific features also resulted in noticeable improvements.

Configuration Management (CM) is useful in many domains, such as software engineering and product evolution and development. It provides a mechanism to treat groups of objects as a unit. For example, a particular software release may consist of a number of modules, makefiles, documentation, etc. which together represent the components that comprise that version of the software. Few object databases, however, support CM directly. Chapter 8 by Meo describes a complete CM system built using Objectivity/DB, taking advantage of its multi-user services, versioning facilities and support for bi-directional associations to guarantee referential integrity between CM components.

Object databases are often associated with engineering applications, although as discussed earlier, the technology has moved into more mainstream commercial use. There is a growing set of examples where object databases are appearing in more "traditional" MIS applications. Chapter 9 by Schlueter and Stahl describes their positive experiences using VERSANT. They particularly emphasize the benefits they found in having a seamless interface between the programming language and the database facilities. They also highlight the importance of understanding product-specific features, such as VERSANT's object-level locking, which influenced their choice of object database product.

A criticism that is often targeted at object databases is that they supposedly do not scale well. The myth is that they are suitable for storing only a few megabytes of data accessed by a small number of users. Chapter 10 by Shiers, however, debunks this myth. Whilst much of what is discussed is "futures", there is also evidence presented to show that object database scalability can be achieved. The two major requirements of the project described are large volumes of data (multipetabyte) and longevity (15–20 years). The example also emphasizes using off-the-shelf solutions for object persistence and adhering to industry standards. These guidelines are adopted in many organizations. Shiers reports on some initial experiences using Objectivity/DB, which look promising for the future. This chapter should also encourage others who are wondering whether object database technology is scalable to truly very large databases.

Brunner, Szalay and Wade describe another project that challenges the claim that object databases cannot scale. Like the earlier chapter by Shiers, Chapter 11 reports upon a system for managing very large quantities of complex data about stars, galaxies, etc. The complexity arises because the data may take a variety of forms, such as text, images, derived parameters, etc. The system is designed to support data mining and when fully operational will be storing tens of terabytes of data. The design is also flexible enough to meet future requirements. The authors additionally describe a geometrical indexing technique that they developed based on Objectivity/DB's container architecture. This particular project was not constrained by existing database technology, since it was started from scratch, and there were no preconceptions about which kind of database management system to use.

5

Flight-Simulator Database: Object-Oriented Design and Implementation

Suad Alagic, Wichita State University

ABSTRACT

The design and implementation experiences from an object-oriented flight simulator database project are analyzed. This specific class of applicative systems is important for aircraft and aviation industry, transportation, defense, and research. The object-oriented technology is shown to be the most appropriate generic database technology for the purpose. The reasons are structural and behavioral complexity of objects in this particular application environment, computational completeness re-

The work that is reported in this paper has been carried out while the author was supported as Faculty Fellow of the National Institute for Aviation Research. In addition, this material is based upon work supported in part by the U.S. Army Research Office under Grant no. DAAH04-96-1-0192. The equipment of the Object-Oriented Research Lab used in this project has been funded by a DOD Research Instrumentation Award under Defense University Initiative, Grant No. DAAH04-95-1-0007.

The author would like to thank Jenny Yen-Li Liew, Robert Harder and Anding Greich for their contributions to the object-oriented flight simulator database project. Their views influenced parts of this paper. It is regrettable that due to their other commitments they were unable to collaborate on this chapter. Svetlana Kouznetsova and Jose Solorzano made a number of comments that improved the final version of this paper.

quired by fairly sophisticated aerodynamic models, and significant gains in software reusability based on an elaborate inheritance hierarchy in the model. The project has been implemented using O_2. Features of O_2 relevant to this project are also analyzed and compared with the emerging industrial standard (ODMG).

INTRODUCTION: WHY OBJECT-ORIENTED FLIGHT SIMULATOR TECHNOLOGY?

This project is believed to be the first in which object-oriented database technology has been applied to flight simulators. Our hope is that our work will have considerable practical implications on how flight simulators will be developed in the future.

There are several decisive reasons why object-oriented technology is particularly suitable for flight simulators. The main advantage of the object-oriented technology is that it offers a suitable general modeling paradigm supported by the underlying software technology. The paradigm is capable of capturing both structural and behavioral complexity of flight simulator systems. It is hard to imagine that any other existing generic technology would be more appropriate. Indeed, the overall environment requires structurally and behaviorally complex models. But it also requires proper technology to manage the complexity of the software system. Further requirements are advanced visualization and database management techniques.

Flight simulators have been developed so far in a large number of specific projects, with ad hoc software techniques and ad hoc data management techniques. The level of reuse of effort of numerous teams has been very low. Object-oriented technology has a major advantage in offering generic solutions that can be used by a variety of teams. Such a generic model and the associated class library will be a specific deliverable of this project. The expected savings in cost and the required time to develop specific flight simulators by tailoring a generic one via inheritance are very significant.

The fact that the object-oriented paradigm is computationally complete is a further significant advantage of the object-oriented technology. Flight simulators are based on fairly sophisticated aerodynamic models. In the object-oriented technology these models can be expressed in a uniform and unified environment. By way of comparison, relational technology could not offer this advantage. In addition, relational technology cannot express properly the structural and behavioral complexity of flight simulator systems.

Modeling structurally complex objects in O_2 for a flight simulator system is addressed in the next section. In the following sections we illustrate other topics, such as single and multiple inheritance as it appears in the conceptual modeling of a flight simulator system. Further aspects of modeling complex structure using polymorphic type constructors of O_2 are discussed. We discuss the underlying type system of O_2 and its implications in this particular application. Modeling of the airplane's control system is discussed, and behavioral, aerodynamic modeling, is the next topic. This is where the operational part of the object-oriented model becomes particularly critical, as well as its computational completeness. The role of object-oriented queries in flight simulator systems, with illustrations in OQL, is also discussed. The model of persistence in O_2 and its suitability for this particular class of applications, is analyzed, and we discuss active database management facilities (constraints and triggers) required for flight simulators and lacking in O2. Finally, we analyze O_2, and compare its features with the ODMG Standard [Cat96]. Two basic conclusions that follow from our experience in this project are given.

Computing Infrastructure

A prototype implementation of object-oriented flight simulator technology [Ala96] has been carried out in a lab equipped with a multiprocessor SUN server workstation, a multimedia SGI server workstation with powerful 3D graphic features, and a collection of high-quality, large-screen NCD X-stations. The software environment consists of an object-oriented programming environment based on C++, a separate, less elaborate object-oriented programming environment based on Eiffel, two object-oriented database management systems (ODE and O_2), and an object-oriented simulation package. Database management aspects have been implemented using O_2 running on all the machines. The graphic package that has been used is OpenGL.

COMPLEX OBJECTS: AIRPLANE MODEL

Structural complexity of objects in flight simulator systems is the first reason why object-oriented technology is much more suitable for this class of applications in comparison with relational technology. An illustration is the airplane object itself. It has complex structure consisting of airframe, control system, a set of instruments, dynamics, position, and orientation. This particular view reflects the requirements of flight simulation. Other models are, of course, possible.

```
class Airplane read type
     tuple(model: string,
           pilot: Person,
           controls: Control_system,
           instruments: set(Instrument),
           frame: Air_frame,
           dynamics: Dynamics,
           position: Location,
           orientation: Orientation)
end;
```

Methods are omitted in the first few samples of classes, and only the structural part is given. The components of the airplane object are themselves complex. For example, components of airframe are wings, fuselage, empennage, and the power plant.

```
class Air_frame read type
     tuple (left_wing, right_wing: Wing,
          fuselage: Fuselage,
          empennage: Empennage,
          engines: list(Engine))
end;
```

This decomposition along has-a relationships proceeds further until the required level of detail for flight simulation is reached.

A distinctive feature of the O_2 data model right from the very beginning [LR89] is that it offers both objects and values. Objects are instances of classes. Objects are equipped with identity and communicate via messages. Values are instances of types. Values may also be complex, but they do not have identity and are thus not shared. The same philosophy has been accepted in the ODMG Standard [Cat96]. In the class Airplane, Location and Orientation would be examples of structured types, rather than classes. Situations in which this distinction is natural appear quite often in this application and also in further sample classes given in this chapter.

Classes in this chapter are typically specified as read types with public methods. According to O_2 access rules, this means that components of an object of such a class can be accessed directly in read-only mode and changed only by the methods of the class. Other options in O_2 are private (default) and public [O2T95b].

Inheritance

Conceptual modeling of flight simulator applications requires both single and multiple inheritance, illustrated in Figures 5–1 and 5–2. The fact that O_2 supports multiple inheritance is a plus.

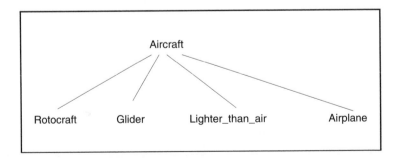

Figure 5–1   Single inheritance.

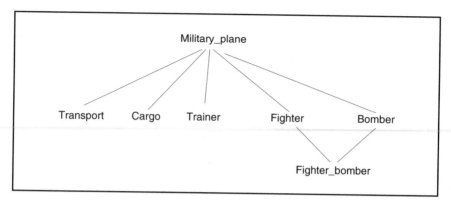

Figure 5–2 Multiple inheritance.

TYPE CONSTRUCTORS: AIRPORT MODEL

In addition to tuple, O_2 offers two polymorphic type constructors: list and set. The list constructor covers list and array constructors of the ODMG object model, set corresponds to bag, and unique set corresponds to the set ODMG type constructors. These types of constructors are essential for the proper modeling of the flight simulator database, as illustrated by the following examples.

```
class Airport read type
     tuple (name: string,
          runways: list(Runway),
          patterns: list(Pattern),
          structures: set(Structure),
          location: Location,
          ramp: Ramp)
end;
```

The components of an airport object are thus its name, a list of runways, a list of traffic patterns, a set of ground structures (such as buildings), the airport's location, and its ramp (a parking area for aircraft). A ground structure has a shape, height, and location.

```
class Structure read type
     tuple(shape: Shape,
          height: float,
          location: Location)
end;
```

A ramp has a shape, a set of aircraft, and methods such as park and taxi an aircraft.

```
class Ramp read type
     tuple(shape: Shape,
           aircraft: set(Aircraft))
     method public park_aircraft(a: Aircraft),
           public taxi_aircraft(a: Aircraft, r: Runway)
end;
```

POLYMORPHISM AND COVARIANCE

In O_2 inheritance coincides with subtyping. The argument types and the result type of a method redefined in a derived class can be both extended covariantly. This is a discipline adopted in Eiffel and it causes some well-known problems [Coo89]. The ODMG object model does not suffer from these problems. But the type system underlying the ODMG object model is not sound either for entirely different reasons [Ala97].

Support for parametric polymorphism in O_2 is limited. It is not available in the schema definition language and certainly not in O_2C. The ODMG object model also has a limited way of supporting parametric polymorphism for collection classes. It appears that other generic classes cannot be defined either. Parametric polymorphism is supported in the C++ bindings of both O_2 and the ODMG Standard.

This limitation is a drawback that shows up in our particular application. For example, Queue cannot be defined as a generic class. A way around this problem is presented below. Queue is defined in such a way that it contains elements of type object, where object is the root of the inheritance hierarchy in O_2. Since subtype polymorphism coincides with inheritance, objects of any type may be placed in the queue. In fact, they can be of different types, which is not the idea behind parametric polymorphism.

A specific queue type such as `Aircraft_queue` is now derived by inheritance from the Queue class. The type of queue elements is necessarily derived by inheritance from the type object. Note that the argument type for the enqueue method is not redefined. Thus an object of any class may be placed in the queue. On the other hand, the result type of dequeue method has been redefined covariantly. The reason for this is that an object dequeued from an aircraft queue had better be of type Aircraft as opposed to being just of type object. By way of comparison, this is not possible in the ODMG object model.

```
class Queue read type
     queue: list(object),
     method public enqueue(a: object),
            public dequeue: object,
            public number_of_objects: integer
end;

class Aircraft_queue inherit Queue
     read type queue: list(Aircraft),
     method public dequeue: Aircraft
end;
```

Two illustrations of using the class `Aircraft_queue` are given below. One of them is modeling runways and the other is modeling traffic patterns.

```
class Runway read type
      tuple(shape: Shape,
            elevation: float,
            heading: integer,
            aircraft: Aircraft_queue)
      method public enqueue(a: Aircraft),
            public dequeue: Aircraft
end;

class Pattern read type
      tuple(shape: Shape,
            aircraft: Aircraft_queue)
      method public enqueue(a: Aircraft),
            public dequeue: Aircraft
end;
```

CONTROL SYSTEM MODELING

The control system of an aircraft is an object that accepts messages that are actuator commands created by moving stick, pressing pedals, changing throttle position, changing flaps' deflections, and so on. These commands affect the positions of airplane's control surfaces (ailerons, elevators, rudder, and flaps). Additional effects include speed brakes and the landing gear positions [Ala+96].

```
class Control_system read type
      controls: Controls,
      method public move_stick(s: float),
            public press_pedals(p: float),
            public change_throttle(t: float),
            public change_flaps(f: float)
end;

class Controls read type
      tuple (aileron_deflection: float,
            elevator_deflection: float,
            rudder_deflection: float,
            flap_deflection: float,
            speed_brake_deflection: boolean,
            landing_gear_position: boolean,
            throttle_position: float)
method public change_elevator_deflection(e: float),
            public change_aileron_deflection(a: float),
            public change_rudder_deflection(r: float),
            public change_flap_deflection(f: float),
            public change_speed_brake_deflection,
```

```
        public change_landing_gear_position,
        public change_throttle_position(t: float)
end;
```

BEHAVIORAL MODELING: AERODYNAMICS

A particularly critical reason for object-oriented technology in this application is that the key object—aircraft—happens to be not only structurally complex, but it also exhibits complex behavioral patterns. For this reason a conventional technology such as relational is simply inappropriate. Behavior of an aircraft is governed by an aerodynamic model, which is expressed by the equations of motion [Gal96]. These equations determine three linear and three angular accelerations represented as the results of public methods of the class Dynamics (see also Figure 5–3). The state components of the dynamics object are complex and contain properties relevant for computing the results of the acceleration methods [Ala+96].

```
class Dynamics read type
        tuple (inertia: float,
              forces: Forces_and_Moments,
              geometry: Geometric_properties,
              observers: Observers)
method public acceleration_X: float,
        public acceleration_Y: float,
        public acceleration_Z: float,
        public roll_acceleration: float,
        public pitch_acceleration: float,
        public yaw_acceleration: float
end;
```

Aerodynamic forces and moments acting on an aircraft change all the time and are thus specified via methods of the class Forces_and_Moments.

```
class Forces_and_Moments read type
        tuple (observers: Observers,
              controls: Controls,
              geometry: Geometric_properties)
method public lift_force: float,
        public drag_force: float,
        public side_force: float,
        public roll_moment: float,
        public pitch_moment: float,
        public yaw_moment: float,
        public weight_force: float,
        public thrust_force: float
end;
```

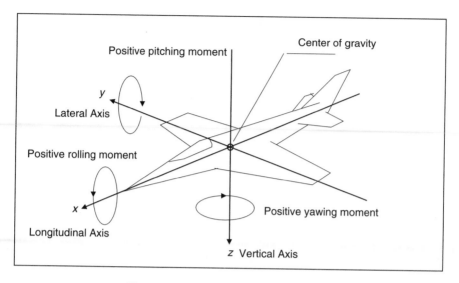

Figure 5–3   Airplane body axis system.

The observers and the geometric properties of an object of the above class and the corresponding components of the dynamics object of the same aircraft object are naturally meant to be shared. Ensuring the associated integrity constraints is not a simple matter, because O_2 supports neither constraints nor triggers (see section below). An alternative approach would be to use relationships as defined in the ODMG Standard. But in O_2 they are supported only in the C++ interface.

Another collection of parameters that enter into the equations of motion are various external manifestations of aircraft behavior. These observable properties also change all the time and are thus represented as methods of the class Observers (see also Figure 5–4).

```
class Observers read type
method public angle_of_attack: float,
       public angle_of_attack _rate: float,
       public sideslip_angle: float,
       public roll_rate: float,
       public pitch_rate: float,
       public yaw_rate: float,
       public air_speed: float,
       public air_density: float
end;
```

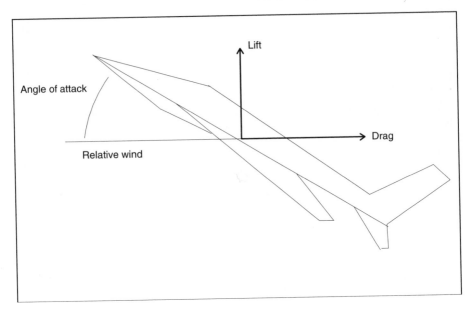

Figure 5–4   Stability axis aero forces.

QUERIES

To our knowledge, query facilities are completely absent in all other existing flight simulator technologies. Yet there are at least two distinct situations in which such facilities are really needed. One of them is the flight simulator design phase, which is necessarily based on querying a suitable database. The other situation is selection of a flight simulator environment, which consists of a particular aircraft type, a ground environment model (for example, an airport), and an air environment model. The air environment model is not discussed in this chapter. Both situations require searching of a suitable object-oriented database. Sample OQL queries typical for this application are given below.

```
select tuple(name: a.name,
      distance: a.location.distance_from(p.location))
from a in Airport, r in a.runways
      p in Airplane,
where r.elevation < 1000
      and a.location.distance_from(p.location) < 200
      and r.heading = 180
      and r.number_of_objects < 3
      and p = my_aircraft
```

```
select p
from a in Airport,
     p in a.ramp.aircraft,
where p.model = "Boeing 777"
     and a.location = my_location

select max(p.frame.left_wing.span + p.frame.right_wing.span)
from a in Airport,
     r in a.runways,
     p in r.aircraft
where a.location = my_location
```

PERSISTENCE AND DYNAMIC BINDING

The model of persistence in O_2 is based on naming and reachability [O2T95b, O2T95c, O2T95d]. Thus an object that is assigned a name becomes persistent. A name is an external handle that allows quick access to the associated object. Components of a persistent object are also persistent (reachability). This well-known model is perfectly suitable for flight simulator applications. For example, making an aircraft object persistent without making all of its direct and indirect components persistent (reachability) would be useless from the point of view of flight simulation.

Unlike the example above, in a sample illustration given below in O_2C, we will assume that the type Airport has been defined as a public type. The implication is that its components can be manipulated directly outside of methods of the Airport class. A named persistent airport object is created first. ICT is persistent because it has a name specified in the schema. A transient building object is then created. This transient object is inserted into the set of the airport's ground structures. Now the inserted object becomes persistent as it participates in a set, which is a component of a persistent object.

The for loop illustrates a situation in which dynamic binding would be important. As there are different subtypes of ground structures, represented by derived classes of the class structure, specific display methods will be chosen depending upon the runtime type of the object referred to by q.

```
run body{ ICT = new Airport;
          o2 Structure building = new Structure;
          ICT->structures + = set(building);

          o2 Structure q;
          for (q in ICT->structures)
             {q->display};
          }
```

CONSTRAINTS AND TRIGGERS

A flight simulator database is naturally an active database. Unfortunately, O_2 lacks declarative constraint and trigger specification facilities. From the viewpoint of this particular application, this is probably the most serious conceptual drawback of O_2, (sample classes that follow are thus not in O_2). They illustrate facilities that are needed in this application. Those facilities include soft and hard constraints, one-time, perpetual and timed triggers. They are all offered by ODE, an object-oriented database management system [GJ91] that has been used extensively in our Lab. But ODE is to our knowledge only a research prototype.

A hard constraint is enforced after execution of every public method. If it is not satisfied, the transaction executing the method is aborted. An example is given below.

```
class Passenger_plane inherit Airplane read type
tuple( ...
     seating_capacity: integer),
method public book_passenger(p: Person),
     public number_of_passengers: integer,
     ...
constraint hard:
     self->number_of_passengers <= self->seating_capacity,
     ...
end;
```

A soft constraint is not enforced immediately after completion of a public method. Rather, it is enforced at transaction commit time. An example is given below. A pilot is assigned an airplane and an airplane is assigned a pilot. The associated constraint cannot be enforced until both assignments are completed.

```
class Pilot inherit Person read type
tuple( ...
     airplane: Airplane),
method public assign_plane(a: Airplane),
     ...
constraint soft:
     self->airplane->pilot==self,
     ...
end;
```

An illustration of a class with three different types of triggers is given below.

```
class Bomber inherit Military_plane read type
tuple( min_fuel_level: float,
       payload: float,
```

```
               target: object),
method public set_target(t: object),
        public at_target: boolean,
        public mount_payload,
        public deliver_payload,
        public return_to_base,
        public fuel_level: float,
        public refuel,
```

```
trigger drop:
        self->at_target ==> self->deliver_payload,
trigger perpetual fuel:
        self->fuel_level <= self->min_fuel_level ==> refuel,
trigger deliver:
        within 120? self->at_target ==> self->deliver_payload
        else return_to_base
end;
```

An illustration of a one-time trigger is drop. When it fires, it gets deactivated. It requires explicit reactivation. The method `mount_payload` activates this trigger. Fuel is a perpetual trigger. It fires when the level of fuel drops below the required minimum. This causes the refueling operation to be initiated. But the trigger remains active, that is, it does not require reactivation. An illustration of a timed trigger is deliver. This trigger is required to fire within a specific time interval, which is 120 minutes. If the trigger does not fire within 120 minutes, the method `return_to_base` is executed.

ANALYSIS

O_2 is claimed to be ODMG-compliant. It is obvious that the ideas behind O_2 have influenced the ODMG Standard, particularly as far as OQL is concerned. The fact is that the core of O_2 has been developed before the ODMG Standard [LR89] and thus differs from the ODMG Standard in many obvious and some more subtle ways. The components of O_2 that are compliant with the ODMG Standard, as much as one can reasonably expect, are OQL and the C++ interface [O2T95a, O2T95c, O2T95d]. None of this played a significant role in this particular application.

The type systems of O_2 and the ODMG object model are different. O_2 adopts a type discipline that is similar to Eiffel. The ODMG object model adopts a type discipline that is based on C++. However, the type system underlying the ODMG object model is different from the type system of C++. Both type systems are unsafe [Ala97]. Both identify inheritance and subtyping, which causes problems in the O_2 type system, similar to those in Eiffel [Coo89]. The typing discipline in O_2 is more natural than in the ODMG object model, but type safety cannot be guaranteed by static type checking. It cannot be guaranteed in the ODMG object model either, but for entirely different reasons [Ala97].

O_2 proper does not support generic collection classes. This is why generic classes do not appear in this chapter. The generic collection classes are supported in the C++ interface of O_2 and the C++ binding of the ODMG Standard. In fact, unlike Eiffel and C++, both O_2 and the ODMG object model lack general support for generic (parametric) classes.

The mapping between O_2 proper and the C++ model is performed by import and export. The fact that the two type systems are really different comes up in this transformation. The ODMG Standard requires that there is a single type system across the programming language and database. It is unclear how this requirement can be fully complied with in O_2. The ODMG Standard suffers from the same problem, mostly because it is intended to be common for languages that are as different as C++ and Smalltalk [Ala97].

There are obvious syntactic differences between classes in O_2 and the ODMG Standard [O2T95b, Cat96]. Relationships are a distinctive feature of the ODMG Standard. They are supported in O_2, but only in the C++ interface.

The limitations that affected our particular application are in fact common to O_2 and the ODMG Standard. The most serious one is the absence of a general declarative mechanism for constraints and triggers. By way of comparison, once-only, perpetual, and timed triggers as defined in ODE [GJ91] are all particularly relevant for flight simulation.

Another problem that we experienced is name space management. Both O_2 and the ODMG Standard are based on a single, flat name space, which corresponds to the entire database. This is very impractical, and the ability to define subspaces and submodels is essential for any multi user or distributed application.

The C++ bindings of O_2 and the ODMG Standard suffer from a common conceptual and practical problem. Quite contrary to the intent of the object-oriented paradigm and much of research in database systems [Atk+89], object identifiers appear as instances of a particular class d_Ref. Thus object identifiers are really directly accessible to the users, contrary to a situation in which they would be hidden and entirely system managed. The reason for this is, of course, C++. As C++ is not a pure object-oriented language, it has references (pointers) explicitly in the language, unlike, for example, Eiffel or Java. Having identifiers of persistent objects explicitly in the language is unsafe and requires a number of complicated rules [O2T95c, O2T95d] in order to prevent errors.

The model of persistence in the ODMG Standard is based on persistence capable classes. This means that there are classes whose objects can only be transient and classes whose objects may be transient or persistent. In the C++ bindings of O_2 and the ODMG Standard, persistent capable classes are derived by inheritance from a specific class d_object. This is a model that appears in several C++ based extensions providing persistence. Multiple inheritance thus plays a crucial role. However, this model is not truly orthogonal as defined in [Atk89].

Indeed, there are still classes whose objects can never be persistent. This feature, and explicit presence of references to persistent objects in the language, produce a model of persistence that is not high-level, so that some low-level details are not transparent to users.

EXPERIENCES AND SUMMARY

Two basic conclusions follow from our experience in this project. The first one is that the object-oriented technology is a superior technology for flight simulator systems. It is hard to imagine that any other currently available software or database technology would be better suited for the task.

The second conclusion pertains to a particular object-oriented database system used for this project. We had problems with consistency, reliability, concurrency, efficiency, and exception handling. Judging from our experience, it appears that object-oriented database technology has quite a way to go to achieve the level of maturity offered by the best relational systems on the market. This is hardly a surprise.

REFERENCES

[Ala+96] S. Alagic, D. Ellis, R. Harder, J. Hutchinson, G. Nagati, U. Rafi: *Object-Oriented Flight Simulator Technology*. AIAA Flight Simulator Technologies Conference, Technical Papers, AIAA, 360–368, 1996.

[Ala97] S. Alagic: *The ODMG Object Model: Does it Make Sense?* Proceedings of the OOPSLA '97 Conference, Atlanta, Georgia, 1997.

[Atk+89] M. Atkinson, F. Bancilhon, D. DeWitt, K. Dittrich, S. Zdonik: *The Object Oriented Database System Manifesto*. Proceedings of the First Object-Oriented and Deductive Database Conference (DOOD) 40–75, Kyoto, Japan 1989.

[Cat96] R. G. G. Cattell (ed.): *The Object-Oriented Database Standard: ODMG-93*. Morgan-Kaufmann Publishers, 1996.

[Coo89] W. R. Cook: *A Proposal for Making Eiffel Type Safe*. The Computer Journal, 32 (4), 305–311, 1989.

[Gal96] R. T. Galloway: *Aerodynamic Math Modeling*. Twelfth Annual Flight and Ground Vehicle Simulation Update. Binghampton University, 1996.

[GJ91] N. Gehani, H. V. Jagadish: *Ode as Active Database: Constraints and Triggers*. Proceedings of the 13th International VLDB Conference, Morgan-Kaufmann Publishers, 327–336, 1991.

[LR89] C. Lecluse, P. Richard: *The O2 Database Programming Language.* Proceedings of the 15th International VLDB Conference, Morgan-Kaufmann Publishers, 411–422, 1989.

[O2T95a] O$_2$ Technology: *OQL User Manual*, Release 4.6, 1995.

[O2T95b] O$_2$ Technology: *O$_2$C Reference Manual*, Release 4.6, 1995.

[O2T95c] O$_2$ Technology: *ODMG C++ Binding Guide*, Release 4.6, 1995.

[O2T95d] O$_2$ Technology: *ODMG C++ Binding Reference Manual*, Release 4.6, 1995.

6

An Object-Oriented Image Database For Biomedical Research

Mahlon C. Stacy, Mayo Foundation
Kurt E. Augustine, Mayo Foundation
Richard A. Robb, Mayo Foundation

ABSTRACT

The primary purpose for the use of a database is to help manage the vast amounts of data generated in today's "information age." The alarming rate at which information is growing in all sectors of society makes the management of data an increasingly critical issue. The medical research world is no exception. Biomedical image data is currently being generated at enormous rates, and shows no signs of decreasing. The large volume of image data has become unmanageable under many current computational systems, including the UNIX filesystem.

Mayo Foundation supports a diverse collection of clinical and biomedical research activities. A significant number of research studies include medical (Computed Tomography, Magnetic Resonance, etc.) and biomedical (Optical Microscope, Confocal Microscope, etc.) images. Research topics range from basic science through clinical diseases. To support research, Mayo provides several common core resources, available to all investigators. The Biomedical Imaging Resource (BIR) is one of these, with a mission to provide expertise and computer resources for advanced image visualization and analysis. The BIR has become a repository for a large number of 2 dimensional and 3 dimensional (volumetric) images.

Some of the current studies supported by the BIR include Nerve Cell studies of the gastrointestinal system [Mil+96], patient specific modeling of the human body [Rob96], applications of virtual endoscopy [SR97], mechanisms of the eye [Mag+92, Cam+96], and longitudinal studies of brain size in relation to epilepsy [Jac+90]. Support for surgery planning, radiation therapy and publication support for both image and non-image based research via dye-sublimation color printing and video production are also provided.

These research activities generate large volumes of image data. For example, gastrointestinal nerve studies which derive images from optical microscopy, typically generate 50–70 images per nerve, each image containing 512×512 8-bit pixels, or approximately 262 Kilobytes each. Similar cell types are imaged using different staining techniques. Several sets of images are collected from different organs in the body, and several different types of animals are under study, resulting in hundreds of sets of raw image data. After the raw data are collected, image processing is used to register, segment, and scale the images into an isotropic volume image. From these volume images, measurements are taken, objects are segmented and various visualization techniques, such as volume and surface rendering, are used to view the cells and understand the 3 dimensional relationships in the data. To date, the BIR has accumulated over 40 Gigabytes of image data for this physiology study, representing approximately 5,500 images.

Problems to Be Solved

Finding the right image: For projects with a small number of images, the UNIX filesystem hierarchy usually provides sufficient organization for management of the data. However, as the number of images grows it becomes impossible for investigators to remember the arcane mnemonics used in naming directories and files, suggesting the need for a better method. Historically, this information has been kept in laboratory notebooks, which impose a project-based organization scheme on the data. These are difficult to search through for specific files which may be created or referenced in other projects. Compounding this difficulty, much of the research is conducted by post-doctoral fellows and graduate students, and the investigator does not personally have the visual memory cues necessary to find a particular image based on another's file naming system. Further, when these fellows and students leave, only the notebooks retain the information about the images, and searching the notebooks manually is difficult.

Capture of data from a dynamic, existing system: While the typical database is intended to store the data, storing all of the Mayo images inside a database would interfere with the existing image processing software which expects to find images in the filesystem. A number of different software packages are used in UNIX, Macintosh, and Windows environments to massage and view these images. Imposition of a database system as the sole interface to the image data would prohibit users from accessing their image data directly. Consequently, the system design needs to include methods to capture image metadata from the filesystem into the database on a regular, but unobtrusive basis, or through user executed programs. The image data itself must remain in the Unix filesystem for free access by all applications.

This "uncontrolled data" design creates other problems. For example, the database needs to retain information about all of the files in the UNIX filesystem in order to capture changes in image files, based on the date of last modification. In addition, users also have no ability to move files without disconnecting the image from its metadata in the database. The design approach taken makes attempts to handle this gracefully, but work remains to provide multilevel storage of image files between magnetic disk, optical disk systems, and tape archives while keeping the images correctly connected to the metadata in the database.

Flexible Attributes: The diverse studies conducted at Mayo generates a variety of research protocols and attendant attributes needed and used to characterize the image information. For example, the researchers on the nervous system are interested in the particular stains used to highlight certain elements of the cells in microscope images, whereas studies on brain volume measurements from MRI data need no such attribute. The design for the database needs to provide flexible attribute naming schemes to accommodate an individual or laboratories' particular needs.

Sharing of images and information: While much research is conducted independently by each laboratory, some research crosses disciplines. Nearly all new research topics in the BIR which come from intramural laboratories involve some related image based research in the BIR. Where longer term collaborations arise, the database system must provide properly balanced control of access to the images and metadata to permit adequate collaboration combined with appropriate security.

Provision for content based queries and selective batch processing: Historically, image analysis in the BIR has been primarily based on ANALYZE [RH95], which provides a highly integrated interactive image exploration environment. Conversion of flexible, interactive research into more efficient production based image analysis is difficult. The database design should incorporate the ability to select a set of images and perform the same image processing tasks on each image in the set. If the results produced by this processing can be measured against predetermined criteria and images from the set accepted or rejected, this operation can be viewed as a content based query on the image set.

When processing images, users usually retain information about the procedural steps necessary to perform particular sequences of image processing steps. If this information can be captured, along with sufficient parametric information, then images selected in the database can be fed to procedures, also stored in the database, to effect batch processing.

The interface tools necessary to perform such queries and batch processing are complex, and highly subject to the underlying image processing software. Since the BIR has packaged the functionality of ANALYZE into a set of C-callable software libraries called AVW, this task is simplified considerably.

To address these and other problems, the BIR has been conducting a research project to develop an image database system dubbed the "Image BOSS" (Biomedical Object Storage System).

IMAGE BOSS SYSTEM OVERVIEW

Software and Hardware

A decision was made early in the design phase to develop the image database on top of a commercially available object-oriented database management system. The database chosen was VERSANT ODBMS [Ver95]. The interface to the ODBMS is standard C++ which eliminates the introduction of an additional language (like SQL). Because the interface language is C++, all standard object-oriented features are supported (inheritance, polymorphism, etc.). VERSANT also provides a useful class library which includes string and date classes, templated collection classes like arrays, lists and sets, and error handling classes with a standard try-catch implementation [Ver95]. Because databases store persistent data, the notion of a persistent pointer is needed. VERSANT implements this through the Link<type> template class. Similar to the Link<type> class but unlike anything found in standard C++ is the BiLink<type> class. This class provides a bidirectional persistent pointer between two related classes which proves to be a powerful tool in creating a robust database system that supports complex relationships between class objects. Related to the Link<type> and BiLink<type> classes are the LinkVstr<type> and BiLinkVstr<type> classes. These can be thought of as variable length arrays of Links and BiLinks.

VERSANT ODBMS supports the use of multiple distributed databases, executes on various platforms, provides typical locking mechanisms (object locking as oppose to page locking) and carries out server side processing, which was an important consideration for our image database system design.

All software directly related to Image BOSS is written in C++. This affords a direct interface to VERSANT's ODBMS without prohibiting use of some of the underlying library routines that were written in C, which include the X, Xt, and Motif libraries as well as the image processing routines found in AVW (see Figure 6–1). While none of the AVW routines are called directly by Image BOSS software, C++ "wrapper" classes called AVW++ have been developed as an interface to the C++ code. Tools.h++, which is a commercially available C++ library from Rogue Wave is utilized as well.

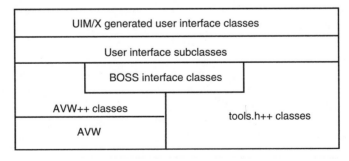

Figure 6–1   Software structure.

The X windows user interface code is based on standard Motif but has been written in C++. To accomplish this, a user-interface management system called UIM/X was used to build the interface and generate C++ code. Each interface is represented by a UIM/X generated class. These classes are then subclassed to create classes that interface with the UIM/X-Motif code on top and the database code on the bottom which successfully separates database interface code from the UIM/X generated code. The image database has been developed to run on SGI workstations running IRIX 5.3 or later and on Sun workstations running Solaris 2.4 or later. Additional platforms are planned to be supported.

Various Applications and Tools Implemented

One of the key features of the Image BOSS is an automated image data capture facility. The goal was to provide a database that works with the UNIX filesystem rather than hiding it from the user. Creating a closed system in which users must interface to the database may be easier to manage but becomes much less flexible for the user. Experience shows that most users work first with the filesystem until their image files become too numerous to manage, then they want to interface with a database. The way Image BOSS is designed, the interface to the user will be an up-to-date representation of the filesystem.

Image Capture

To capture the image file data for Image BOSS, a simple database administration tool is required. "Scavenge" is the name of the image data capture application which is executed on a regular basis. The frequency of "scavenges" depends on the size of the filesystem and how quickly users need to see new images reflected in the database. A typical frequency is once per day, after normal working hours if possible.

Image Browser/Organizer

The primary purpose for Image BOSS is to provide the user with a means for managing complicated sets of image data. The main user tool that provides this service is the image browser/organizer. Derived from the way researchers tend to organize their data, this tool utilizes a bookcase/workbook metaphor as its primary interface (see Figure 6–2).

The goal was to provide a way for the user to browse, search and organize images in a way that is already familiar to them. A user may "page through" any one of a number of workbooks in search of a particular image or set of images which are represented by a "thumbnail" version of the image. Images may be organized on a per page basis, or at a higher level by creating specific sets of workbooks. To bring up the browser/organizer tool the user executes the "db" command, which pops up their personal bookcase window. Here the user sees all of their personal workbooks, the first of which is a primary workbook, followed alphabetically by secondary workbooks. The primary workbook is generated and updated automatically by the

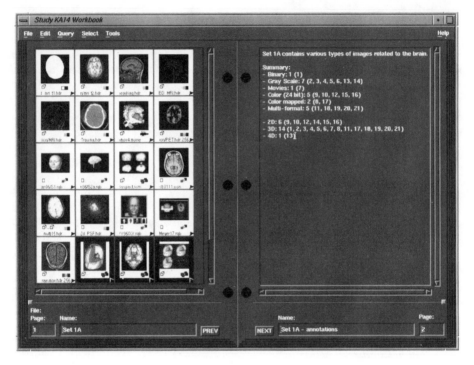

Figure 6–2   Image browser/organizer.

scavenge program along with several other database administration tools. It is meant to be a current representation of all the user's images found in the filesystem and is therefore, essentially read-only. Each page is associated with a directory in the filesystem and contains thumbnails representing all images within that directory that are owned (in the UNIX sense of ownership) by the given user. The secondary workbooks are created by the user and can contain two types of pages: image pages and text pages. Any image thumbnail may by placed on the image pages, including thumbnails representing images that are not owned by the user. Principally, this is accomplished through the drag and drop feature. Queries may be carried out based on image attributes. The text pages are used to annotate image pages or for any other purpose as determined by the user.

External Tools

A variety of other tools and applications may be accessed directly from the db tool as well. If a user sees an image thumbnail they believe represents the data they want, they may view it in full scale and color resolution (accuracy of color resolution depends on visuals available on workstation). This is accomplished by drag and drop to the image viewer tool called "iv".

One of the key features of Image BOSS is its facile integration with Analyze$_{AVW}$. If a user wishes to analyze or process an image but is not sure where the image is in the filesystem, they can find it in a workbook, drag the thumbnail onto the Analyze$_{AVW}$ window and have it loaded into that application.

IMAGE BOSS DESIGN

Data Abstraction

The key to understanding and managing large amounts of data is to abstract the useful information from the original data. This must be done in a way that minimizes the amount of information provided to the user but not to the point of rendering it useless. The UNIX filesystem offers a form of image data abstraction by using filenames and directory structures which are very efficient from a data volume management standpoint. The problem is that too much information about the image file is hidden. As the number of files grows, it is increasingly difficult to search and differentiate one image set from another. Typically, some type of naming convention is implemented to aid in image file management. In research, this technique inevitably breaks down at some point, prohibiting efficient utilization of image data. In some cases, utility can be extended through "file managers" which hide some of the operating system detail, but these offer little additional information about the image file.

Thumbnail Abstraction

Visual cues are a powerful tool to aid in recognition, differentiation and management of information. This is especially true for image data. A primary abstraction of image data should therefore include some representation of the image itself. The most common form of image data abstraction is a small representative image called a "thumbnail" (see Figure 6–3). A thumbnail of a two-dimensional image is typically a scaled down version of the original. In Image BOSS, this implementation is a 64 pixel by 64 pixel image, dithered to 64 predefined colors. For three-dimensional (multiple 2-D slices) images, these thumbnails default to the middle slice of the volume image. The exception is the case where the image data set is actually multiple disjoint 2-D images (e.g., set of slides for a slide presentation) in

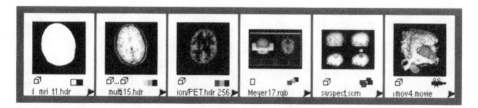

Figure 6–3   Example thumbnails.

which case the first image in the set is used for the representative thumbnail. The size of a thumbnail was chosen to have optimal impact on the database. Larger thumbnails provide more detail but the number of bytes stored increases as the square of the dimensions of the image. A size of 64×64 was chosen as a reasonable trade-off. The 64 color dimension was selected to enable thumbnail presentation on low color resolution displays.

While image thumbnails provide a useful form of data abstraction, there is significant information remaining hidden. For this reason, additional information is abstracted from the original data which is helpful in managing the image data. A primary interface to the actual image data is still the UNIX filesystem, so the full pathname associated with the data is displayed with each thumbnail. Since the thumbnail is a 2-D representation, the user must have a simple way to determine the dimensionality of the dataset. This is accomplished with a small icon attached to each thumbnail. Because of the scaling and dithering that takes place to produce the thumbnail from the original image data, users are not able to determine the format of the image (binary, gray scale, color mapped, true color) so an additional icon representing the image format is attached to the thumbnail.

Attribute Abstraction

Each of the above image data abstractions are always provided and visible to the user because they are common to all images. The user that obtained or generated the image data may wish to associate other information with an image which would require user-specified abstractions. Researchers often associate characteristics with their sets of images that are unique to their particular discipline. This calls for a way of assigning data abstractions that are unique to each user. For example, a biologist may wish to assign a "stain" attribute to the images where as an anatomist might wish to assign an "anatomical structure" attribute. This feature is provided in the form of text based image attributes. Associated with each thumbnail is a set of fifteen attributes which the user is free to define in any way s/he sees fit. This set of information, while considered an abstraction of the original data is accessed through a secondary dialog interface to minimize clutter on the thumbnail.

Class Hierarchy

The current database hierarchy is shown in Figure 6–4. From an implementation standpoint, containment relationships and "Link to" relationships are carried out through the same mechanism, namely the Bi-directional Link (BiLink) structure referred to earlier. Conceptually, it makes sense to say workbooks contain pages and thus *Workbook* objects have access to a *Page* object through the BiLink (actually, a BiLinkVstr is used here because of the "1 to n" relationship—there are many *Pages* in a single *Workbook*). On the other hand, it is important that a *Page* object "knows" which *Workbook* object it is part of. This illustrates the power of the Bi-Directional link. In a similar fashion, image pages naturally contain images but it is also useful for an *Image* object to be able to access any or all *Page* objects within

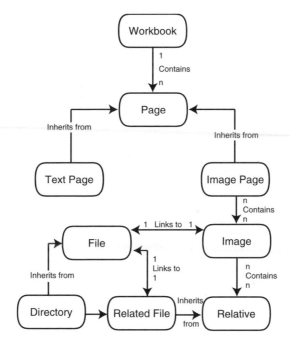

Figure 6–4   Current database hierarchy.

which it is contained, thus the need for a BiLink. *File—Image* links and *Image— Relative* links are considered to be more of a peer to peer relationship and therefore do not fit the containment model. Here the BiLink association seems more natural (i.e., a *File* object must know if it is an image type and an *Image* object must know about the attributes of the file in which it is found—one does not contain the other).

The inheritance found among Image BOSS classes is fairly simple and quite natural from a user point of view. *Text Pages* and *Image Pages* are a kind of *Page*, a UNIX *Directory* is a kind of UNIX *File*, and a *Related File* is a kind of *Relative*. This last set of classes requires a brief description at this point. An image may have many other types of information or data directly associated with it, such as transformation matrix files and/or related statistics files, or data not stored in files, such as descriptions of a subregion of the image. In either case, the data is considered to be a *Relative* of the *Image* and therefore contained within it. A *Related File* is just a specialized *Relative*, thus the inheritance relationship between the two classes. At this point, these two classes have not been utilized in Image BOSS but are included in the design for future enhancements. Image BOSS utilizes an additional persistent class which does not appear in the hierarchy chart. A *User* object is generated for each user and is referenced by Image BOSS applications but is not related to any of the other persistent classes. The *User* class contains personalized Image BOSS user interface information.

Future Design Plans

Currently, the primary contents of the image database is image information/objects and all other data required to support image management. There is another type of class needed which is related to an image object but conceptually quite different. Users not only wish to store and manage images, but they also want to store and manage the procedures carried out on images. Often a researcher needs to recall the image processing steps carried out to produce a particular derivative image. Once the steps are refined, recall of the procedure at a later time provides an efficient way to reproduce the processing step so they can be carried out again on the same or other images, possibly a large set in batch mode. This enhancement promises to distinguish Image BOSS from conventional image storage and management systems— an integrated package that enhances image processing and analysis as well as store and retrieve images.

Another area planned for future consideration is that of "image query by content." There has been considerable study done in this area [GR95], [Fli+95], [OS95], and certainly the user community is eager to have it. To date, no system has been able to provide truly useful, general purpose query-by-content capability. As this function has been considered in the design of Image BOSS, future implementations will include this important capability.

JUSTIFICATION FOR SELECTING OODB

In 1992, when this project was being proposed to internal Mayo funding committees, the merger of relational and object oriented database systems was still futuristic. Some prototyping for this project was done using the public version of Postgres [SR86] from Berkeley. During the prototype phase, it was determined that the ability to modify the behavior of the database manager, and the ability to create new, complex datatypes would be valuable in the final design, particularly to accommodate the custom needs of the many research entities who might make use of the database. The ability to create complex bi-directionally linked object relationships was not anticipated in the original design, but the nature of the data in Image BOSS and its need to adapt to the changes in the UNIX filesystem have made this an important feature.

Another strong argument for an OODBMS was made based on the need to associate functions with the objects in the database. For example, many BIR projects make use of 3 dimensional images, which are usually organized as a set of 2 dimensional slices. Many 3-D image processing functions operate on such images slice by slice. This requires methods for extracting a single slice from a 3 dimensional volume image in storage, and similar methods that would write a modified slice back into a volume image. These functions are available in the AVW library and accessible through AVW++ as methods to operate on *Image* objects. Such subregion handling capability was not available in Binary Large Objects (BLOB's) in relational databases at the time.

Another factor which led to the adoption of an object-oriented design was the variety of files and data which are created in relation to images. For example, an analysis project might begin with a set of Computed Tomography (CT) images, which are scaled into an isotropic 3 dimensional volume image. Renderings of this volume would produce subregions of interest. Volume objects may be defined in the image, resulting in a separate ANALYZE objects file.[1] Linear distances, areas, and volumes may be measured within the 3-D images and reported to statistics files. Two images from separate modalities (i.e., MRI and CT) may be registered to each other by finding the proper transformation matrix to align the images to the same 3-D axes. Associated files from one image may be applied to another for correlation. Tracking all of the associated files and linking them between one image set and another are ideal candidates for object oriented mechanisms such as containers provided in the selected OODBMS.

PROBLEMS ENCOUNTERED

Integration of Other Tools

Early in the development cycle of Image BOSS a decision was made to program the user interface using Motif. To speed this process, it was decided that a GUI builder would be used. UIM/X was chosen, in part because it supported both C code generation (majority of developers in BIR are C programmers) as well as C++ code generation (this project was to be written in an OO language, namely C++, for reasons stated earlier). VERSANT ODBMS was chosen as the underlying database management system. Both products are well developed and comprehensive packages, but integration of the two was challenging. The most significant problem was that UIM/X generates standard C++ code, while VERSANT required modified C++ to support persistent objects (a restriction removed in a recent release). This, along with UIM/X's built in C interpreter made for frustrating development. Most of the problems were solved when the user interface code (UIM/X generated code) and the database interface code (VERSANT compliant C++ classes) were separated into independent layers connected through a common API. This was accomplished through an interesting technique presented at the November, 1994 UIM/X Developer's Conference by Berdych [Ber94] in which he described a way to remove all C++ code from the GUI builder code. To do this, each UIM/X generated C++ interface class is subclassed. These subclasses now act as the interface to the database classes below and have access to any user interface attributes (through inheritance) from above, without the C interpreter in UIM/X interfering.

---

[1]ANALYZE uses "object" files (not related to Object Oriented Design) to mark and display regions of an image. These object files are 3-D bitmaps of the original image, with up to 8 objects in each bitmap. One use of these object files is to map one element, such as the skull bones, in a modality which renders bones most easily (CT) onto another image after the two images have been co-registered.

Another problem is the mismatch between operating system (OS) versions each product supports. This means that development must be carried out on the earliest OS version which eliminates incorporation of new features and software bug fixes.

Rogue Wave's tools.h++ class library and the AVW library were integrated into the project which added further complexity.

Archiving

Inactive image files from completed projects may be moved off-line or to archival storage. Such relocation of image files poses a problem since the images no longer appear in the filesystem referenced by the database. This has been handled to the extent that *Image* objects are not deleted if the file is moved or removed (associated *File* objects are deleted). If the file is later restored and the image owner has not explicitly removed the *Image* object, nothing is lost. If a user is moving many files, this could cause considerable confusion (Is this file archived? Is it really deleted? If it is archived, where is it?). A set of BOSS aware programs to move files have been started, but development has been postponed until the final BIR archival storage solution is in place.

Filename Translation

Another major problem which added considerable complexity to the system is the issue of pathname translations required for all filenames. The need to translate pathnames is based on BIR's client/server file sharing environment and the ability of users to create soft links (aliases) to files. An elegant strategy has been devised to solve this problem, but this is outside the scope of this chapter.

Locking

In general, locking is a problem encountered by anyone designing a complex, multi-user database system. Image BOSS is no exception. The locking problems tend to arise only in unusual circumstances. For example, consider the case where a single user has two instances of the same workbook open at the same time because Image BOSS was started twice (opening two identical bookcases) and then the same workbooks from each bookcase were opened. Proper locking will eliminate corruption of the database but results from attempted changes to both workbooks may be unpredictable.

Queries

At the outset of this project, VERSANT ODBMS had rather limited selection (query) facilities. For example, queries could not follow links (attributes of linked objects were not accessible to the query), and predicates could only be combined with the AND operator. The latest release of the ODBMS supports enhanced query capabilities (e.g. OR and NOT included as logical operators) which will be reflected in the Image BOSS query interface in the future.

Server Crashes

Because of the tremendous stress placed on the BIR's servers, the storage system was implemented with third party hierarchical file systems that were not tested under similar circumstances. Consequently, the server for the files and the database has crashed numerous times during the development and early deployment of Image BOSS. This has repeatedly corrupted the database, requiring repeated database restorations. Restoring a BOSS database to the state just before the crash can be very time consuming and frustrating (especially if the server crashes in the middle of a restoration!). This only highlights the critical need for robust backup systems for both image data and the database itself.

PRIMARY APPLICATIONS OF IMAGE DATABASE

Development of the full functionality of Image BOSS will continue into the future, as several important functions have yet to be implemented. The project is now in beta release internally at Mayo, and feedback provided by users will generate bug fixes and enhancements to the software. Development of a network based image processor which can perform the batch processing functions is still early in the prototype stage, though special networks have been installed to support the high bandwidth necessary to implement such processing.

The early implementors are using Image BOSS for the following research projects: 1. Cornea Research, 2. Spatial Physiology, 3. Slide File Management, 4. BIR Development and Demonstration. Each of these are discussed below.

1. **Cornea Research.** A collaborative project is being undertaken by Dr. Leo Maguire in collaboration with the BIR. Corneal images have been collected with a digital keratoscope on approximately 100 normal patients, and over 30 patients with keratoconus and post radial keratotomy. These images reflect on the regions measured and reported as digital values by the keratoscope. Research assistants collect this data, and apply measurement information from the images as attributes into the metadata information in the database. Ophthalmology researchers may then select corneal images based on the attribute information and view the results of their selections rapidly using ANALYZE, Analyze$_{AVW}$, or the Image Viewer tools provided with the database.

    The nature of the data applied as attributes to these images could have been recorded in a standard relational database. However, inherent in the project was the relationship to the actual image data. The use of Image BOSS makes access to these images immediate while selecting the information. In addition, the workbook metaphor is setup such that each page in a book represents a set of exams on a single eye, and each book represents a study. This organization pre-sorts the information for the investigator and provides rapid access among the many sets of images.

2. **Spatial Physiology.** Dr. Joseph Szurszewski, in Mayo's Physiology Department, is performing Gastrointestinal (GI) Neurological research, studying the locations of receptor sites on GI neurons throughout the GI system. Neuron cells are prepared using a variety of photoflourescent materials, and images are collected using a Zeiss Laser Scanning Confocal microscope, with typical field widths of 400 microns. After capture, the images are transferred to the BIR image server system. Hundreds of cells have been thus captured.

Critical to the research is the spatial distribution of the receptor sites on the cell soma body and/or dendrites. Localization of these sites traditionally has been difficult, until procedures developed by Dr. Szurszewski permitted direct visualization of them using ANALYZE.

Preparation of materials is painstaking, and careful attention is paid to the wavelengths of specific photoflours and conjugation of photoflours to antibodies specific to the receptor sites. As the project progresses, these techniques are refined to produce better results. The work thus builds upon itself, and depends on accurate determination of prior methods to use or avoid. Such information is stored in lab notebooks, remembered by lab personnel, or found through literature searches. None of these methods can recall the image itself, and thus Image BOSS provides a practical and important link in the process to help speed the process and avoid errors.

Since there is no digital specimen attribute information provided with the images at capture time (other than an encoded filename), research assistants enter the related information for each image in the database. Separate secondary BOSS workbooks will be organized to represent Papers, Meetings, Anatomical, Photoflours, and Scanning Techniques. Using the query methods of the current Image BOSS, the images can further be selected based on keywords in the user defined attributes grouped for: Cell Codes, Species, Organs, Tissues, Photoflour, Receptor-Transmitter Type.

It is expected that future enhancements to Image BOSS will speed this work further, by accelerating the rate at which images can be selected and loaded for additional analysis or visualization, and by permitting the creation of sequences of processing steps which are discovered to provide more meaningful visualizations of the resulting image data, through the batch processing techniques.

3. **Slide File Management.** Publication of results in a diverse medical research environment such as Mayo's utilizes a variety of media. Image research presents unique problems to internal printing departments, since the images are produced in a wide variety of formats, and the specific requirements of the various publications and granting institutions are varied. To accommodate the need for color slides, color prints, and video presentations, the BIR has accumulated various equipment and software to produce such media.

Color slides and video present unique storage requirements. While slides can be viewed from a stack, in hand, or on a sorting table, when the volume of slides is significant, such techniques break down, particularly for investigators such as the Director of the BIR, as he is involved in a variety of image based collaborations that cut across a selection of disciplines. Presentations for such meetings often involve collecting and reorganizing slide presentations from recent presentations is similar or perhaps completely different disciplines.

To address this need, in early 1996, the BIR media staff began storing slide images in directories that are captured by Image BOSS. These directories are collected into a slide presentation workbook in the database. The lab director may now select slides for new presentations by opening his database browser on his workstation, collect the images desired, place them on a new page in the database, and then the entire set can be sent to Mayo's Visual Information Section film recorder cameras. A permanent record of the images selected for each presentation is then made in Image BOSS. Of course, the investigator can select previous film copies of slides if s/he has kept them in order so that the existing copies can be referenced from the BOSS. As often as this can be done, however, small but usually significant changes have to be made to each image for the new presentation.

4. **Biomedical Imaging Resource Development and Demonstration.** As would be expected of a dynamic multidiscipline core support function based on exciting visual information, the BIR is called upon to provide presentations to visiting doctors, researchers, and various public groups. In such presentations questions often arise in which the ideal image to illustrate the answer to the question exists, but it cannot be found quickly enough to present it to the interested party. A small but comprehensive collection of raw image data, processed data, visualization data sets, annotated image and movie files can be selected from various pre-organized workbooks, representing different "views" of the same data. For example, one workbook represents the "software" view, in which images highlighting related algorithms are on the same page. Another workbook represents the "disease" view, where the table of contents accelerates a user to various disease related images. Another workbook is organized by anatomical regions, permitting rapid location of hearts, brains, etc.

CONCLUSIONS

The Image BOSS project provides new and advanced capabilities for support of imaging science investigators in a large research organization which generates copious amounts of images and image related data. While the development of the system is still in progress, sufficient work has been done to demonstrate the feasibility and power of the approach. A number of problems encountered with this technique have been solved. Users are provided with intuitive interfaces and useful tools to collect and organize their images and related image metadata. As the images remain in the native filesystem, all existing software systems are unaffected. The use of icons organized into workbooks give users intuitive visual cues to image content, which can be organized into classical sets in a familiar lab workbook metaphor. Duplication of images is avoided since an image may have many icon representations pointing to the same (raw) image. Sharing of image information is enabled through the sharing of workbooks.

Work remains to be done on the implementation of content-based queries and batch processing methods. The current system infrastructure is designed to incorporate these features. Additional areas of study include simplified methods of archive storage and the definition and implementation of collections of image related files.

REFERENCES

[Ber94] J. Berdych: *Using UIM/X with C++*. UIM/X Developer's Conference, 1994.

[Cam+96] J. J. Camp, et al.: *3-D reconstruction of aqueous channels in human trabecular meshwork using light microscopy and confocal microscopy*. SCANNING, 1996.

[Fli+95] M. Flickner, H. Sawhney, W. Niblack, J. Ashley, Q. Huang, B. Dom, M. Gorkani, J. Hafner, D. Lee, D. Petkovic, D. Steele, P. Yanker: *Query by image and video content: The QBIC system*. Computer, 0018-9162, pp. 28–32, 1995.

[GR95] V. N. Gudivada, V. V. Raghaven: *Content-based image retrieval system*. Computer, 0018-9162, pp. 18–21, 1995.

[Jac+90] C. R. Jack, M. Bentley, C. K. Twomey, et al: *Temporal lobe seizures: lateralization with MR volume measurements of hippocampal formation*. Radiology, 176, pp. 205–209, 1990.

[Mag+92] L. J. Maguire, J. J. Camp, R. A. Robb: *Informing interested parties of changes in the optical performance of the cornea caused by keratorefractive surgery—a ray tracing model that tailors presentation results to fit the level of sophistication of the audience*. Proceedings of Visualization and Biomedical Computing, Chapel Hill, North Carolina, 1992.

[Mil+96] S. K. Miller, M. Hanani, S. M. Kuntz, P. F. Schmalz, J. H. Szurszewski: *Light, electron, and confocal microscopic study of the mouse superior mesenteric ganglion*. The Journal of Comparative Neurology, 365, pp. 427–444, 1996.

[OS95] V. E. Ogle, M. Stonebraker: *Chabot: retrieval from a relational database of images*. Computer, 0018-9162, 40–48, 1995.

[Rob96] R. A. Robb: *VR assisted surgery planning using patient specific anatomic models.* IEEE Engineering in Medicine and Biology, 0739-5175, pp. 60–69, 1996.

[RH95] R. A. Robb, D. P. Hanson: *The ANALYZE^{TM} software system for visualization and analysis in surgery simulation.* Computer Integrated Surgery, eds. S. Lavallee et al., MIT Press, Cambridge, Massachusetts, 1995.

[SR97] R. M. Satava, R. A. Robb: *Virtual endoscopy: application of 3-D visualization to medical diagnosis.* PRESENCE, January, 1997.

[SR86] M. Stonebraker, L. A. Rowe: *The design of POSTGRES.* Proceedings of the 1986 ACM SIGMOD International Conference on Management of Data, Washington, D. C., pp. 340–355, 1986.

[Ver95] Versant, *Versant ODBMS C++/Versant reference manual.* Versant Object Technology, Menlo Park, California, 1995.

7

The OSEF (Object-oriented Software Engineering Flow) Framework

Stefan Fäustle, Siemens Nixdorf, Italy

ABSTRACT

At Siemens Nixdorf Informatica (SNI) Italy, in partnership with Alitalia, we have developed an OO framework based on C++ on a UNIX platform (HP/UX) with X/Motif, with the major goal of testing interoperability between commercial tools supporting different phases of OOP, in order to obtain an automated SW production cycle. Commercial tools involved are Rational Rose/C++ as a CASE front-end and Objectivity/DB as ODBMS back-end. Source code management (editing, searching, navigation, versioning, etc.) and makefile dependencies are handled by SNiFF+. Purify and PureCoverage are embedded for debugging. GUI classes were obtained using Builder Xcessory, XRT/table, and XRT/graph.

Besides customized commercial tools, the framework consists of a set of utilities and filters (mainly implemented in Perl) needed as glue between the tools, and a foundation class (FC) library, implementing an object metaschema on top of Objectivity's base classes. Starting from the FC library, the target domain can be modeled in the usual terms of classes, attributes, and relationships. Attributes, however, are not implemented as C++ members of classes but as dynamic associations between *ApplicationClass* objects and *Attribute* objects, thus permitting an evolutionary object schema approach with automatic data migration at schema modifications. An application is designed specializing and relating framework FCs using Booch or

OMT notation (supported by Rational Rose). Framework FCs take the burden of managing object persistence, transaction handling, database locking, and encapsulation of problem-solving algorithms and event-driven procedures, permitting the application developer to concentrate on the actual problem domain.

The application is automatically generated together with a standard GUI consisting of type-specific data entry and DB browsing dialogs. Further, a built-in Gantt chart is available for graphical manipulation of time scheduled tasks.

SNI itself intends to use the framework as a rapid application development environment to deploy end user applications in the Decision Support System (DSS) area, as well as to sell the framework as a programming environment for its software developing customers.

The project was partially financed by the ESSI program of the European Community. This chapter outlines the architecture of the resulting environment, with a particular focus on the integration of Rational Rose on one side and of Objectivity/DB on the other.

OSEF ARCHITECTURE

One of the aims of the OSEF project was to set up an integrated environment for the development of applications based on commercial tools. All of these tools have to follow the object-oriented (OO) paradigm, supporting the software engineer's work from the initial phases of analysis and design. The resulting environment should demonstrate that a framework-based OO approach in software development can lead to substantial reuse of design and code. Further, Siemens Nixdorf and Alitalia want to introduce OO know-how acquired during this project into their software development process.

General Criteria

At start of the project, in early 1994, the following guidelines were fixed:

- Select the most popular object-oriented language: C++.
- Hardware independence: The tools must be available on the most common UNIX platforms.
- Product support: Evaluate the quality of the support provided by the vendors.
- Runtime licenses: Avoid, when possible, products with a runtime license.
- Popularity: Select the most used tools, avoid young and unknown products.
- Cohesion: All the tools selected must allow for connection, in some way, in order to obtain a software production chain.
- Effectiveness: Each tool must simplify the life of the developer.
- Coverage: The toolset should cover the whole production cycle from analysis and design to performance tuning and testing.

Software Development Method

During the last decade many methods have appeared, including the work of Jacobson, Rumbaugh, Coad and Yourdon, Costantine, Shlaer and Mellor, Martin and Odell, Wasserman, Goldberg and Rubin, Embley, Wirfs-Brock, Goldstein and Alger, Henderson-Sellers, Firesmith and Booch.

We've surveyed many of these methods, interviewed developers and managers who have applied them, and when possible tried tools that supported some of these methods. We've read some formal and informal comparison papers, observing that some interesting trends are emerging. Specifically, virtually all such comparisons have rated Booch and Rumbaugh's OMT as the "best" notations, by whatever criteria each comparison establishes, and most rate the expressiveness of these notations so closely to be statistically insignificant. Recently, Booch's and Rumbaugh's methods have been merged yielding the Unified method.

Our choice fell on the Booch method, which takes an iterative approach for system development.

This incremental iterative approach encourages making a quick model of the system, analyzing it, and then refining it, exploiting the increased understanding of the problem. Iteration on this process continues until the desired completeness and correctness of the analysis is achieved.

BOUGHT COMPONENTS

The project was developed on UNIX workstations. All the tools we chose are available at least on Sun, Hewlett Packard, Siemens Nixdorf, and Silicon Graphics platforms. Following the indications given by Alitalia, the selected vendor has been Hewlett Packard, and the OSEF framework was developed on an HP 712/80i model with HP/UX 9.05 and HP C++ compiler (based on USL 3.0 standard).

CASE Tool

For analysis and design support we've considered several CASE tools, and, according to the consideration made above, the most suitable tool seemed to be Rational Rose (Rational Software Corporation), whose most recent release supports both Booch and OMT notations. Rose is a language independent tool for which C++, Ada, and Smalltalk code generators are available. Other tools we evaluated were OMTool (originally created by General Electric and now distributed by IDE) and ObjectMaker (Mark V systems).

Database Management System

For data persistence we wanted a distributed, multi-user ODBMS with a C++ API. We selected Objectivity/DB (Objectivity, Inc.) that seemed to be one of the emerging products in this field. Objectivity/DB is a high-performance storage system shipped on the widest range of platforms. For this kind of tool, we've stressed hardware independence, because it belongs to the framework kernel and not only to the development environment. The other major competitors, ObjectStore (ODI) and VERSANT (Versant, Inc.) weren't available on Siemens Nixdorf and Silicon Graphics platforms, when we started our projects.

The CASE tool and the ODBMS mentioned above constitute the backbone of the OSEF development environment. Some other tools were also loosely integrated into the SW production flow. Their presence, however, albeit useful, is not strictly required for the development environment to work. Here is a short description of them:

Source Code Administration Tool

We used SNiFF+ (TakeFive Software Gmbh) for source file editing and administration. SNiFF+ is a tool, derived from public domain software, that provides browsing, cross-referencing, design visualization, documentation, configuration management (based on SCCS, RCS or other), and editing support. The main goal of SNiFF+ is to provide an efficient and portable C++ programming environment that makes it possible to edit and browse large software systems, both textually and graphically. Further, a useful feature of SNiFF+ is the maintainance of makefile dependencies.

Debugging and Tuning Tools

For debugging and performance tuning we have selected Purify and PureCoverage (Pure Software). Purify detects runtime errors, identifying memory leaks, reading or writing beyond array bounds, reading or writing to freed memory, reading uninitialized memory, freeing unallocated memory, and so on. PureCoverage maintains a counter on each line of source code, a useful aid evaluating the coverage of tests and the identification of possible performance bottlenecks.

GUI Builder

Finally, we chose Builder Xcessory, integrated with the XRT/table and XRT/graph widgets, to develop GUI classes. The Builder Xcessory is a GUI builder tool implementing the Douglas Young method to wrap the Motif C API obtaining C++ classes.

BUILT COMPONENTS

The integration of the tools mentioned above into an organic environment required the implementation of some ad-hoc components, tools, and utilities.

Framework Class Library

In the OSEF development environment, the application developer does not implement each new application from scratch. He or she starts from a predefined class library, the framework class (FC) library, which is reusable throughout all applications. The FC library implements an object metaschema on top of Objectivity/DB's base classes. Specializing the FC library, the target domain can be modeled in the usual terms of classes, attributes, and relationships. Attributes, however, are not implemented as C++ members of classes but as dynamic associations between application class objects and attribute objects, thus permitting an evolutionary object schema approach with automatic data migration at schema modifications. The implementation of the dynamic attribute relationships relies heavily on Objectivity/DB's association classes, which provide higher level capabilities (e.g., propagation of some actions) than simple pointers.

Framework classes take the burden of managing object persistence, transaction handling, database locking, and encapsulation of problem-solving algorithms and event-driven procedures (daemons), permitting the application engineer to concentrate on the actual problem domain rather than reimplement basic features. Further, framework classes provide also a standard GUI behavior for each class or attribute type (which, of course, may be redefined).

Developing a great number of prototypes in different problem domains, we found out that approximatively 60 to 70 percent of the functionalities can be implemented at framework level, thus being effectively reusable across applications.

Rational Rose Metaschema Model

Starting a new application, the developer finds the framework classes mentioned above represented in a Rational Rose metaschema model. The application is designed specializing and relating framework classes using Booch or OMT notation, thus instantiating the generic metaschema into the actual object schema of the problem domain. Generally, we found no need to define from-scratch classes, the target domain can be completely modeled by specializing metaschema classes, as shown in Figure 7–1.

Perl Filters and Preprocessors

Rational Rose is able to generate C++ code, which is actually a subset of Objectivity/DB's Data Definition Language (DDL). By customizing Rational Rose's code generation property sets, it was possible to generate code very similar to DDL, but some syntactical elements (like "<->" for the representation of bidirectional relationships or declare/implement macros of variable size arrays) could not be obtained, so it was necessary to write filters that perform some pattern substitution and filtering in the generated code.

Further, we implemented a preprocessor that generates a set of built-in member functions (delivering basic database and GUI services) for each class defined in an OSEF application, according to its type.

Filters and preprocessors were initially implemented using UNIX shell and awk scripts, but as the project grew and parsing requirement became more complex,

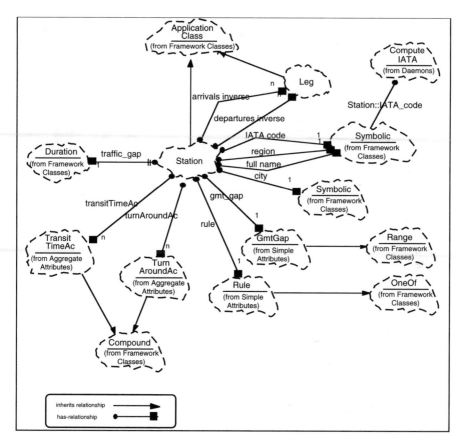

Figure 7–1 Specialization of the metaschema to an actual object schema (in this example from the air transportation domain).

they were re-implemented in Perl 5.0. The invocation of all filters and preprocessors is managed by makefiles, which are reusable for each new OSEF application.

OSEF Runtime Kernel and Application Control Interface

The OSEF runtime kernel includes the daemon manager, the data consistency manager, the solver manager, and an Application Control Interface (ACI) shown in Figure 7–2. The latter is a class, either graphical or ASCII based, providing a virtual "main" function that is responsible for the layout of the application's main window (if the application has a GUI). This class can be redefined by the application, if needed. By specializing the ACI class of the runtime kernel, multiple application control interface classes can be defined, each with its own "main" function. This way it is possible to deploy more than one application that can be executed against the same federated database.

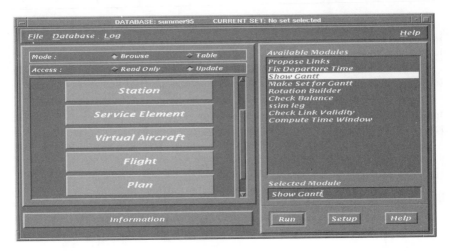

Figure 7–2 The default Application Control Interface.

THE DEVELOPMENT CYCLE

The development cycle of an application in the OSEF environment is composed of the following steps, executed iteratively:

A *Modeling of the target domain using Rational Rose:* The application developer analyzes the target domain of the application using Booch or OMT notation on top of the framework classes, starting from the metaschema Rose model.

B *Code generation and (possibly) implementation:* The application developer implements possible redefined (or new defined) methods of application-specific classes.

C *Compilation and usage of the prototype:* The generated makefiles permit the developer to compile code generated by Rational Rose directly into an executable prototype.

After step C, the application developer returns to the analysis of the domain (step A), but in this task he or she is now supported by the prototype application obtained during the previous iteration. The prototype application can now be populated with sample data.

To obtain a first prototype, a few hours of analysis suffice, and it is not necessary to write any code (step B), since basic behavior, as well a GUI, are inherited by application-specific classes from the framework classes. In fact, during the first iterations, the developer normally focuses on data structures that are typical of the target domain and is not concerned with the implementation of particular functionalities.

We found that the immediate availability of a usable prototype facilitates the involvement of final users, reducing dramatically the risk of misunderstood requirements and augmenting the commitment to the resulting application.

The architecture of an OSEF application, based on a static metaschema (the FC library) on top of which a dynamic data schema of the target domain is built, is well suited for the iterative process because it allows for an evolutionary approach. The same set of sample data can be maintained across many (possibly all) iterations, even if the data schema changes (new attributes, deletion of attributes, modification of attribute types and/or relationship cardinalities). If a unique transformation is possible from the old schema of an object to the new one, then the object will automatically migrate towards the new structure and no data will be lost or corrupted.

STEP A: MODELING

Among the steps seen above, step A (modeling) outweighs the others, especially at the beginning of the development. Modeling consists of four complementary activities:

A1 Determination of classes/relationships/attributes: The application developer determines classes, type/cardinality of attributes, and type/cardinality of relationships among classes. Classes as attribute types are directly or indirectly derived from framework classes.

A2 The application developer extends the public interface delivered by each class defining new methods (i.e., public member functions, in C++), in addition to those inherited from its base classes.

A3 The application developer defines daemons and associates them to classes/attributes and triggering events. Possible triggers are modification of attributes, creation/deletion of objects, and so on.

A4 The application developer defines solvers and their input/output domain.

Note that at least in the first iteration, activity A1 is mandatory, while A2/3/4 are optional throughout the whole cycle. In fact, a prototype obtained through activity A1 only has complete data entry and database navigation facilities.

The main goal of activity A1 is to capture syntactical relationships between real-world entities of the target domain. When the syntactical structure of the target domain is well defined and understood, activities A2/3 become more and more predominant. Daemons are mainly used to introduce those semantic relationships that cannot be captured syntactically during activity A1, such as dependencies between attributes or constraints on attribute values.

With activity A4, finally, an application engineer can introduce problem-solving algorithms into the application. This normally occurs after activities A1/2/3 have delivered a relatively stable syntactical/sematical model of the target domain, and it typically is the main activity to transform the prototype into a fully functional application.

STEP B: IMPLEMENTATION

In step B of each iteration, methods, daemons, and solvers defined in activities A2/3/4 have to be implemented. For each method, daemon or solver, Rational Rose or the OSEF preprocessor generates an empty stub where an implementation has to be supplied. This implementation is preserved when code is successively regenerated. To implement functionalities, the application developer uses API functions belonging to several layers:

> Layer 0:   Objectivity/DB and X/Motif API. These APIs are wrapped by the layer 1 OSEF API, therefore the application developer is not encouraged to use them.
>
> Layer 1:   OSEF API. This API hides details of the underlying database management and windowing system and further delivers basic services of each framework class. The OSEF API delivers most types of interaction with the database system, such as creation, deletion, and access/manipulation of objects.
>
> Layer 2:   The class methods defined in activity A2 constitute layer 2. This is an extension of layer 1. While layer 1 delivers all those functionalities common to all application domains (framework level), this layer introduces all domain specific functions (application level).
>
> Layer 3:   Daemons and solvers defined in activities A3/4 can be implemented directly on top of layer 1. Nevertheless, it seems to be good programming practice to try to define an application level layer and use it for daemon and solver implementations, obtaining a more maintainable and reusable code.

The resulting layered functional architecture is depicted in Figure 7–3

RATIONAL ROSE/C++

Rational Rose/C++ is produced by Rational Software Corporation, Santa Clara, California. Rose is a graphical object-oriented software engineering tool supporting Booch, as well as OMT notation for object-oriented analysis and design. In particular, it provides a C++ code generator. In the OSEF development environment, all design level decisions involved in building an application (e.g., definition of classes and their attributes, user-defined attribute types, and relations between classes) have to be taken within Rose.

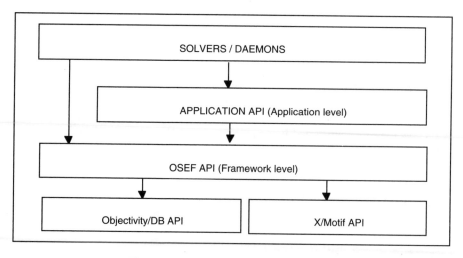

Figure 7–3 Functional API architecture.

A Rose model is an abstraction of a system's organization and behavior. It is organized as a collection of diagrams, classes, relationships, modules, and so on that together should deliver a complete and consistent description of the system to be built. Typically, a model consists of graphical and textual information, the diagrams, and the specifications. Rose models are stored in ASCII format (MDL) files.

Diagrams

Every Rational Rose model is organized as a collection of diagrams. Every diagram represents a view of the model. Entities (e.g., a class) can appear on multiple diagrams, but exist only once in the model. Diagrams can be related among each other to form a hierarchical structure. The following diagram types are supported by Rose:

Class diagrams: Show relationships between classes (association, inheritance, has and uses relationships). Classes can be arranged in class categories.

Object diagrams: Show interactions between objects, such as sent messages, etc.

State diagrams: Represent states and transitions to describe the behavior of classes having event-ordered behavior.

Module diagrams: Show physical dependencies between modules, packages, tasks, and the arrangement of modules into subsystems.

Process diagrams: Depict processors, processes, devices, and connections.

The graphical items that can be used to draw a diagram are available from a palette of icons. Among them, the most important are several kinds of classes (represented in a cloud-like fashion in Booch notation, or as rectangles in OMT notation) and different types of relationships (represented by arrows or edges). Graphical items can be cut and pasted from one diagram to another.

Each graphical entity has two kinds of textual information associated with it: the *specifications* and the *code generation properties*. The former contain specific information about the item, like documentation, attributes, and operation definitions; the latter contain information that influence the style of generated code. While specifications are target language independent, properties are tightly related to the programming language and provide a mapping from the model to the target language (C++, in our case). Specifications and properties can be modified within dialog boxes.

Since a model may be composed of many different diagrams, Rose offers search and cross-reference functions to trace usage of a given item.

Exportation/Importation of Items

All or part of a model can be exported into a text file, called petal file (PTL). PTL files can be imported into other models, hence they constitute a way to exchange information between models.

Code Generation Property Sets

The code generator generates C++ source code files from information in the model. The source code generation style can be customized by the means of the code-generation properties mentioned above.

Different sets of properties are provided for different entity types (classes, relationships, modules, etc.). Property sets are defined on a system-wide scope with default values and can be customized and attached to model entities. In C++, for example, an operation corresponds to a member function, and operation properties permit defining whether the member function should be `virtual`, `friend`, `static`, and so on.

Preserved Code Regions

After class skeletons have been generated, implementations must be supplied into the empty function bodies. The C++ generator inserts specially marked code regions, such as the following:

```
//##begin <region_label> preserve=yes
    your implementation code...
//##end <region_label>
```

Code regions (if "preserve" is set to "yes") are preserved when the file is regenerated. Implementations are not lost when the Rose model is modified.

Tool Evaluation

Overall, Rational Rose has proved be to a valuable tool for analysis, design, and project administration. Our framework kernel model actually contains about forty classes, divided into approximatively fifteen categories and about fifty modules arranged in nine subsystems, not counting the Gantt and ODBC extensions. Further, we have defined over 100 customized property sets. The resulting Rose model (MDL) file is about 55,000 lines long.

Release History

At project start-up we installed release 2.0.15 of Rational Rose for SunOS and for Windows. This version had some problems with NFS-mounted filesystems: If a timeout occurred due to heavy LAN traffic during the saving of a model, Rose sometimes crashed, leaving the model file in corrupted state (release 2.0.15 saved models in a binary format called DSN). Also, pressing accidentally certain keys (e.g., the ESC key within some documentation fields) caused Rose to crash.

When we moved to version 2.5.26, many of these problems were fixed. Upgrading from release 2.0.15, we had to rewrite partially our preprocessors and filters, since code generation style was slightly different, especially concerning code region markers. A further difference was that models were no longer stored as binary DSN files but as MDL files in ASCII format (the "Petal" format). A new feature of release 2.5.26 was multiuser support. A model could be split into units, and each of them can be locked and administrated with SCCS (in the UNIX version of Rose). A useful functionality introduced in release 2.5 and missed in release 2.0 was the "relocate" function that permits a class to be moved from one category to another.

When we moved to release 2.7.1, we noticed further improvements in performance and robustness. This time we had no problems with generated code, since the code generator didn't change from release 2.5.26.

The most recent release of Rational Rose we have used is 3.0.2. Besides a slightly redesigned GUI, a notable new feature is the support of OMT notation. Each diagram can be created and visualized either in Booch or in OMT notation. Further, in respect to all release 2.x versions, user manuals have been substantially improved.

OBJECTIVITY/DB

Objectivity/DB is a distributed client/server object database management system (ODBMS) produced by Objectivity, Inc. Objectivity/DB provides full database functionality with a distributed architecture that supports networks of heterogeneous platforms.

Data Definition Language

The data schema of a persistent application is specified within one or more DDL (Data Definition Language) files. DDL is a superset of C++. DDL files mainly contain class definitions in the usual C++ syntax, extended with some Objectivity/DB-specific syntactical features (e.g., <-> to express bidirectional associations). If a class is derived from one of the four storage classes below, it is persistent. For each persistent class Objectivity/DB generates a set of member functions and parameterized "proxy" classes (`ooHandle`, `ooRef`, and `ooItr` classes), which are used to access objects of that class.

Storage Classes

To be persistent within an Objectivity/DB database, an object must be instance of one of the four storage classes:

> *Basic Object:* is the fundamental unit of storage. It is represented by the class `ooObj`.
>
> *Container:* is a collection of Basic Objects, physically clustered together in memory pages and on disk. Pages are further subdivided into slots. Containers are represented by class `ooContObj`.
>
> *Database:* is a collection of Containers. Physically, each database is stored in a file on disk. Databases are objects of class `ooDBObj`.
>
> *Federated Database:* logically contains all defined databases and the data schema. It has an object of class `ooFDObj`.

Objects of the four storage classes continue to exist after the application that created them terminates. They can be shared among applications, with locking managed by Objectivity/DB. Except for federated databases, all persistent objects can be created and deleted dynamically by an application program.

To identify persistent objects, Objectivity/DB uses an Object Identifier (OID), which is unique in a federated database (a collection of databases sharing the same data schema). An object identifier is a string with format "#D-C-P-S," where D, C, P, S are integers identifying respectively the database, the container, the page, and the slot on the page. For example #2-3-123-45 corresponds to an object in slot 45 of page 123 in container 3 of database 2.

References and Handles

Objectivity provides several parameterized classes used as proxies to access persistent objects: object references (`ooRef`) and object handles (`ooHandle`). Both `ooRef` and `ooHandle` are type-safe classes that redefine many of the operators (e.g., ->) available on C++ pointers, in addition to Objectivity/DB-specific database operations. A corresponding handle class is created automatically by the DDL process for every persistent class found in the schema headers. Handle classes provide member functions to test validity and open/close/lock status of a reference to a persistent object and to set locks on a persistent object.

Iterators

Iterator classes, implemented by the class `ooItr`, enable an application to navigate through collections of persistent objects, filtering for those objects that:

1. Belong to a particular class or its subclasses
2. Belong to a one-to-many association
3. Are one level lower in the logical storage hierarchy (e.g., all containers in a database, all objects in a container)

Associations

Objectivity/DB provides a set of parameterized classes, called associations, that provide higher level capabilities than simple pointers for modeling and managing relationships between objects. Associations can be unidirectional or bidirectional, and their cardinalities can range from one-to-one to many-to-many. Associations are implemented through the parameterized class `ooHandle` (`ooRef` since version 3.5). For each declared association, Objectivity/DB generates a set of member functions used to manipulate objects linked by the association.

Further, associations can be used to propagate copy and lock or delete operations along association chains. A valuable feature of bidirectional associations is referential integrity. Bidirectional associations are the main mechanism used to implement the metaschema mentioned in the previous section. Defining attributes as associations instead of C++ members and exploiting their characteristics, OSEF is able to manage schema transformations dynamically. Associations were also used to establish links between daemons and attributes and between solvers and their input/output domain variables.

Navigation along associations has proven to be very efficient, especially if objects were clustered conveniently.

Variable-Size Arrays

Objectivity provides two parameterized classes representing persistent or transient variable-size arrays, the classes `ooVArray` and `ooTVArray`. Although these classes are useful, we have missed the possibility of defining persistent arrays, whose items are handles. You can define persistent arrays of base types (int, float, fixed length strings, etc.), but only transient arrays (`ooTVArray`) can have elements of type `ooHandle`. Fortunately, it was possible to find a workaround for this problem, implementing such a variable-size array class on our own.

Physical Clustering of Objects

Persistent objects are created using the (redefined) "new" operator. An object can be created "near to" another object. This is done specifying a cluster as an argument of the "new" operator. A cluster may be a database, a container, or another basic object. If clustering is requested, Objectivity/DB tries to locate the new object onto the same memory page of the cluster, thus reducing substantially the number of disk reads for objects that frequently have to be accessed together. Clustering was found to have a great impact on performance, especially navigating associations. To use clustering effectively, you must know how data are used by an application. In fact, when we moved from default clustering to explicit clustering, we saw a performance improvement up to 50 to 60 percent in algorithms that made heavy use of association navigation.

Note that Objectivity/DB recognizes a null pointer as a special clustering directive. In that case the created object is transient, that is, it doesn't go into the database. Transient objects, however, cannot have associations with other objects.

Indexes

Indexes provide fast access to basic objects by sorting objects of a particular class according to the value in one or more members of the class. To maintain a class, a `ooKeyDesc` object must be created for the class, and a `ooKeyField` object must be created and added to the `ooKeyDesc` for each indexed member. Indexes are persistent and can be created and deleted during runtime. Once created, indexes are kept up to date by Objectivity/DB. In version 3.0, indexes were limited to a given container, but this limitation has been overcome in newer releases (3.5 and 3.8). `ooKeyDesc` and `ooKeyField` objects cannot be specialized.

Transactions and Locking

As is usual in DB management systems, all Objectivity/DB database operations occur within a transaction. When a transaction completes successfully and is committed, the modifications are actually written into the database and become visible to other applications. If a transaction is aborted, the database is left in the state of the previous commit. A transaction can be started either in read or update mode.

Objectivity/DB provides MROW (Multiple Readers, One Writer) access to databases. Objectivity/DB supports multiple concurrent update transactions on a database. As soon as someone wants to modify an object, this has to be locked. This happens either implicitly or explicitly (calling the "update" function on the handle referencing the object). The locking granularity is the container. When an object in a container is locked, the whole container is locked.

When a transaction is aborted, locks are released, and all handles in virtual memory are invalidated. This gave us some problems with Motif: GUI components have associated destroy callbacks. These are triggered at transaction abort time (when a transaction is aborted, all GUI components, except the main window, are destroyed), but the X server actually calls them only after the abortion has completed, that is, outside a legal transaction. Since client data we pass to these callbacks also contain handles, these handles are invalidated, but we found no secure method to test this. We finally solved this problem with a boolean variable stating if there is a current active transaction.

A transaction can also be commited or commited-and-held. When a transaction is committed, locks are released and the current transaction is closed. After restarting a new transaction, handles should be still usable, but we found handles remaining in an undefined (and untestable) state. After invoking the "close" function on them, they can be used again. A possible solution could be to call the "close" function prior to each handle usage, but since every database interaction is performed through handles, this seemed to have too negative an impact on performance, besides giving us a "multiple closed objects" diagnostic from the `ooRunStatus` utility (a function that may be registered to be called at exit time of the process and to give a report of database activity during the process lifetime). Finally, we identified all code portions that can access handles directly after a commit and closed handles there. We would have appreciated it if Objectivity/DB had closed handles for us (not out-of-scope handles are registered by the DBMS, so probably it would have been possible. For compatibility reasons with our customer, we are still using version 3.0, maybe newer releases of Objectivity/DB can do this job).

A commit-and-hold action writes modifications to the database and maintains the current transaction, and the handles in virtual memory are still valid. Thus, this seemed to be the solution of our problems with handles after a commit. This action, however, doesn't release any lock, so it is not suitable for a multiuser concurrent environment.

Objectivity/DB Classes in the OSEF Rose Metaschemia Model

In the OSEF metaschema Rational Rose model, Objectivity/DB's base and parameterized classes, like storage classes, handles, iterators, and variable size arrays, are available as classes or class templates belonging to the "Objectivity/DB classes" category, as shown in Figure 7–4.

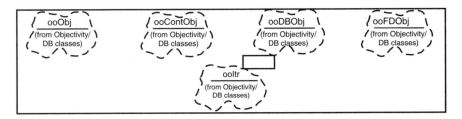

Figure 7–4   Some of Objectivity/DB's base or parameterized classes in the Rose model.

DATABASE ARCHITECTURE OF OSEF APPLICATIONS

All applications developed in the OSEF development environment share a common database structure: for each modeled domain a federated database is created. The federated database contains the static part (like inheritance hierarchies) of the data structures typical of the target domain. Many applications that access the same federated database can be deployed (defining multiple application control interface object, as seen in the previous section).

Each federated database can contain an unlimited number of databases (disk space is the only limit), all sharing the static part of the data schema.

Each database contains five containers:

Schema Container: This container holds the dynamic part of the domain specific data schema. Actually, it holds exactly one object of each class type or attribute type defined in a given application. This object (that we call "default object" of the class) is used as a representative of its class. When new objects are created, they have the same structure (attribute links, daemon links, etc.) as the default object.

Daemon Container: Contains all daemon objects. Daemon objects encapsulate procedures triggered by events.

Solver Container: Contains all solver objects, which encapsulate algorithms.

Temporary Container: This container contains persistent objects that have the lifetime of a session. This container is created when a database is opened and is destroyed, together with all objects it contains, when the database is closed. The creation of temporary persistent objects for session-specific data is suggested by Objectivity, because transient objects (they can be created with a null clustering directive) cannot deal with things like associations or indexes.

Data Container: Contains actual data. When a user creates new objects, they are created inside this container. Note that since creation of default objects, daemon objects, and solver objects is handled by the runtime kernel, the data container is the only one the application can control explicitly. If no clustering directive is given in the application, the data container is assumed to be the default cluster. This means that if the application does not explicitly indicate an object near to which a new object has to be located, the OSEF runtime kernel will create it somewhere in the data container.

The database architecture is determined by the Application Control Interface class, whose partial structure is shown in Figure 7–5.

Performances and Tuning

At the beginning we had some performance problems with the pilot application that performs aircraft scheduling for the long-range fleet of Alitalia. Initially, we

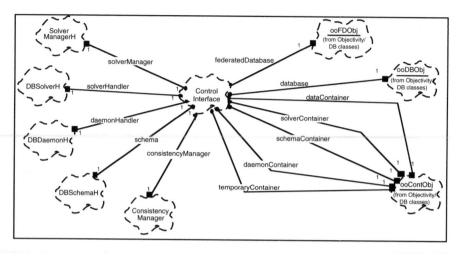

Figure 7–5   OSEF database architecture managed by the Control Interface class.

thought this could be due to the heavy dynamic metaschema on top of which every OSEF application is built: many associations have to be traversed in order to access attributes, call daemons, and so on. In our relatively small sample database (about 10,000 objects), the execution of a problem-solving algorithm may cause millions of association traversals. A closer analysis, however, revealed that almost all of the bottlenecks were because of inefficient algorithms or inexperience in the use of database features. For example, we could achieve notable performance increases through extensive use of the clustering directive (up to 60 percent), minimizing re-sizings of variable-size arrays, and systematically passing handles by reference in-stead of value.

To improve and analyze performance we found the runtime statistics that Ob-jectivity/DB can print out at process exit a valuable source of information.

Overall, we were able to decrease response times of the pilot application by approximatively 10 to 20 times from the first prototype to the actual release. A solver that initially took as long as half an hour—the *rotation builder*, which as-signs flights to aircrafts, producing the actual timetable—now runs in about 2 min-utes, and there is still some code that has not been critically revisited.

Evaluation

Objectivity provides a number of utilities to administrate databases within a feder-ated database. A federated database is a collection of databases sharing the same schema. The catalog of databases in a federated database can be seen with the oodumpcatalog utility. Most of the functionalities provided by utilities are available as API functions, too. Currently, no "save-as" utility exists (this can be obtained combining the `oocopydb` and the `ooattachdb` utilities). From a program, you have to issue a system call on a shell script invoking those utilities. Further, each database file has a unique ID (a small integer) within a federated database, which is preserved by the `oocopydb` utility, so that an ID conflict arises when `ooattachdb` tries to reattach the copied database file to the catalog of the federated database. We found a workaround by writing a set of shell scripts to detach, copy, and attach database files to a federated database, but problems sometimes still arise (what this means is that you may lose an entire database). As far as we know, release 3.8 did not fix this problem, but the technical support team told us that they are working on it.

Objectivity has a backup utility (`oodump`) that dumps the contents of a database into an ASCII file. With version 3.0, performing a dump is a very long task and the resulting file is very large (approximately 100 MB for our sample database containing about 10,000 objects. A dump file can be reloaded with the `ooload` utility, but we had some problems with name clashes between inherited and none inherited members.

Another minor problem we had was that some of Motif's header files were not processable by the DDL preprocessor. This happened for files containing definitions of "enums" containing particular expressions. We could work around this problem by revisiting the header inclusion architecture, but it took us some time.

Release History

At start of the project, in early 1994, Objectivity's current release was 3.0. Our project partner Alitalia and ourselves began working with that release.

During 1995 we received release 3.5. This version requires a slightly different DDL code syntax (e.g., `ooHandles` have to be replaced by `ooRefs` in association declarations), but this gave us no problem, since we used handle and reference classes through Rational Rose's property sets (we simply had to systematically redefine all association code generation property sets). Further, the DDL preprocessor of release 3.5 is called `ooddlx` instead of `ooddl` and supports different options, so our makefiles had to be rivisited. Overall, we had no problems upgrading from 3.0 to 3.5, but since our partner did not perform the upgrade, we continued working and deploying applications on release 3.0.

By the beginning of 1996, we were told by Objectivity's technical support team about the availability of release 3.8 and of version 4.0 for the third quarter.

Database Browsing and Inspection

Objectivity/DB provides several tools for viewing and modifying a database. These tools can be started through the tool manager (`ootoolmgr`), a graphical user interface including a type browser and a data browser.

Unused Features

Other features offered by Objectivity are the following:

System Names: A system name uniquely identifies a persistent object. System names are mandatory for federated databases and databases (they correspond to their filenames); they are optional for containers.

Dictionaries: The dictionary class, `ooMap` provides a hash table, where each element consists of an object name and an OID.

Versioning: Versioning allows you to maintain many copies of the same basic object. We didn't use this feature because in our database architecture, the target domain's schema was modeled through associations instead of C++ members, allowing us to manage object "versions" dynamically.

C++ Pointer Interface: Using this interface it is very easy to transform a non-persistent C++ application into a persistent one. At the simplest level, only two steps have to be performed:

1. Classes that have to be persistent must simply be derived from the `ooObj` class.
2. The file extension of header files containing the declarations of persistent classes has to be changed from .h to .ddl.

Actually, the transformation is done in a very short time. Obviously, persistent code obtained this way does not exploit all of the facilities offered by Objectivity/DB, like associations, handles, iterators, and so on. These can be introduced into the source code as needed.

Autostart Package: Objectivity/DB provides the `ooAutoStart` package, which automatically performs the steps necessary to manage a transaction: it initializes Objectivity/DB, it begins a transaction, it opens the federated database, and finally, after execution of the application, it commits or aborts the transaction. This feature is useful when beginning to work with Objectivity/DB, because it permits the novice user to create and use databases without having to deal with transactions. In fact, our first protoype used the autostart package, but as we needed to grant concurrent access, we had to move to explicit transaction handling.

EXPERIENCES AND SUMMARY

The OSEF project has revealed that a framework-based approach to software development can bring up to 60 to 70 percent of effective design and code reuse from one application to another. During the project's lifetime, the two major products involved in the environment's architecture—Rational Rose and Objectivity/DB—have maturity to make them more useful products.

Rational Rose, in particular, has proven to be a highly powerful and customizable CASE tool, where almost all of the design decisions can be taken and documented.

Further, we found that an ODBMS like Objectivity/DB is well suited to support framework-based persistent applications, where performance issues are particularly important due to the overhead introduced by the framework level.

Issues currently under investigation are the inclusion of automated test scripting tools (e.g., Segue QA Partner) and object distribution tools, as well as porting to Windows.

8

Using Objectivity/DB in an Application for Configuration Management

Rosa Meo, Politecnico di Torino

ABSTRACT

A well-known OODBMS—Objectivity/DB—has been used to develop a new configuration manager (CM). By means of this, code and related documents such as design and specification documents, can be stored and retrieved, changed, versioned, and shared by the members of a software development team. The new configuration manager has been developed in C++, extended to the Data Definition Language of Objectivity/DB. By virtue of an object-oriented data model, the methods developed can be used as configuration management services by higher-level applications.

CONFIGURATION MANAGERS
AND OBJECT-ORIENTED DATABASES

This chapter, proposes a general model for configuration management based on an object-oriented (OO) model for both product and process data concerning software projects. A layer has been created on top of an OO database to take advantage of the

---

I would like to thank Maria Letizia Jaccheri for her advice in research development.

OO technique. In this way, adopting the perspective of reuse, OO methods can be viewed as services provided by this CM application to higher level applications.

Requirements of a Configuration Manager

A configuration manager (CM) can be defined as a process-centered software development environment used as a process engine coordinating the work of developers and maintaining consistency between their documents. This happens in a distributed fashion. So a CM must also provide a model that simultaneously represents the process model, the subdivision of the work to be fulfilled, the organization of the project team, and the product itself.

In addition, since the project team may be composed of many members, a CM must provide mechanisms to manage sharing of the project components, such as product components or tasks, partial views on the complexity of the overall system, and mechanisms or grades of priority and privileges. Incremental updates and flexible access to shared documents are needed to coordinate common work. Moreover, fine-grained documents are required to maintain document references and manage consistency. Finally, the policies adopted should not be predefined but flexible and dynamically adapted to the evolution of the project itself.

Database Requirements

According to Emmerich and colleagues [Emm+92] "suitable databases for process-centered environments do not yet exist." The data definition language must cope with complexity and be provided with the features needed to manage encapsulation of information, inheritance, and specialization, as well as definitions of operations applicable to each of them and facilities for the navigation on the related graph. Moreover, a concept of versioning must be adapted to graphs, and a suitable check-in/check-out mechanism is required to support a multi-user environment. According to Estublier [Est94], this is the most important topic in database support to software engineering environments. The database should be able to hide the versioning dimension of objects, while still distinguishing object constraints on the particular version, or following rules related to versioning. From the structural standpoint, sometimes the OO databases suffer from the so-called *granularity problem* posed by the different dimensions of the objects forming the units of cooperation between developers. Granularity unity often coincides with the file or has the document boundaries and so the system cannot efficiently manage objects of different sizes. A second difficulty is the need for support in creating opposite views of portions of the system and a third is the lack of a transaction scheme suited to the particular project structure. Lastly, few environments support distribution of databases or distributed access to centralized data. The database should propose, not impose, the cooperation strategy because that which will be adopted depends on the tools, the type of objects, and the schema of data available. All these elements constitute a sub-database that forms the frame to operate in, whereas the policies and mechanisms adopted by each database are not predefined, and the communication protocols between the sub-databases remain customizable [Est94].

USING OBJECTIVITY/DB TO IMPLEMENT A CONFIGURATION MANAGER

Objectivity/DB is an object-oriented federated database, which is an aggregation of databases sharing the same object organizational scheme. It is suitable for a CM because of its support for distribution, versioning, and aggregation of objects, as well as searching and querying using an SQL-like language and management of transactions. Besides, it allows effective organization of the entire data in a distributed environment. In fact, each group of work can share the same local database, reducing the overhead of remote logging.

The database is equipped with many graphical tools to facilitate database maintenance. In particular, the *data browser* is used to inspect the content of any object in a database and its links, the *type browser* views and navigates the hierarchical relationships between the object classes, the *debugger* views and alters database contents and also *instantiates* objects and their links. Finally, the database *statistics panel* is useful to inspect how the tool manager accesses the federated database.

Organization of a Federated Database and Related Limits

A federated database is composed of databases containing objects represented on a common schema stating their properties. Each database contains composite objects that are called *containers*. A container groups together *basic* objects. These can contain no other objects and are the smallest unit of *storage, encapsulation* and *inheritance* in the system. The order of containment between objects is defined according to the containment relationship in Figure 8–1. An object can contain no other object characterized by the same order of containment.

Containers are suitable for modeling the *working environment* of each software developer; in fact, each of them works with software objects, tools, or software modules that are shared with other developers and are characterized with some specific access privileges. As we will see, we will be able to model the complex objects belonging to working environments as a web of basic objects connected by relationship instances. In addition, we will associate access privileges with each software object with respect to each working environment (by means of *name scopes*).

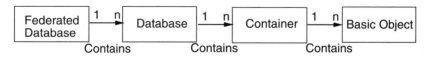

Figure 8–1   Order of containment between objects in Objectivity/DB.

Object Constraints

Any object is subjected to constraints specifying the types of its attributes. Some types such as, for example, integer, float, or boolean, are predefined in the database and automatically checked by the system. Other types are specified and verified by the developer by means of suitable methods, such as `ooValidate()` automatically invoked at creation time, or `Update()` in modifications. Indeed, this method is common to all the classes, it being inherited from the root class. The attribute of an object must not be another object. It must always have a value from a primitive domain (such as, for example, the domain of integers or boolean). This limitation will raise some problems in specifying containment relationships between composite objects.

Property of Associations

In Objectivity/DB, relationships between objects with single or multiple cardinality are available and are called *associations*. As will be seen later, an association can have a *propagation property* of operations on objects.

Locks

Generally, a federated database provides multiprocessing and multiple access to data. To ensure data consistency, access rights are restricted through the use of locks, either *read locks,* which allow a plurality of processes to read the same data, or *update locks*, which allow a single process to read or write data. The management of lock conflicts between processes can be dynamically adapted according to the choice of the user. Three alternatives are possible when the access of data is not allowed: give it up; wait and retry after a fixed period of time; stop in a lock waiting state until the resource is available. A facility is offered to detect the presence of deadlocks, as well. In order to prevent a deadlock, an explicitly locking methodology is offered, which does not guarantee the consistency state of the database itself.

Granularity

A container is the minimum granularity of lock. If you lock the container, no other process is admitted to any basic object contained in it. Also, if you lock a basic object, its container is locked and all the other basic objects in it as well. Moreover, as will be seen later, an operation of lock can "propagate" along associations.

MROW (Multiple Readers, One Writer)

This methodology allows a container to have multiple readers and one writer in a transaction. It is advantageous if you want to improve concurrency in your system when there are some other transactions that want to acquire access to the same objects. In this manner, a single writing process is allowed while some others are allowed in reading the last committed version. If you receive a notice that your container has been changed, you can issue an operation to refresh.

Transactions

Transactions are not overlapping or nested. The transaction is the length of time that all the locks and the established behavior (MROW and waiting for locks policy) last. A process has a unique active transaction, and a unique federated database. So each transaction operates only on the objects contained in a well-established scope in time and space.

Check-In and Check-Out Facility

Objectivity/DB extends the access privileges to an object beyond process boundaries for an extended period of time: this is the way to obtain working environments built on a pool of shared objects. In fact, when you wish to acquire access to an object for a period of time extending beyond a single transaction, you first invoke a *Check-Out* operation on that object. This forbids others from acquiring access to it. When you finish your operations on that object, you can release it to the developer community by the opposite operation, called *Check-In*.

Versioning

The database itself associates an object with a version concept and inserts it in a version hierarchy called *genealogy*. The database supports a *linear* evolution of versions. This implicitly identifies them as the consecutive *revisions* of an object due to an improvement process. So a version that already has a revision cannot be updated any more but only consulted. Two successive revisions are linked by an instance of association called `PrevVers` ↔ `NextVers` with single cardinality. Otherwise, a version can be submitted to the operation of creating a *variant*, in order to produce a ray arrangement of the versions. This permits the acquisition of parallelism between the cooperating processes of version acquisition and updating and implies an independent evolution of them. Two variants are linked by an instance of association called `Derivatives` ↔ `DerivedFrom` with multiple cardinality.

Scope Name and Name Scope

Scope names are used to identify objects for the purpose of their retrieval. A scope name, say `AfromB`, is the name that uniquely identifies an object A, from the point of view of another object B. B is called the *name scope* for that scope name. A scope name must be unique inside a given name scope. Scope names can be dynamically created or removed.

As previously mentioned, we used scope names to implement a mechanism of access rights. In fact, if A is the resource object whose access is restricted, then call B all the containers representing a *working environment* of a developer who is granted access to A. The scope name `AfromB`, used as a mechanism to retrieve A, is communicated only to those developers, working in their container, who are allowed access to A. In this way, the pool of containers is the name scope B.

Scan to Retrieve Objects on SQL-like Predicates

A pool of objects identified by determining characteristics based on the values of their attributes can also be retrieved by issuing queries in a SQL-like fashion. These predicates are interpreted and an "iterator" pointing to the result of the query is returned. In this way, more sophisticated conditions and constraints can be evaluated on a set of objects. All of these features supply a system with a wide variety of data models and policies to operate on.

THE PROPOSED CM MODEL

The starting point from which to approach this model is a configuration item (CI). A CI may have different origins, nature, and contents. It can be an atomic element or an aggregate of other CIs when it is the result of a composition described by the use of relationships, so that configuration extensibility is assured. As will be illustrated later, configuration development may be carried out by the addition, subtraction, or development of CIs. Development of a CI creates a version graph of the CI itself. Versioning is captured by relationships and each version graph produced is identified by the presence of a node of genealogy.

To control configuration development, a relationship is introduced to model dependency between several CIs. The semantics of the dependency are not fixed. The configuration status is established according to dependencies of its configuration components. Different versioned CIs may be logically linked together by a change imposed by a member of the development team. Labels for identification of a group of versioned CIs are provided in the definition of the versioned CI, as well as other attributes concerning the development team.

Main Design

The OO model is used to generate CM methods on a pool of basic elements characterizing the project: developers (each with a working environment), the basic product structure, and their links.

The product structure consists of documents and software objects, each being composed in terms of the others in a recursive fashion. The schema stating these composition associations and the nature of each configuration component grasps the relative dependencies between objects, and these are designed to be both general and customized. Last, each object is captured in its temporal development in the shape of successive versions that form a historical versioning graph.

The schema presented consists of five basic classes: `SoftwareObject`, `Document`, `VersionedItem`, `Composite`, and `VersGene` (Figure 8–2).

SoftwareObject

This class embodies the concept of file or a software unit characterized by the attributes of `AccessMode` (access mode) and the position in a file system of the distributed DBMS, or `Collocation`. For example, a value of the attribute

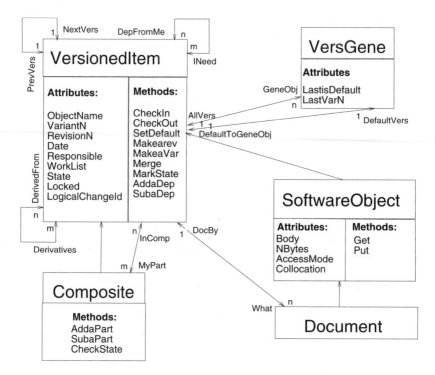

Figure 8–2   Detailed schema of the classes.

AccessMode might be Read Only and a value of Collocation might be the concatenation <NodeNumber,FileSystemNumber, PositionInThe-FileSystem>. The file content is stored in the attribute Body, while its length in bytes is stored in the NBytes attribute.

Document

This is a SoftwareObject subclass and represents the collection of textual descriptions and information needed to describe the semantics of other objects. For example, project specifications and established requirements are contained in a Document instance. We shall see later how to use instances of the class Document for other purposes.

VersionedItem

The instances of class SoftwareObject can be versioned, in the sense that a SoftwareObject instance may have one or more versions. VersionedItem class is therefore the class of the versions of each SoftwareObject (and each object of the class Composite, which will be defined later). The SoftwareObject class is a subclass of VersionedItem class.

As discussed below, this class is characterized by two attributes, `RevisionN` (Revision Number) and `VariantN` (Variant Number), used to identify versions in a version graph, and two methods, `MakeaRev` (Make a Revision) and `MakeaVar` (Make a Variant), that exploit the versioning relationships to create a version history. Besides, it presents the attribute `LogicalChangeId` (Logical Change Identifier) to identify different CIs joined by the same logical process of change.

Composite

A composite object can be composed of software objects or other composite objects, according to a recursive definition. CM check is carried out by the `Check-State` method of this class. Note that `Composite` is a subclass of the `Ver-sionedItem` class. This implies configuration versioning.

VersGene

There is also the `VersGene` class, which is used to identify an entire object-versioning genealogy. In other terms, an instance of `VersGene` is associated with a set of instances of the class `VersionedItem` connected by the relationship `AllVers` ↔ `GeneObj` (Figure 8–3). Note in Figure 8–3 that a version may be either a revision or a variant, as will be explained later.

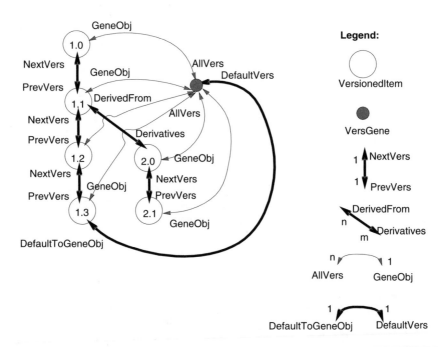

Figure 8–3   An object of VersGene class is associated with a graph of versions.

The database interface enabling the user to insert in the database a new software object is shown in Figure 8–4. In the upper part of the window we choose among the defined classes, and in the lower part we inspect the attributes and relationships defined for that particular object.

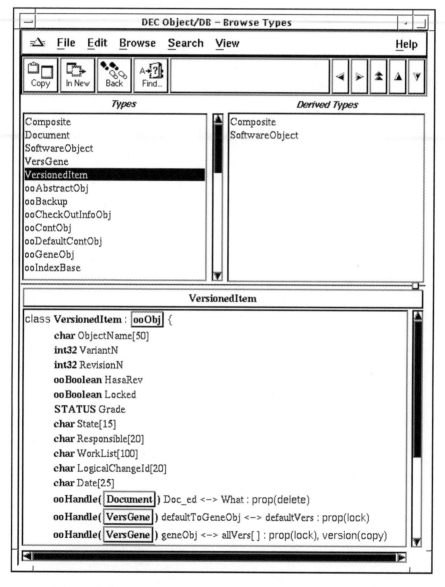

Figure 8–4 The database interface showing the browser of classes.

As is common practice in CM, we shall distinguish two dimensions for versioning. The first is associated with the concept of *variant*. A variant of a CI is the origin of a new subgraph associated with a different development line in a CI generation process. The second is the concept of *revision*, which normally denotes a new version produced during debugging.

An example of a versioning graph is shown in Figure 8–5, where each node label is indicated by the number of the variant, followed by a point and the number of the revision of that variant. The instances of these classes can be linked together by relationships, called *associations* in the OODBMS used for implementation of our CM.

A `Composite` object may be connected to a `VersionedItem` object by an instance of relationship `MyPart` ↔ `InComp` with cardinality m:n. Thus all the parts of a `Composite` object are identified.

Besides, a `VersionedItem` object may be connected to another by an instance of relationship `DepFromMe` ↔ `INeed`, which specifies the dependency links between CIs. For example, a software object that is an "include" file (such as `header.h`) is needed by all the software objects (such as `module1.c`) using it. We model this dependency by the two relationships `module1.c` → `INeed` `header.h` and `header.h` → `DepFromMe` `module1.c`.

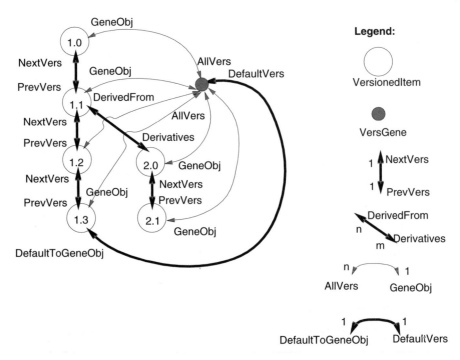

Figure 8–5   An object of VersGene class is associated with a graph of versions.

The CM Schema

VersionedItem

This class encapsulates the attributes and relationships pertaining to the notions of both version and component, or CI. Each instance presents:

- An `ObjectName,` which is the name of the CI
- A `DateOfCreation` of the version
- An identification of the developer `Responsible,` who is concerned about the change requests issued by the components of the project team
- The `WorkList` attribute, used to manage component access rights, all the developers who wish to have access to the component item must be registered in this `WorkList`
- The pair of `VariantN` and `RevisionN` attributes containing information used to identify a version in the genealogy graph (Figure 8–4)
- The `Locked` boolean attribute specifying the version availability to the project community
- The attribute of `State` containing the information of the configuration baseline[1] progress. Its values are orthogonal to the version `Locked` attribute, in the sense that every combination of values of `State` and `Locked` attributes is possible. For example: State value="Obsolete"; Locked value="false"
- `LogicalChangeId` specifies the reason for a modification generally involving several CIs—this attribute will be used for retrieval operations relative to a set of CIs characterized by correlated changes

In addition to `MakeaRev` and `MakeaVar` methods already discussed, other methods for versions are:

- `SetDefault,` which is a method to explicitly choose the default version in the genealogy. The default version is usually the last to be developed, but it could also be a well-tested preceding version.
- `CheckIn,` which locks the specified CI and delivers it to the developer, and `CheckOut,` which unlocks the specified CI and allocates the new version. They guarantee the persistence of changes issued on the component and make the concurrent ones sequential.
- Our CM permits the operation of `Merge,` to reunify two branches of independent evolution of versions: this might require the explicit intervention of the developer `Responsible.`
- `AddaDep` (Add a Dependency link) creates an instance of relationship `DepFromMe` ↔ `INeed;` `SubaDep` (Subtract a Dependency link) eliminates

---

[1]A configuration baseline is a milestone in the configuration development process.

it. Note that dependency links are not automatically determined by the existing links in the previous versions. A change set of modifications, in fact, may have generated more than one version and also changed the semantics determining the dependency links. So, whenever possible, these links can be determined from information found in the document instances, but the complete set of dependencies must be explicitly stated by the developer who carried out the changes.

VersGene

Each version history is specified by an instance of this class, for which associations are defined to access all the versions or the default. The policy by which the default version is determined in the version graph can be either dynamically established by an attribute of this class (LastIsDefault) that states that the default version is the last created, or explicitly defined by using the SetDefault method in class VersionedItem.

Composite

As the VersionedItem class has methods for the addition or subtraction of a dependency to a CI, the Composite class embodies primitives to add or subtract a part from a composite object: AddaPart and SubaPart. Moreover, since the status of a composite object is determined by that of all its parts, a method is needed to check the state of a CI, where state denotes the milestone reached in the development process, such as "Specified," "Allocated," "Tested," or "Obsolete." Check-State recursively navigates MyPart ↔ InComp associations between the components of an aggregation of objects: if they are in the same state, their composite object will also be placed in that state.

Software Object

A software object can be implemented as a file. SoftwareObject class encapsulates two methods called Get and Put.

- Get is a mechanism that translates the content of files stored in a compressed and versioned form from the file system itself into a SoftwareObject instance. It uses the Collocation attribute to retrieve files in the file system and stores their content in the attribute Body, which is effectively a stream of bytes forming the logical content of the software object.
- Put offers a service that is exactly the opposite of Get. It can use a hierarchy of versions and operators, such as UNIX diff, to obtain a version representation in terms of a compressed version difference.

Lastly, the attribute NBytes stores the length in bytes of the file content, while attributes AccessMode and Collocation provide the file-system information regarding the software object.

Document

A document is naturally an object containing textual information about a configuration item or version. The relationship DocBy ↔ What links every document to a set of version items (the items illustrated by that document).

In addition, a suitable document can be introduced to illustrate an instance of the INeed ↔ DepFromMe relationship. The mechanism adopted to introduce a document relative to a relationship instance is illustrated in Figure 8–6. As already mentioned in a previous example, it is the software module module1.c → INeed header.h and header.h → DepFromMe module1.c. The software object, module1.c of Figure 8–6 may be associated with an intermediate document (example: docu7), and this in turn is associated with the related software object header.h. The document connects the former software object to the latter. Thus, the relationship DepFromMe ↔ INeed (introduced for the sake of simplicity in Figure 8–2) is implemented as shown in Figure 8–6a.

Similarly, a document illustrating an instance of MyPart ↔ InComp, has been introduced with two associations Doc ↔ InComp and Doc ↔ MyPart as shown in Figure 8–6b. Note that the method AddaPart encapsulated in Composite automatically instantiates these two relationships.

Figure 8–7 shows the database interface enabling the user to navigate between two software objects connected to each other by means of an intermediate document object and by several instances of Doc ↔ InComp and Doc ↔ MyPart relationships. The document object is named 4-3-3-42 and shown in Figure 8–7 in the central

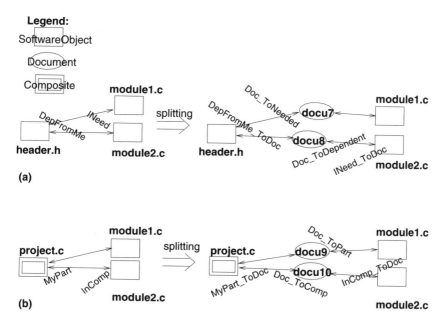

Figure 8–6   Embedding information for associations in a Document object.

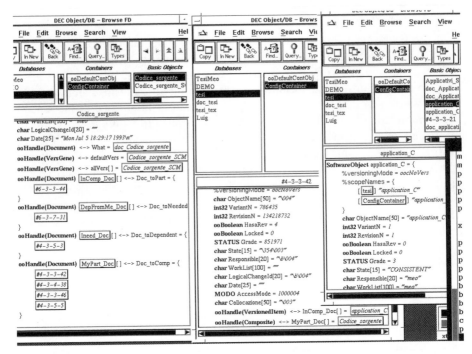

Figure 8–7   The database interface showing a software object with one of its parts and the document describing their relationship.

window. The composite object is shown in the left window while the component object is shown in the right one. In each window we can inspect the attribute values and navigate the relationship links (shown in the lower part of each window).

Similarly, the method `AddaDep` automatically instantiates the relationships `Doc` ↔ `INeed` and `Doc` ↔ `DepFromMe` that implement the relationship `INeed` ↔ `DepFromMe` with the intermediary of the document.

Modeling Information Inside Associations

This technique for the attribution of information to associations through an intermediate object (typically, an instance of class `Document`) requires care.

- A one-to-one association instance between two objects splits into a one-to-one association instance between the first object and one document and another between the document and the second object.
- A one-to-many association between two classes splits into a one-to-many association between the first class and the `Document` class, and a one-to-one association between `Document` class and the second class, as shown in Figure 8–6.

- A many-to-many association between two classes splits into a many-to-one association between the first class and the Document class, and a one-to-many association between the Document class and the second class (Figure 8–8a).

This solution has been adopted because of its conceptual simplicity. However, even more complex models exist, such as the splitting of a many-to-many association into either a many-to-many association between the first class and the Document class and a one-to-one association between the Document class and the second class (Figure 8–8b), or in the limit case, into two many-to-many associations.

FINAL CONSIDERATIONS ABOUT OBJECTIVITY/DB

Objectivity/DB presents the *automatic association generation* and the *propagation property of associations* characteristics, suitable for getting to an efficient implementation of a configuration manager. We discuss them in this final section to better understand their implications on all the components of the configuration manager.

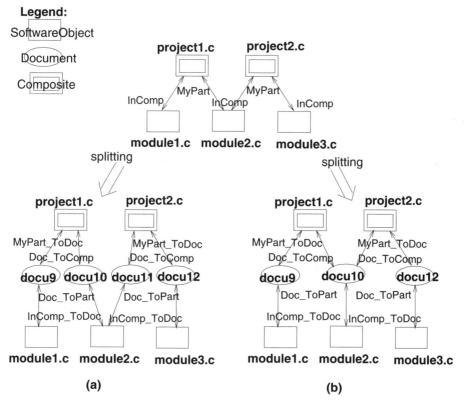

Figure 8–8   Various ways of splitting associations.

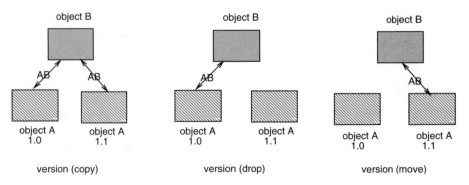

Figure 8–9 Versioning semantics with respect to the associations.

Automatic Association Generation in Versioning

Objectivity/DB makes it possible to automatically transfer predefined associations to a new version, which is a useful option in versioning. Three needs may occur for these associations:

1. In Figure 8–9, version 1.0 of object A is linked to an instance of B by a link[2] of AB. If association AB is declared using `version(copy)`, making a new version of A implies creating another link of AB by connecting the same instance of B to the new version of A. So if `version(copy)` behavior of an association is needed, a link of that association is automatically generated for both the previous and the last version of object A.

2. With reference to Figure 8–9, if `version(drop)` behavior is predefined in B for the association AB, versioning object A does not generate a new link of AB.

3. If `version(move)` behavior is chosen, the link of AB is moved from the previous to the newly created version of A. This behavior means that an association is only present for the last version.

The `version(copy)` behavior automatically duplicates the association links between the parts and a version of the composite object. It is chosen when all the components of the composite object are to be shared by all its successive versions. The `version(drop)` behavior, on the other hand, requires specification of the new parts for the composite object (for example, because the number of parts or their choice is changed with respect to the older version). `version(move)` still attributes the same components to the new version, but involves "stealing" the components from the previous version. This eliminates direct access to the components for the previous versions. This behavior enhances system management time and re-

---

[2]A link is an instance of an association.

duces the memory space used by associations. However, it considers the previous versions only useful for determination of the version history of an object and expects to make access to each of them less frequent than access to the last. Moreover, it implies that the choice of the components does not change with respect to the versioning process.

When versioning a part, the situation is different: `version(copy)` has no interesting meaning, while `version(drop)` waits for explicit developer intervention to determine whether the new version of the part can be included in the composite configuration. `version(move)` expects the last version to be always the one chosen in the composite configuration and assumes that development of a new version improves the composite configuration state. Analogous considerations (with minor changes) apply to the dependency association. Finally, note that `version(move)` is useful when objects A and B are versioned at the same time.

Propagation Property of Associations

Objectivity/DB makes it possible to automatically transfer most database operations, such as copying, deleting, locking, and so on, from a single object to all the objects connected to it by an association, if a suitable *propagation property* has been defined for that operation and for that association. For example, this property can be used to repeat each operation issued on the composite object on all its parts. Significant examples follow:

Lock Operation

When an association AB between object A and B is declared as `prop(lock)`, an operation of lock issued over A also determines locking of B. The propagation behavior of the lock operation along the association `MyPart` ↔ `InComp` will determine whether the shared components are accessible during access to their composite object. If the lock operation is propagated along the links from the parts towards the composite object, all the parts are inaccessible to other processes during access to the composite object. The same occurs for delete and copy operations.

Delete Operation

When an association AB is declared as `prop(delete)`, an operation of delete issued over A also determines deletion of B. This behavior answers the problem of `dangling references` or similar integrity constraints. If a delete operation is propagated along `MyPart` ↔ `InComp`, deletion of a `Composite` object also deletes all its parts.

Copy Operation

Analogous considerations apply to copy propagation.

EVALUATION OF THE CM MODEL

We believe that the CM model discussed above allows the effective management of
a software development process as stated by the requirements presented at the beginning of the chapter and illustrated in the following.

Identification of the Configuration Elements

This is achieved by means of the attributes of the class `VersionedItem` and the
relationships that identify the set of versioned components belonging to a given
configuration (`MyPart` ↔ `InComp`). From the semantic point of view, each of
these relationships is provided with an instance of the `Document` class that may be
used to specify the requirements of the related components. As regards the complete
identification of a configuration, the default version identification is provided for
all the components by means of the association (`defaultVers` ↔ `defaultTo-
GeneObj`) and the method (`SetDefault`).

Change of Configurations

This is obtained by means of the versioning of each configuration component (and
even the configuration itself). As regards composite components, the properties discussed in the previous section allow a variety of different criteria for their identification during the development process of their parts and are suitable for different
policies.

   Other design elements, such as the attribute `LogicalChangeId`, are used
to identify a logical unit of change and to report the state of each component
(`State`). Finally, change is safe if considered in a concurrent context of development since it is executed in a transactional environment in which a high parallelism
level is possible.

Status Accounting

This is achieved by means of the method `CheckState` of the `Composite` class
that recursively checks the value of an opposite attribute (`State`) for all the configuration components. Finally, whether any particular need arises to validate the state
of an object, the virtual method `ooValidate()` may be specialized to implement
the particular constraint validation.

Granularity

The granularity of the objects used as units of cooperation is not imposed or fixed
by the model. The `SoftwareObject` class presents some methods (`Get` and
`Put`) that work as intermediaries between the physical storage of the file and the
logical content. Therefore, the borderline between the units of work may be fixed
on the logical content and not on the physical allocation.

Support in Views

This is possible with the use of the containers and the scope names. A new container may be created as soon as a view on a set of objects is required. These objects may be explicitly chosen or retrieved by means of a scope name.

A prototype based on the designed model has been effectively used at Politecnico di Torino as a support to the development and documentation of software in the students thesis (at public disposal from `ftp://ftp.polito.it/pub/e3/DECDB.tar.gz`).

In addition, this CM is going to be used as the basic repository tool for the project E3 (Environment for Experimenting and Evolving process models) [Bal+94, JG92, RM87] developed at Politecnico di Torino.

CONCLUSIONS

A new Configuration Management Architecture was presented, based on object-oriented design concepts and characterized by model independence of linguistic implementation, environment and model extensibility, easy customization, and instantiation.

REFERENCES

[Bal+94] M. Baldi, S. Gai, M. L. Jaccheri, P. Lago: *Object Oriented Software Process Model Design in E3*, in *Software Process Technology*, in B. A. Nuseibeh (ed.). Research Studies Press, 1994.

[Est94] J. Estublier: *What Process Technology Needs from Databases*. Proceedings of the European Workshop on Software Process Technology, Grenoble, France, February, 1994.

[Emm+92] W. Emmerich, W. Schaefer, J. Welsh: *Suitable Databases for Process-Centered Environments Do Not Yet Exist*, in J.-C. Derniame (ed.). Springer Verlag LNCS 635, Trondheim, Norway, September, 1992.

[JG92] M. L. Jaccheri, S. Gai: *Initial Requirements for E3: an Environment for Experimenting and Evolving Software Processes*, in *Proceedings of EWSPT'92* J.-C. Derniame (ed.). Trondheim, Norway: Springer Verlag LNCS, pp. 99–102, September, 1992.

[RM87] M. Rozier, J. L. Martins: *Object Oriented Software Process Model Design in E3*. Berlin: Springer-Verlag, 1987.

9

Using an OODB for an MIS Application

Bernd Schlueter, pc-plus COMPUTING GmbH
Harald Stahl, pc-plus COMPUTING GmbH

ABSTRACT

In this chapter we want to share our experiences in working with an object-oriented database management system (OODBMS): we employ VERSANT as the central data repository for a Management Information System (MIS). Development of the product began in 1993; today it contains about 170,000 lines of code and runs at several customer sites in 24-hour, 7-days-a-week environments.

This chapter briefly introduces the company pc-plus and gives an overview of its products and its MIS system. We also elaborate on how we use VERSANT for MIS, including the reasons why VERSANT was chosen, the OODB's impact on MIS architecture and some hints on software development using an OODB. We conclude that VERSANT has been a wise choice for MIS and state our wishes for the future.

pc-plus AND ITS PRODUCTS

pc-plus COMPUTING is a telecommunication software company specializing in telephone operator applications and directory assistance (DA) and networking platforms. The German-based organization has subsidiaries in Switzerland, the United Kingdom, and the United States.

Figure 9–1 shows that pc-plus offers a wide range of DA related applications and the Operator Services Architecture (OSA), which is the framework for all DA-related products.

The following list of products is meant to provide the context of the MIS application:

- IDIS (International Directory Inquiry System) provides access to different kinds of worldwide directories, using standard protocols or native converters to specific databases. IDIS provides operators with uniform screens in their native language and simulates a standardization among internationally inconsistent spellings, abbreviations, and communication protocols.

- NDIS (National Directory Inquiry System) is a database system specifically designed for fast retrieval of telephone listings from very large volumes of data. The system's functions include phonetics, demerit, reverse, and neighborhood searches.

- QST (inQuiry Support for Telecom operators) is a general purpose reference database specifically designed for DA operators. Its repository consolidates the large amount of supplementary information used in DA, such as frequently called or hard-to-find foreign numbers, time zone tables, and language dictionaries.

- ADIS/tx (Automatic Directory Inquiry System for Telex) provides automatic processing of incoming subscriber inquiries over telex machines. The subscriber database handles inquiries with any order or number of user-defined search criteria and houses all existing telex subscriber numbers worldwide.

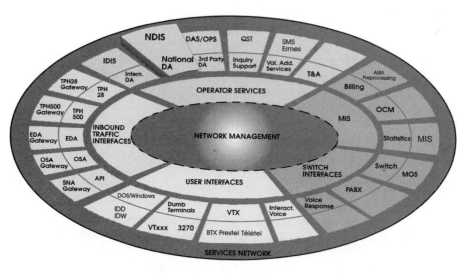

Figure 9–1 pc-plus products.

- A CTI (Computer Telephony Integration) application integrates DA with toll and assist functions to provide, for example, call completion, number announcement, and an automatic call distribution interface. Switch integration is achieved either by directly implementing the data protocol or by integrating a toll and assist application into the inquiry desks.

- IVP (Intelligent Voice Peripheral) performs all voice processing applications. It adds audio functionality to any DA solution, supporting different levels of automation and various services, such as automated call completion or intercept with voice announcement.

- RDIS (Reverse Directory Inquiry System) finds and announces the name and address of a listing, given the telephone number. Callers simply dial the number of the RDIS service, are guided through an automated dialog, and receive the corresponding name and address via speech synthesis.

- Multimedia DA supports both white and yellow page inquiries, adding multimedia capabilities to the NDIS database. In connection with an online service, it provides sound, graphics, animation, and video, allowing customers to actually see and hear the information they need.

- MIS (Management Information System) provides management, statistical, and billing reports. The system collects data sent online from the production systems, merges them and thus allows analysis of the complete system, for example, operator team efficiency, record access auditing, and database access cost per call.

A Directory Assistance Call Scenario

To understand the MIS application and its requirements, it is important to have an idea of the production system delivering data to MIS. Therefore, we sketch the events related to a single directory assistance call within a simple configuration.

The workstation of a directory assistance operator mainly consists of an extended telephone, which is connected to a switch providing automatic call distribution, and the inquiry desk providing access to the directory databases. Both worlds are linked together by the CTI application.

When a customer calls, the switch sends a message to the CTI application. More messages follow when the call is queued, routed to an operator, and accepted by him or her. Now the operator talks to the customer, asks for search arguments, and starts a database inquiry. The database response is listed on the screen. The operator may select an entry and initiate an automatic number announcement. This request is sent to the switch via the CTI application.

If the customer wants to request another number, he or she stays on the line after the number announcement and is reconnected, possibly to a different operator. On receiving the respective message from the switch, the CTI application resets the inquiry desk of that operator to the state of the last inquiry made for this customer.

When the customer hangs up, the CTI application deletes all information held for this call.

MIS receives copies of all these events and stores them in a VERSANT database for further analysis.

The MIS Application

From the user's point of view, MIS is a true management information system. It provides all data necessary to manage a directory assistance call center:

- Call center utilization in terms of
  * Telephone calls
  * Operator workload
  * Database system load
- Operator team efficiency
  * Average call handling time
  * Database search strategy
  * Number of database inquiries per call
- Figures relevant to billing
  * Call counts
  * Database inquiry counts
  * Listing access counts
- Database monitoring
  * Database response times
  * Search argument statistics

From a more technical point of view, MIS is not a typical application in the field of management or executive information systems, as it does not manipulate high-level numbers (money in most places) gathered from high-level business applications. The technical requirements resemble those of typical factory data aquisition systems, where decentralized production systems output low-level operational data:

- Data may not be collected on demand, but are sent in a steady stream.
- The daily amount of data reaches several hundred megabytes, which have to be processed virtually online.
- Different production system components provide different kinds of data.
- A lot of knowledge about the production systems is necessary to interpret and compute the data.
- For some purposes, like operator team efficiency measurement, integrated views on all production system components are required.
- Since MIS reports are used for billing purposes, single transaction traces have to be available on demand. This, in turn, requires that detailed data must not be deleted after data aggregation.

USING VERSANT FOR MIS

MIS Architecture

From the perspective of other pc-plus products, MIS acts as a data sink. Indeed, the processes involve functions as a data pipeline, with persistent buffers between them, transforming low-level messages into user reports. The OODB and its contents, a prominent persistent buffer, closely reflect the problem domain, and we will give an example of that further below.

Process Model

The MIS software is made up of several modules, which constitute the process architecture: Notify, Collect, Msg2Db, and Report, as shown in Figure 9–2.

First, data or events are simply detected and sent to MIS by the respective OSA application (e.g., IDIS and MOS) using the Notify module. This module consists of a library, which is linked to the application. It is lean and fast in order not to impair the production process. Notifications are atomic rather than cumulated, that is, OSA applications do not send tickets with a complete set of related events but send each event separately.

Next, Collect receives messages sent from different applications and performs consistency checks. Most importantly, the system clocks of all machines running Notifying applications must be synchronized very accurately.

Msg2Db feeds all events into internal state machines and thus is able to connect related events not only from a single source, but from different sources and applications. This is another reason for the atomic notifications. If, for example, the CTI application collected all events for a certain call, it would be impossible to map different parts of the call to different operators. Msg2Db then stores all information into the database. The object model of the database is a one-to-one model of the atomic events, reduced by any redundant information that is present in the messages to provide context and consistency criteria, and extended by links modeling relations between events.

Today, application-specific Report programs directly access the event object model to calculate relevant data, which is written to ASCII files. In the future, data processing will be controlled in three different ways: calculation of intermedi-

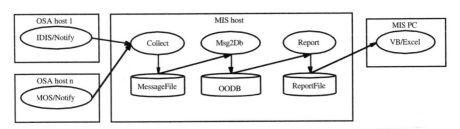

Figure 9–2   MIS process model.

ate results will be controlled data driven, that is, certain events will trigger the con-
densation of several events, eventually reducing the amount of stored data. Further
calculations of concrete results for reports may be triggered by user interaction (request driven) or scheduled regularly (batch driven). Calculation dependencies will
be described in an object model with pre- and postcondition predicates.

Visualization of reports like translation into different languages and formatting of tables and charts is done by spreadsheet applications (MS Excel). A Visual
Basic (VB) application provides easy access to the large amount of available reports
in the form of ASCII files and starts Visual Basic for Applications (VBA) macros to
control the spreadsheet application.

Persistent Object Model

The OODB stores the input for Report programs and serves as a central data
repository. Objects in the database mirror the problem domain to be flexible if new
reporting requirements arise; the database contains classes like `Call`, `Session`,
`Operator`, and `DatabaseTransaction`. Instances of these classes are interconnected with links indicating relationships, as shown in Figure 9–3.

This is a simplified part of the MIS persistent object model: `SessionEvent`
is an abstract class, which needs refinement, class `CallEvent` has additional subclasses, and many other classes are not shown at all.

Why VERSANT?

The decision to use an OODB instead of an RDB was made quite early in the project. There were two major reasons: some of the people involved in the decision had
just completed another project in which the gap between OOP (C++) and an RDB

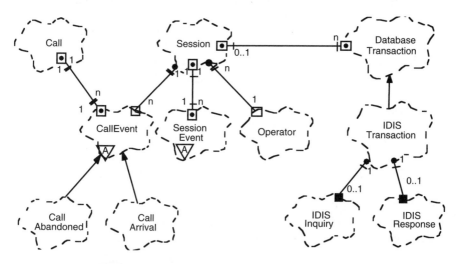

Figure 9–3   Part of the MIS persistent object model.

had become obvious. They also had learned that even mature relational products have bugs. Secondly, OODBs promised to be the technology of choice for a company committed to OO technology and looking for a technological advantage over its competitors.

Various products were considered. VERSANT was finally chosen because:

- It provides object level locking. We were willing to accept performance penalties to reduce unnecessary locking problems that occur in page locking systems. From today's point of view, locking is not a major issue for MIS, since historical data tends to be very stable and is rarely modified. In fact, the MIS reporting executables can safely operate in NOLOCK mode.
- It provides maximum database server concurrency by creating one server process per application and database. This is sometimes cited as a drawback (too many processes), but MIS has a limited number of concurrent processes (one writer and fewer than five readers).
- Its C++-API supports both selective and navigational data access.
- It promised to deliver flexible reporting facilities: An initial version of VERSANT's ToolSet had an OQL interface, a report writer, and a GUI builder integrated with the OODB. Sad to say, but VERSANT ToolSet never really materialized and has been withdrawn. The same happened to VERSANT/M, an SQL interface.

The OODB's Impact on the Architecture

The withdrawal of the ToolSet had a rather dramatic effect on MIS, since the data visualization and reporting facilities were suddenly gone. We decided to develop special purpose reporting executables producing plain text output, and an MS Excel-based front end to display the output. Developing the reporting executables is costly and time consuming, but moving to MS Excel has turned out to be a good idea, since our users tend to be familiar with spreadsheet applications.

Originally we thought that we could develop a single process combining data collection (Collect) and database update (Msg2Db). However, back in the early days we observed software stability problems that eventually led to the decision to separate data collection from the database update. That was VERSANT 2.1.0 and 2.1.4 on AIX, and things have improved a lot in recent releases. But we still retain the lightweight data collection process, since its robustness has saved our lives so many times.

MIS was designed to store fairly large amounts of data on a single machine, anything between 20 MB and 1 GB per day, over a three- to four-month period. VERSANT has the capability to store data in several system volume files, but we thought that this was insufficient and that these amounts of data would be better distributed among multiple databases, one for each day. This design is more scalable in terms of system limits on a single database size. It also speeds up daily report generation, since the data is located in a few smaller databases. VERSANT's transparent cross database links were essential for this to work.

The design of a fault tolerant MIS, which is currently being developed, has also been influenced by the OODB. In stage one we are developing software that ensures that a message sent to MIS will sooner or later arrive in the database. This is important if MIS is used for billing purposes. We are not using VERSANT's fault tolerance options at this stage. Stage two focuses on the availability of reporting facilities, and we intend to use VERSANT's database replication facilities for this purpose.

Alternatively, we considered using VERSANT to send data from other pc-plus products to MIS, so that a larger part of the communication would have been VERSANT's responsibility. We did not do that in the end, since we wanted to make use of redundant communication lines in a single application process and wanted to be open to communication load balancing requirements among pc-plus products and to other communication protocols than TCP/IP. Existing pc-plus communication facilities already had these properties. Having to install VERSANT on all hosts at customer sites was another obstacle.

Software Development using the OODB

When we set out to use VERSANT/C++, we were surprised by its ease of use. A programmer really gets a benefit from the tight language binding between C++ and the OODB! A good C++ programmer with some database background will need little training before he or she can start to use VERSANT.

However, things sometimes look deceptively simple. Based on our experience, we recommend that you gain a thorough understanding of VERSANT's memory and lock management. When you start to design your classes, you should know what happens to your objects in client and server memory when you commit, dereference a link, or enable object swapping. Your class design has to deal with these issues.

You should also understand that only `PDOM::resetoct()` frees all dynamically allocated VERSANT memory, and since it invalidates all links, you might want to introduce root or hook objects, although VERSANT does not strictly require them. These root objects serve to recreate the application's state as it was before the `resetoct()` function call. This is particularly important for daemon processes such as `Msg2Db`, which have to put a limit on memory size.

We found a few other hints and guidelines useful in our project:

- Put all persistence capable classes (classes derived from `PObject`) in a single directory and library.
- Try to keep persistent classes simple, for example, attempt to restrict member functions to simple data member access, avoid access to other classes:

If you put all persistent classes into one library, all executables using the database need one and the same library for the complete database schema. This increases your chances for consistency and keeps makefiles simple. If the classes are simple, you will not need to link other libraries referenced by the persistent classes. Finally, schema generation can be restricted to a single makefile in one directory, and you can create one file that contains all schema definitions, that is, O_CAPTURE_SCHEMA invocations. Today, MIS has some 65 persistent classes.

- Write your own application specific wrapper classes for VERSANT's API:

VERSANT's API covers several areas, e.g., session handling (beginsession(), endsession()), database handling (connectdb(), disconnectdb()), queries (select()), and as is stated in VERSANT's Concepts and Usage Manual: "Versant provides a lot of features. It is up to you to decide how best to use them for your needs." Since the MIS executables all have similar requirements in these areas, we found it useful to write wrapper classes that capture these requirements, that is, DatabaseHandler, SessionHandler, Selector<class>.

For example, a DatabaseHandler object knows which databases should be connected at any given time and it knows which errors to ignore when attempting to connect to several databases. A SessionHandler object knows the name of the session database and the type of session to start. A Selector object restricts the options of VERSANT's select() function to our application's needs and—perhaps more important—keeps track of the resulting LinkVstr memory and provides consistent tracing and error reporting for all selections (e.g., how many objects were selected in which database?)

These wrapper classes hide VERSANT complexity from application classes. For example, writing programs whose only purpose is to test given classes is easy and fun with these building blocks, and even programmers with little VERSANT knowledge can use them.

Actually, the wrapper classes do not know anything about the persistent classes. We put them into a separate library and directory, too.

- Integrate PError into your exception class hierarchy:

Error handling is an important issue in every application. C++'s exception handling is a valuable feature and we employed it extensively (including throw specifications) and successfully for error handling purposes. VERSANT's C++-API also uses exceptions and throws instances of class PError. The use of exceptions has helped us locate errors that otherwise would have been difficult to detect.

We decided that all objects that can be thrown in MIS should be derived from a common superclass called MisError, so that the meaning of a catch(const MisError&) statement is fairly close to catch(...), and most throw specifications consist of a simple throw(const MisError). We integrated VERSANT's PError class into this hierarchy by writing a class `DbmsError: public MisError` with a `PError` data member. Classes close to the database software layer catch `PErrors` and convert them to `DbmsErrors` (or something else). The benefit of this procedure is that many classes do not need to know the existence of `PErrors`, or even `DbmsErrors`, although they indirectly use database software.

- Porting from AIX to HP-UX:

    AIX/Cset++ is MIS' primary development platform, but at the end of 1995 we had to deliver the product on an HP-UX 9.0/HP-C++ platform—and that turned out to be a problem. The ODBMS did not support HP-C++ compiler native exception handling for HP-UX 9.0. It used `setjmp/longjmp` based macros instead, and these macros worked only on instances of class `Perror`. They did not work on application classes, such as `MisError`.

    At runtime, this means that stack unwinding does not take place when an exception is thrown, so that some objects will not be deleted, acquired resources will not be released in object destructors, and memory leaks will occur.

    This is critical for the MIS `Msg2Db` daemon process. However, since `Msg2Db` can be stopped without loss of data, it can be restarted periodically. Luckily, that solved our runtime problems. The most important MIS daemon process, the data collector, does not rely on OODB software and can be compiled with compiler native exceptions.

    At the source code level, we had to write a second set of macros that expand to VERSANT's macros on HP and to native C++ syntax on AIX. The situation today is that pc-plus are beta-testers for a new C++ compiler for HP-UX, and we hope that VERSANT will support native exception handling for that compiler in the future. The sooner we get rid of these macros the better. Apart from the exception handling problem, we did not encounter other VERSANT portability problems between AIX and HP-UX 9.0.

- Platform specific support:

    Based on this and some other experiences, we recommend a careful check of supported platforms and compiler requirements when you select an OODB product. If your company compiles with GNU-C++, you might have a problem. You should also be aware of the fact that different platforms/companies have different importance to the OODB vendors. You might have trouble getting bugs fixed or finding online support for some platforms. Do not hesitate to ask if your OODB support company has the hardware and operating system that fits your needs. AIX is different from HP-UX, and problems with the OODB software will sometimes be specific for that platform.

- Dealing with collection classes from different class libraries:

    Other class libraries we are working with also provide collection classes and we had to define a boundary between these classes and VERSANT's. The choice between extensive or restricted use of VERSANT's collection classes was made in favor of a restricted use, even at the price of having to copy collections or define iterators in a class interface to hide VERSANT collections.

Naturally, all persistent classes use VERSANT collections, but only a few nonpersistent classes do.

Also, some objects are used in different contexts, which leads to different requirements on the class definitions. For example, classes sent from other applications to MIS consist of simple data members with no PObject overhead. But they are, on the other hand, candidates for persistency. Here, too, we opted for separation, that is, converting objects from one class to another, so that the applications sending the data classes did not need to know VERSANT and its libraries, and the classes could be optimized for their use in a database or communication context.

- Schema evolution, advantages of a problem domain persistent object model:

    Perhaps surprisingly, schema evolution facilities have been of little practical importance for MIS until today. Objects created at a given point of time have no relevance for objects created four months later, and applications do not have to access them concurrently. In fact, we could have changed the object model every few months without any difficulty.

    On the other hand, the persistent object model has proved to be remarkably stable. Apart from new class definitions, there has been just a single major revision that led to incompatibilities between successive MIS releases. We think this is because the persistent classes model aspects of the problem domain do not change frequently. Very careful requirements analysis and subsequent design also help.

    An object model that closely reflects the problem domain also simplifies the process of error location or debugging, since it becomes much easier for the programmer to map his or her understanding of the problem domain to the program's structure. A mapping from classes to relational tables adds another layer of complexity. We believe that the OODB has helped us improve software quality because of the reduced complexity. At least we have had very few bug reports.

- Finally, a remark that is obvious for database people, but may be of interest to OO-people: if you need a high database performance, the commit/rollback policy may be different from what you may think is intuitive. For example, the Msg2Db process does not commit after it has converted a message to a persistent object and updated a few related objects (a logical unit of work). You need to understand the DBMS's mechanisms and consider them in the application's design.

EXPERIENCES AND SUMMARY

Using an object-oriented database management system met our expectations: a tight language binding and the homogeneity of the programming paradigm make it very intuitive to work with persistent data.

VERSANT's architecture matches MIS' requirements. This is a point that has to be evaluated anew for every new project; most of the evaluation effort should be devoted to it. It does not make sense to assess OODBs without weighing their features for the respective application.

VERSANT's quality and stability are as good as those of ObjectStore, Informix, or Oracle, to name only those products being used in other projects at pc-plus.

Most of our needs remain unsatisfied in the area of backend tools. We have to expend a lot of effort, because no report generation tool is available. From our customers' point of view, a standardized query language interface would be desirable.

A dream would come true if an OLAP (OnLine Analytical Processing) frontend became available. The multidimensional data model and visualization techniques of the OLAP concept are essential in the field of management, or executive information systems and data warehouses. Why don't OODB vendors invest in this profitable field? Objects with possibly multiple links may model multiple dimensions much easier than two-dimensional relational tables do and are more flexible than optimized multidimensional databases (MDDB).

10

Building a Multi-Petabyte Database:

The RD45 Project at CERN

Jamie Shiers, CERN

ABSTRACT

The European Laboratory for Particle Physics, CERN, straddles the border between France and Switzerland near Geneva. CERN is building a new particle accelerator, the Large Hadron Collider (LHC), which is scheduled to commence operation in 2005. This machine, which will be used by physicists from around the world, is being built to help answer fundamental questions concerning our understanding of the universe in which we live, including issues such as the observed dominance of matter over anti-matter, and the origins of mass. There will be at least four experiments taking data at the LHC, three of which will accumulate over 1 Petabyte (PB, or 10^{15} bytes) of data per year. The total volume of data, both "real" and "simulated," that must be stored each year will be between 4–5 PB, and the experiments will probably run for fifteen to twenty years. Thus, our requirement is for a solution that will scale to at least 100PB—orders of magnitude beyond what is traditionally referred to as a very large database (VLDB). This chapter describes an ongoing research project that is attempting to identify solutions to the data management problems posed by the LHC.

INTRODUCTION

The next generation of High Energy Physics (HEP) experiments at CERN will be larger in every respect than existing projects in HEP. Each collaboration will consist of up to 2000 physicists from of the order of 100 institutes in some tens of countries. The detectors employed will themselves be vast: 25–30 meters in each direction with hundreds of thousands of channels, and will generate enormous amounts of data. We currently expect to have to store some 5 PB of new data per year (summed over the four different experiments), giving rise to a total volume of about 100 PB over the expected twenty-year lifetime of the project. This volume of data exceeds by many orders of magnitude what has traditionally been termed a very large database, or VLDB. Today, 1 TB is considered large—one of the experiments at the LHC will be storing 1 TB *every 10 minutes*!

Faced with such a major challenge, an R&D project was established at CERN in early 1995 to look for solutions to this vast data storage and management problem. Given the time-scales involved, much of what is described in this chapter refers to future work—we do not expect to hit the TB mark until the end of 1997. Currently, our largest test database is 0.5 TB, and to enter the TB region we need to incorporate transparent access between the ODBMS and a Mass Storage System (MSS). Basically, we expect to increase the maximum size of the database by approximately one order of magnitude per year, until a number of pre-LHC experiments enter production in 1999–2000. Already at this stage, hundreds of TB of new data will be produced per experiment per year. If *all* of the HEP experiments starting at this time adopt a common solution, then we will be generating several PB of new data per year by the year 2000.

This project has focused on industry standard solutions—a significant departure from the route previously followed in our community, where the software has traditionally been written in Fortran and solutions to the data management and persistency problem have always been developed in-house. Relational databases have been used with limited success for handling meta-data, but even here, significant problems have arisen from the mismatch of data models—the relational model is simply not a good fit for our problem domain.

In recent years, we have seen a move towards an object-oriented approach to HEP software, and the current focus is primarily on C++, although, along with the rest of the industry, there is growing interest in Java. This naturally leads to the possibility of using an Object-Oriented Database for persistence, and indeed this is the line that is currently being pursued in the RD45 project. Of course, simple persistence is only a small part of the problem—we need essentially all of the functionality provided by an ODBMS (and perhaps more).

Initial investigations have confirmed that an ODBMS approach is viable, and the main focus of our activities is now on understanding the issues of scalability and performance. To this end, we are building a multi-TB testbed, which will slowly grow to the ten and hundred TB region, before finally reaching the PB domain as the LHC collider becomes operational. At the time of writing, we are at the level of a few hundred GB of disk storage, but expect to reach 500 GB of disk and 5 TB of tape by the end of 1997, and 1 TB disk and 10 TB tape by mid-1998.

This chapter describes our experience with object databases so far as well as our longer term plans.

THE RD45 PROJECT

As described above, the RD45 project was initiated at CERN in early 1995, with the goal of finding solutions to the problem of handling the multi-PB of event data (assumed to be objects), that would be generated at the LHC. At the time that the project was approved, "conventional wisdom" within the HEP community was that our requirements were simply beyond the scope of both existing and future database products. Indeed, today one rarely finds deployed ODBMSs that handle more than a few tens of GB, although there are a growing number of projects in the short (months) and medium (1–2 years) terms that call for a few hundred GB to a few (tens of) TB. Within our own community, there are projects that will need a solution for the storage and management of a few hundred TB around 1999, so we see a relatively steady, albeit steep, increase in the total volume of data that must be stored between now and the beginning of LHC.

The project was initially approved with the following milestones to be completed by the end of the first year, although the first milestone was subsequently amended, as noted below.

1. [Produce a] requirements specification for the management of persistent objects typical of HEP data together with criteria for evaluating potential implementations.
2. Evaluate the suitability of ODMG's Object Definition Language for specifying an object model describing HEP event data.
3. Starting from such a model, develop a prototype using commercial ODBMSs that conform to the ODMG standard. The functionality and performance of the ODBMSs should be evaluated.

As can be seen from these milestones, the project was given clear instructions to focus on industry standard, commercial solutions. In addition, it was stressed that the project should concentrate on event data, that is, the high-volume data, although we had hoped to "cut our teeth" on ODBMS technology using relatively less demanding data, such as calibration data for the detectors, which is expected to be in the 100 GB/year range.

Milestone 1 was subsequently amended as follows:

1. Produce a "Statement of Probable Capabilities" for a HEP persistent object manager system based on commercial ODBMSs and large-market mass storage systems.

As is described in more detail below, we felt that we had identified a potential solution to the problem after only a few months. The proposed solution is based on using distributed databases, which of course appear to the user as a single logical database. There are a number of constraints on the size of the physical databases that make up the logical databases—our current thinking is to limit this size to around 100 GB. This, we suspect, will be a relatively modest size for a physical database in approximately ten years from now, indeed, they are a reality today. Our main reasons for limiting the physical databases to this size are to permit the inactive databases to be stored on tertiary storage, perhaps magnetic tape, or hopefully a slightly more modern and user-friendly medium, such as Digital Video Disk (DVD), and using similarly conservative estimates for the capacity of commodity tertiary storage volumes, we arrive at a limit of some 50–100 GB. More importantly, we need to define a convenient sized "chunk" for moving to/from tertiary storage and perhaps even over the network.

Given a physical DB size of 100 GB, we need 10^4 databases to reach 1 PB. This is well within the architectural limits of existing, deployed products. Of course, many open questions still remain, primarily related to performance and scalability. These issues are reflected in the milestones of RD45 for 1996, namely:

1. Identify and analyze the impact of using an ODBMS for event data on the Object Model, the physical organization of the data, coding guidelines, and the use of third-party class libraries.
2. Investigate and report on ways that Objectivity/DB features for replication, schema evolution, and object versions can be used to solve data management problems typical of the HEP environment.
3. Make an evaluation of the effectiveness of an ODBMS and MSS as the query and access method for physics analysis.

These milestones have now been completed, and detailed reports can be obtained through the Web from the CERN Web server. The main conclusions are as follows:

- The use of an ODBMS for persistence implies minimal code changes and introduces no arbitrary restrictions on consistent object models.
- Replication, schema evolution, and object versioning are all powerful techniques for solving HEP data management problems, and should be considered mandatory for any eventual solution.
- The performance of an ODBMS-based solution is at least equal to that of existing, home-grown solutions, while offering significantly more flexibility and functionality. In the case of significantly selective queries, dramatic performance improvements over existing HEP tools can be seen.

We are now embarking on our third year of investigation, where issues more directly related to deployment and end-users are being discussed. The three principal milestones to be investigating by March 1998 are as follows:

1. Demonstrate, by the end of 1997, the proof of principle that an ODBMS can satisfy the key requirements of typical production scenarios (e.g., event simulation and reconstruction) for data volumes up to 1 TB. The key requirements will be defined, in conjunction with the LHC experiments, as part of this work.

2. Demonstrate the feasibility of using an ODBMS + MSS for Central Data Recording, at data rates sufficient to support CMS test-beam activities during 1997 and NA45 during their 1998 run.

3. Investigate and report on the impact of using an ODBMS for event data on end users, including issues related to private and semi-private schema and collections, in typical scenarios including simulation, (re-)reconstruction, and analysis.

Progress reports on these issues will be available through the CERN Web site.

OBJECT DATABASES AND STANDARDS

One of the first issues that we investigated was that of standards. In a project that will last decades and will be fully distributed, one cannot assume that the same system will necessarily be adopted at all collaborating institutes, nor that the same system will be used for the entire lifetime of the project. Indeed, there is no guarantee that the product that we are using today will even exist when LHC starts up, let alone when it completes—perhaps in the year 2025!

The promise of the Object Database Management Group (ODMG) standards for ODBMSs, whereby applications can (in principle at least) be moved from one product to another by a simple recompile and where there is even a standard interchange format, is clearly very attractive (although perhaps a little unbelievable). We know of cases when large applications have been moved from one product to another (due to a significant performance advantage), where the porting was completed in a few weeks. This was prior to the release of ODMG-compliant interfaces for the products involved. Our own experience in moving from a vendor-specific interface to an ODMG-compliant one confirms that the move can be relatively smooth, if not completely transparent. In reality, one will only change vendors either if there is a large performance advantage, or if there are major problems with the product or vendor, such as a buggy release, or a buyout resulting in a significant change in direction, so a porting exercise lasting a few weeks or even months is acceptable.

At present, the ODMG standards are not sufficiently complete for many applications—a number of important database features are not covered, such as object versioning, schema evolution, and data replication. These may be included in future revisions of the standard, but it could then take several years after these features are standardized before they appear (in a standards-conforming way) in more than one product. For example, although revision 1.1 of the standard followed 1.0 quite closely (August 1993 and February 1994), there was roughly a two-year gap before version 1.2 became available. Assuming one more year before the features are widely implemented, we cannot expect V2.1 conforming products (V2.0 being the current release) until around the year 2000!

Perhaps more important, particularly for VLDB applications, is a standard interface to Mass Storage Systems, such as the High Performance Storage System (HPSS), being developed at the National Storage Laboratory, hosted by Lawrence Livermore National Laboratory. However, it is not clear that the market, at least today, is sufficiently large as to warrant such an interface, and advances in storage may even render such systems obsolete.

Historically, the ODMG has been driven by the vendors. This has been particularly important in the timely production of the initial version of the standard and the subsequent minor releases. As ODMG-compliant products move into the mainstream, we feel that more user involvement will be essential. How this is achieved is far from clear. There are no secrets to standardization—if you really want to get something through, then you must be sufficiently committed to devote the time that is required. This is seldom easy for user organizations, particularly when the bulk of the meetings take place on a different continent! On the other hand, a standards body cannot afford to ossify if it is to maintain usefulness—the rapid emergence of Java and the ODMG's response to it is a testimony to the need for rapid response to new requirements.

Finally, if the ODBMS market really does take off, it is not clear if there will still be sufficiently strong motivation for the vendors to continue to work on the standards, or whether it would be better for them to further differentiate their products.

CHOOSING AN ODBMS

In choosing an ODBMS for our current activities, we have deliberately not tried to address which system we will eventually use from 2005 on. There are simply too many unknowns for anybody to reliably predict the state of the market nearly one decade hence. As will be explained in more detail below, our primary requirements are for scalability, performance, and heterogeneity. In particular, we were looking for an architecture that, at least theoretically, was capable of scaling to the multi-PB region.

In fact, our initial investigations were not restricted to ODBMSs—we also investigated other mechanisms for providing persistence, including language extensions and so-called "lightweight" object managers.

We list below some of the high-level requirements for a persistent object manager for LHC-era experiments at CERN.

The Object Manager must:

- Not impose any arbitrary restrictions on the Object Model of the collaborations. For example, the full C++ Object Model must be supported by the Object Manager

- Work in the fully distributed, heterogeneous environment
- Appear to the user as a single, logical system, even if composed of multiple physical instances running on a variety of platforms
- Be capable of supporting a variety of different computing models, perhaps even concurrently
- Be capable of supporting the evolution of such models
- Be capable of providing access to the services and/or data of individual objects in a single, logical multi-PB system

The only systems that we know of capable of satisfying this initial list of requirements are full Object Databases. Thus, we do not believe in and have not investigated further into so-called lightweight (or limited functionality) persistent object managers.

Assuming that our persistent object manager is based upon an ODBMS, we then list the requirements for the ODBMS as below.

The Object Database (ODBMS) must:

- Support all eleven mandatory requirements listed in "The Object-Oriented Database Manifesto"
- Comply to the bindings defined by the Object Database Management Group (ODMG) in terms of Object Model, C++ and ODL bindings
- Provide replication of user data
- Support schema evolution and object instance migration (both *eager* and *lazy* modes)
- Be capable of supporting and exploiting parallelism, for example, parallel load and parallel query
- Provide a mechanism for transparently integrating the ODBMS with a Mass Storage System that is site-configurable
- Support individual physical databases of at least 100 GB by 1997, and individual databases of at least 1 TB by 2000
- Provide a mechanism whereby a single, logical database can be built out of multiple physical databases, distributed across multiple, possibly heterogeneous, database/file-servers spread across a wide area network. At least 2^{16} physical databases per logical database must be supported in 1997 and at least 2^{32} by 2000
- Impose no arbitrary limits on the number of classes, number of attributes per class, or the number of instances of individual classes. Should such architectural limits exist, then they should in no case be less than 2^{32}, a higher limit such as 2^{64} being strongly preferred
- Impose no arbitrary limits on the number of simultaneous clients; should such limits exist, then they should exceed 2^{16}

- Offer scalable (i.e., constant or linear) performance characteristics
- Represent a "small" (e.g., 10 percent) overhead related to the raw performance offered by the underlying file-system or raw devices

THE ODBMS MARKET

It was predicted that the ODBMS market would take off during 1995. This did not happen, but a number of important events did occur:

- ODBMSs "arrived." They are widely used in production (at least hundreds of thousands of deployed licenses), particularly in the telecom market.
- The market has "crystallized," in the sense that the various vendors have carved out niches, rather than compete head-on.
- The ODMG-93 standard has achieved industry wide recognition. The bulk of the market, both true ODBMS and ORDBMS, now claim conformance to the ODMG standard.

More recently, we have seen a strong focus by many of the companies on the World Wide Web and on Java. The ODMG formed a Java working group in early 1996, and some vendors already announced bindings—even before the standard was finalized! Will this provide sufficient impetus to drive the long-awaited take-off of the industry? We certainly hope so, as we rely on the availability of healthy, competing products in this domain. Today, we can identify at least two products that we believe we could use in the production phase of LHC. There are other products that could evolve sufficiently as to meet our requirements, but it is equally possible, if not likely, that one or more of today's products will not survive the move of ODBMSs into the mainstream.

Today, our primary candidate, and the product that we are using for all of our prototyping activities, is Objectivity/DB. This product has a scalable architecture that fits well with our requirements. Detailed tests of its scalability and performance have been made and are reported upon below.

HEP EVENT DATA

Although the volume of HEP data is very large, it is essentially write-once, read-many—in fact, largely, in terms of volume, read-rarely. It is also hierarchical in nature, with the bulk of the data (roughly 90 percent) being rarely accessed, and additional levels with varying reduction factors being accessed more frequently. The basic unit of granularity is the "event," which corresponds to the interaction of two particles and the final state products. Each event is independent—there are no relationships between individual events, although they are typically grouped together in larger collections, corresponding to some time-slice, which historically was often defined by the capacity of a tape! An event itself can also be viewed as a collection of collections with varying access frequencies. Combined, these characteristics lead to a fairly natural way of clustering the data. Frequently accessed objects from frequently accessed events can be clustered together, with less frequently accessed data residing on media with different performance characteristics—perhaps even offline, on tape. The "hot" components of individual events will typically be clustered by event type, corresponding more or less to a specific physics analysis channel (although these channels may overlap).

DATA PRODUCTION AND ANALYSIS

In the classical model, data production, where the digitizing readout from the detectors are reconstructed into tracks and clusters corresponding to the particles resulting from the event that occurred, is presumed to be performed in pseudo real-time. The data that is added at this stage represents perhaps 10 percent of the raw data problem, that is, some 100 TB per year. Reprocessing occurs infrequently, perhaps once a year at most, when new detector calibrations or reconstruction algorithms are developed.

EARLY PROTOTYPING

Our initial prototyping activities used existing data. These data exist in HEP-specific formats and were not generated according to an object model. In most cases, however, a DDL description of the data existed, and we were able to write a simple conversion program that mapped data structures to classes, made the appropriate schema definitions, and then loaded the data into the ODBMS. We also wrote a small routine to permit legacy applications to access data from the database, simply as a check that our conversion was indeed correct.

This early prototyping allowed us to make some preliminary performance measurements, which were encouraging, particularly as the object models produced by this more-or-less blind conversion were by no means optimal.

- Read and write performance was measured to be comparable to existing (Fortran-based) systems.
- The overhead of the database with respect to the data volume was found to be very small.
- Access to individual objects was possible with performance that corresponded directly to the volume of data read/written.

These initial results were very encouraging, although still performed at a relatively small scale. What was clearly required was an existing experiment that was prepared to take the plunge and use an ODBMS in production. Fortunately, we were able to find such an experiment, NA45, that had taken the decision to move to C++ and was looking for a solution to the persistency problem.

PRODUCTION USE OF AN ODBMS FOR HEP EVENT DATA

The CERN NA45 experiment is studying electron-pair production in heavy ion collisions. The experiment had attempted to move from Fortran 77 to Fortran 90, but ran into problems, mainly related to the lack of native F90 compilers—the compiler that was being used first translated the code to C and then compiled the latter. As a result, not only was debugging extremely complex, but performance was far lower than would be expected from a native compiler.

Having started to use the extended features of Fortran 90, the collaboration felt that it would be hard to go back to Fortran 77 and preferred to move forward to C++. As such, they had the task of redesigning and reimplementing their software in a very short time period—two to three months—before a production run scheduled for the spring of 1996.

The total data volume involved was around 600 GB. This corresponded to 12 million events, each around 50 KB in size. From these data, some 200 GB were then extracted with relatively loose cuts for various systematic studies. Finally, some 1 million "good" events—around 60 GB in total—were expected to be stored in the ODBMS and used as input to the analysis stage.

The production itself was to run on the CERN Meiko CS-2. At the time, this machine had 64 nodes, each dual-processor HyperSPARC running at 100 MHz, with 64 MB of memory. The nodes were connected by a high-speed (50 MB/second), low latency (<10 microsecond) interconnect. The operating system itself was based on Solaris 2.3, with special patches for the TCP/IP.

Although this platform was not supported by the version of Objectivity/DB that we had at the time (3.5), we were able to use the ODBMS with the Advanced Multithreaded Server (the NFS option did not work out of the box, but the AMS is in any case preferable for performance and other reasons).

The NA45 reconstruction software consisted of around 30 K lines of code and over 700 classes. This code, which was developed on HP/UX, was originally designed without persistency in mind, and we were able to learn some important lessons from "back-stitching" persistency into an existing transient application. Almost all of the problems encountered, however, were related to the lack of functionality in the then-current C++ compiler on HP/UX, rather than any database issues.

The database design was based on the Objectivity/DB federated database concept. There were a total of five sorts of databases, all part of the same federation. Two of these (sets of) databases were kept offline on tape, corresponding to the raw data and information related to trigger settings and configuration data. The remainder were disk-resident and contained the results of the reconstruction (hits, rings, tracks, etc.), event, burst and run objects, and their associations to other objects, and the so-called "tag database"—high-level event classification information and persistent event selections.

The NA45 code was ported without major problems to Objectivity/DB, including the modeling of relatively complex objects in Objectivity/DB's DDL. This was done with little impact on the code. We were able to run multiple (up to 32) jobs in parallel on different nodes, writing into the same Objectivity-federated database, which resided in a parallel file-system. NA45 continues to work with the database, and currently plans to store some 20 TB of data in the system in 1998.

THE INTERFACE TO MASS STORAGE SYSTEMS

Given the vast volumes of data involved, it is far from clear that a solution that involves storing all persistent data on disk will be viable. Hence, we are investigating an interface between Objectivity/DB and the HPSS mass storage system. This interface would be performed at the level of the Objectivity (page) server and would be completely transparent to client applications. The granularity at which data would be migrated/staged to/from tertiary storage would be that of a few GB, seen to HPSS as a file and to Objectivity/DB as a database—one of 2^{16} possible in a Objectivity/DB federated database. Agreement has been reached between Objectivity and the HPSS collaboration for such an interface to be developed, and a prototype will be demonstrated at SuperComputing '97. The requirements for this prototype are as follows:

- The Objectivity/HPSS proof-of-concept prototype should provide transparent client access to an Objectivity/DB federated database stored in HPSS-managed storage.
- The prototype should provide client-transparent migration/staging of databases to/from tertiary storage, that is, the disk pool should be smaller than required for the entire federation.
- The prototype should permit both sequential and random read and write access as well as creation and deletion of databases.
- Access should be possible from both UNIX and NT clients.

It is anticipated that this interface will be used in production at the 100 TB/year level on a number of HEP experiments from 1999 on.

PERFORMANCE AND SCALABILITY MEASUREMENTS

As part of a risk analysis of the current RD45 strategy, we have identified and tested the limits and scalability of the Objectivity/DB architecture. With a few small exceptions, our tests showed that the product behaved as documented and could indeed be used to build databases up to the PB region. No significant problems were encountered. The largest federation that we created contained 13,000 databases—the maximum currently being 65,536. The maximum size of a federation was 0.5 TB.

POSSIBLE STORAGE HIERARCHY

Although it is clearly far too early to predict what sort of storage will be in use in a decade's time, it is important to consider possible models—even if only to verify that they would be technologically possible and financially affordable. In fact, a simple extrapolation of the systems used for the 1 TB testbed suggest some interesting possibilities. First, using relatively conservative projections, it is likely that we will be able to build and afford large disk farms of several hundred terabytes in size. Second, this will be possible using a number of servers that will be easily manageable—between 10 and 50. Assuming a disk farm of some 500 TB in the initial stage, one can then store a very healthy fraction of the data online—the raw data, which is rarely accessed, can reside off-line, although even here some interesting possibilities arise. Traditionally, sequential media such as magnetic tapes have been used for archive storage. The imminent arrival of medium-high capacity, random access devices, such as the Digital Video Disk (DVD), could cause a revolution in this market. The distinction between secondary and tertiary storage becomes immediately blurred, resulting in a significant decrease in complexity.

No one can safely say whether DVD will really take off. The market is certainly there—both as a computer peripheral and in the home entertainment area. The ability to read existing CD-ROMs potentially means that all future PCs will be shipped with a DVD reader, and that DVDs will replace CDs for software distribution. As the WORM and rewritable devices become available, DVD could displace tape in the PC backup market. Finally, it has great potential both in the video and games market.

USE OF VERY LARGE MEMORIES

Even more exciting are the prospects offered by the use of very large memories. GB memories exist today—100 GB memories are almost certain in ten years, if not TB memories. 100 GB of memory in fifty servers gives 5 TB of memory; 1 TB per server gives 50 TB. Provided that an appropriate caching strategy can be employed, the database will simply run from memory, offering enormous performance gains.

It is too soon to be certain that such capabilities will exist, but it is important to consider them. The possibilities that are opened up by having random access to any object in multiple PB, with varying latency appropriately mapped to the "heat" of the individual objects, are huge.

Many of these things we plan to model, based upon our experience with the 1 TB testbed (where we will probably have a few tens of GB of memory—an even more generous ratio than we are predicting for the future!).

EXPERIENCES AND SUMMARY

We have demonstrated the feasibility of using standards-conforming, commercial solutions for handling HEP event data. Current tests have been limited to the order of 1 TB, but will be extended into the 10 TB region and beyond. At least one HEP experiment already plans to store several hundred TB of data using Objectivity/DB and HPSS starting in 1999 and we expect to be storing many PB of data from 2005 on, if not before.

11

An Astronomers View
of Object-Oriented Databases

Robert J. Brunner, The Johns Hopkins University
Alexander S. Szalay, The Johns Hopkins University
Andrew E. Wade, Objectivity, Inc.

ABSTRACT

Throughout recorded time, people have been intrigued by the nighttime sky, wondering about the origin and evolution of the universe. Eventually, individuals began to perform their own personal observations, producing reams of detailed notes. Until relatively recently, this observational technique has been the main methodology used by astronomers. Unfortunately, data gathered in such a fashion are not of optimal scientific value for subsequent reuse, due to differences in calibration and personal biases. More recently, large sky-surveys were made using photographic plates in an attempt to produce uniform data sets that would help eliminate some of these problems. This approach, however, had inherent problems due to the nature of

We would like to thank the rest of the SDSS Science Archive team at the Johns Hopkins University: Kumar Ramaiyer, Andrew Connolly, Istvan Csabai, Gyula Szokoly, and Steve Lubow. We also wish to thank Robert Lupton, Don Petravick, Steve Kent, Jeff Munn, Brian Yanny, Tom Nash, and Ruth Pordes of the SDSS project for stimulating discussions. In addition, we would like to acknowledge the Sloan Digital Sky Survey for providing funding for this project. A.S. has also been supported by the Seaver Institute. The Digital Equipment Corporation has provided a generous research grant, which started us down the road toward object databases; special thanks are due to Jim Rye of DEC. Our friends and colleagues at Objectivity, Inc., especially Dave Hentchel, have provided invaluable support and a lot of enlightening, fun discussions.

photographic astronomical plate data; detections are analog, and the plate response is nonlinear.

To overcome these deficiencies, a consortium of universities have embarked on a project to digitally map the Northern Galactic Cap (approximately one quarter of the night-time sky) using five different filters that span the spectrum from the ultraviolet to the near infrared that will detect more than 200 million objects. Simultaneously, distances will be measured to the brightest 1 million galaxies. This project, the Sloan Digital Sky Survey, hereafter the "SDSS," will revolutionize the field of astronomy, increasing the amount of information available to researchers by several orders of magnitude. Essentially, this project is the astronomical equivalent of the Human Genome Project.

The resultant archive that will be used for scientific research will be large (exceeding several Terabytes) and complex: textual information, derived parameters, multiband images, and spectral information. The catalog will allow astronomers to study the evolution of the universe in greater detail and is intended to serve as the standard reference for the next several decades. As a result, we felt the need to provide an archival system that would make "data mining" much easier and also shield researchers from the underlying complex architecture. In our efforts, we have invested a considerable amount of time and energy in understanding how large, complex data sets can be developed and deployed in an object-oriented framework. Here we discuss the road we have taken in order to create the next generation astronomical reference archive.

INTRODUCTION

Astronomy is an observational science, and ground-based observations are heavily affected by the weather and by the atmosphere. In addition, all astronomical observations are affected by differences in calibration procedures, instruments, and the lack of a uniform reference survey. Thus, creating large, homogeneous data sets between diverse groups of astronomers can be difficult. During the 1950s, the National Geographic Society and Palomar Observatory produced a sky survey using photographic plates, providing a reference catalog that was distributed in the form of film, glass, and paper copies of the original plates. Recently, this survey was digitized [Dgo+92]; however, the accurate calibration of this photographic data has remained a problem.

The Sloan Digital Sky Survey [GK93] is a multi-institutional collaboration designed to produce the next generation optical sky survey. As a fully digital survey, the SDSS is designed to overcome many of the problems that plagued earlier sky surveys. In particular, both the photometric (incident energy flux) and astrometric (physical coordinate) calibrations will be significantly improved. The SDSS will also detect objects that are more than ten times fainter than in previous sky surveys and create several interrelated data products.

We believe that astronomy is about to undergo a major paradigm shift with data sets becoming increasingly larger and more homogeneous, for the first time designed in a top-down fashion. In a few years when an astronomer needs an observation to complete an analysis, it may be much easier to electronically "dial-up" a part of the sky, rather than wait for several months or a year to access a (sometimes quite small) telescope. With several other projects in other wavelengths under way, such as the 2MASS [Kle+94] (infra-red) and the FIRST [Bec+95] (radio) projects, the concept of having a "digital sky," with multiple, TB-size databases interoperating in a seamless fashion is no longer an outlandish idea. A growing number of catalogs will be added and linked to the existing ones, query engines will become more sophisticated, and astronomers will have to be just as familiar with mining data as with observing on telescopes. The SDSS is the first of these projects, and we therefore did not have any paths to follow.

As part of our contribution to the SDSS collaboration, the Johns Hopkins University is producing the science archive software for use within the project. Part of the design requirement has been that the final system be easily extended into a public archive, which is the ultimate goal of our project. As a result, we have developed a three-tiered system that provides maximum flexibility and isolates potential portability conflicts. The system uses a geometrical indexing scheme with several novel features to provide both fast access to the data and feedback on the estimated size and execution time for a submitted query. The query results are extracted from the data repository and returned to the user in a customizable fashion. We utilize Objectivity/DB as the persistent storage mechanism, since our geometric indexing scheme is based upon data containerization/clustering that uniquely fits within Objectivity/DB's storage hierarchy. Queries are interpreted and executed by a multithreaded query support layer that uses POSIX threads for networked process communication. Except for the graphical user interface (which uses Tcl/Tk), the entire system is written in C++.

The first part of this chapter discusses the Sloan Digital Sky Survey in greater detail, including the project participants and both the hardware and software required for the successful completion of the survey. The next section introduces the two constituent archives: the operational archive and the science archive, including a detailed discussion of the design and implementation of the science archive. The third section discusses our geometrical approach to viewing data storage and querying. Our goal with this chapter is to outline the road we have taken towards creating this archival system, and how many of the hard decisions have been answered through the use of object-oriented technology.

THE SLOAN DIGITAL SKY SURVEY

The Sloan Digital Sky Survey is a collaboration between the University of Chicago, Princeton University, The Johns Hopkins University, the University of Washington, Fermi National Accelerator Laboratory, the Japanese Promotion Group, the United

States Naval Observatory, and the Institute for Advanced Study,[1] with additional funding provided by the Sloan Foundation and the National Science Foundation. In order to perform the observations, a dedicated 2.5 meter Ritchey-Chrétien telescope was constructed at Apache Point, New Mexico, USA. This telescope is designed to have a large, flat focal plane that provides a 3° field of view. This design results from an attempt to balance the areal coverage of the instrument against the detector's pixel resolution.

The survey has two main components: a photometric survey and a spectroscopic survey. The photometric survey is produced by drift scan imaging of 10,000 square degrees centered on the North Galactic Cap using five broadband filters that range from the ultraviolet to the near infrared. The photometric imaging will use a CCD[2] array that consists of 30 2K x 2K imaging CCDs, 22 2K x 400 astrometric CCDs, and 2 2K x 400 Focus CCDs. The raw data rate from this imaging camera will exceed 8 Megabytes per second. The spectroscopic survey will target over a million objects chosen from the photometric survey in an attempt to produce a statistically uniform sample. This survey will utilize two multi-fiber medium resolution spectrographs, with a total of 640 optical fibers, of 3 seconds of arc in diameter, to map the images of 640 galaxies simultaneously onto the slits of the spectrograph, that provide spectral coverage from 3900—9200 Angstroms. The telescope will gather about 5000 galaxy spectra in one night. The total number of spectra known to astronomers today is about 50,000—only 10 days of SDSS data! Whenever the Northern Galactic Cap is not accessible from the telescope site, a complementary survey will repeatedly image several areas in the Southern Galactic Cap to study fainter objects and identify any variable sources.[3]

Most of the hardware components are currently being assembled. Integration will begin shortly after the submission of this chapter. After several months of commissioning and testing, the scientific validation of the instruments and the software will begin, with the observations expected to start in the middle of 1997, and then operate for five years. The total amount of raw data that needs to be processed is currently estimated to be about 40 TB. Such a large amount of data can only be dealt with in an automated fashion; consequently, the software required for the operation of the survey is quite extensive, including the telescope control systems, the data acquisition system, the reduction and analysis software, as well as the archival software. An additional constraint is the short turnaround required by the data reduction software as the spectroscopic survey is dependent on the data acquired from the photometric survey. This reduction process involves several pipelines that communicate via an operational archive. In order to utilize existing project personnel expertise, as well as existing code bases, the majority of the software for the project is written in C with a Tcl shell that simplifies testing and analysis. The one main exception is the science archive, which is written in C++.

---

[1]Located in Princeton, New Jersey.

[2]Charge Coupled Device: a solid state imaging device that produces an electronic signal that is linearly related to the incident energy flux.

[3]e.g., Supernovae or Black Hole Candidates.

The collaboration will release the data to the public after an initial verification period. The actual distribution method is still under discussion. This public archive is expected to remain the standard reference catalog for the next several decades, presenting additional design and legacy problems. Furthermore, the design of the SDSS science archive must allow for the archive to grow beyond the actual completion of the survey. For example, the SDSS may be extended to cover a larger area of the sky (i.e., the Southern Galactic Cap). Also, as the reference astronomical data set, each subsequent astronomical survey will want to cross-identify its objects with the SDSS catalog, requiring that the archive remain dynamic.

As no comparable astronomical data sets are currently available, there has been no relevant knowledge base that we could have utilized in our design. This fact has proven beneficial, since one of our goals has been to encourage the user to explore the multidimensional parameter space provided by the SDSS. This ability to perform data mining is heavily dependent on both a novel geometrical indexing technique that we developed and Objectivity/DB's data containerization strategy.

THE SDSS ARCHIVES

Due to the effort required to design and produce the hardware required by the survey, as well as the reduction and analysis software, it was quickly realized that the survey data needs to be organized beyond flat files, thus the concept of a "mythical database" emerged within the project. This "black box" database would accept all the data that we could feed into it, up to several Terabytes, and then magically allow us to quickly extract data in useful formats. We soon realized that no such "off-the-shelf" system existed. At that point the project began a systematic analysis of exactly what would be needed to satisfy the requirements for a project archive. We entered into the database field with little prior knowledge or experience. This proved to be both a hindrance, in that we had to learn the basics before we could begin to tackle the archive design, and yet we remained open to new ideas and technologies that we otherwise might have rejected out of hand.

As part of the early project work on archival implementation, Fermi National Accelerator Laboratory (FNAL) evaluated several relational, object/relational, and object-oriented database systems (OODBS) primarily with regard to system performance. The general consensus was that OODBS provided the best performance as well as the best implementation model for scaling to the Terabyte regime. An initial choice of an OODBS vendor was made with the idea of reevaluating the project's database vendor in two years when the OO market would have matured (which it certainly has!). From the beginning, a major concern with object-oriented technology was the volatility of all the vendors, and a resulting design requirement that emerged was to limit the reliance of the archival software on a particular vendor's product. The main tool for satisfying this requirement was the use of Paradigm Plus, a commercial object data modeling and multiple target code generation software. We chose the Rumbaugh/OMT [Rum+91] method as it satisfied the majority of our modeling needs.

Overall, the survey archive began to devolve into two orthogonal functionalities with two correspondingly distinct components: an operational archive, where the raw data is reduced and mission critical information is stored; and the science archive, where calibrated data are available to the collaboration for analysis and are optimized for such queries.

In the operational archive, retained data are reduced, but uncalibrated, since the calibration data are not necessarily taken at the same time as the observation. Calibrations will be provided on the fly via method functions, allowing several versions to be simultaneously accessible. The science archive will contain only calibrated data, reorganized for efficient scientific use. If a major revision of the calibrations is necessary, the science archive and its replications will have to be regenerated from the operational archive. At any time, the master science archive (see Figure 11–1) will be the standard dataset against which all verifications will be made.

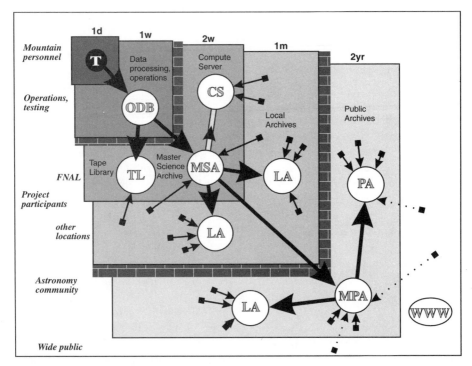

Figure 11–1   A conceptual data-flow diagram of the SDSS data. The data are taken at the telescope (**T**) and shipped on tapes to FNAL, where they are processed within one week, ingested into the operational archive (**ODB**), protected by a firewall, and accessible only to the personnel working on the data processing. Within two weeks, data will be transferred into the Master Science Archive (**MSA**). From there data will be replicated to local archives (**LA**) within another two weeks. The data gets into the public domain (**MPA, LA**) after two years of science verification and, if necessary, recalibration. These servers will provide data to the astronomical community. We will also provide a WWW-based access for the general public, which will be defined in the near future.

This devolution process initially resulted from a design goal to provide optimal performance for sweeping queries in the multidimensional coordinate system that describes the SDSS data. Eventually, other benefits of this approach appeared; most notably, the ability to ensure the integrity of the operational data during the execution of the survey. This approach also guarantees that the scientists are provided uniformly calibrated data. The responsibility for developing each of the archives was divided: FNAL took responsibility for the operational archive, which interacts with the reduction software, and JHU began the conceptual design of the science archive.

During this initial design period, one of us (AS) received a research grant from Digital Equipment Corporation. As a result of this grant, we received DEC Object/DB, a DEC-bundled version of Objectivity/DB, which we then began to evaluate in addition to another product. In such a way, a substantial expertise has been built up within the project, which was not tied to a single vendor. There was a very strong feeling within the collaboration that even though the two archival systems are separate, we should use only a single vendor. After the two-year evaluation period had expired, we developed a set of internal benchmarks and criteria with which to choose a single vendor. These included not only performance-related issues, but also multiplatform support and platform interoperability, which was a major concern given the diversity of the eventual target "customers"—the astronomy community at different universities and observatories. As a result of the detailed evaluation/benchmarking process, the project decided to switch to Objectivity/DB as the OODBS platform.

The Data Products

The SDSS science archive will consist of four main data products: a photometric catalog, a spectroscopic catalog, images, and spectra. The photometric catalog is expected to contain a minimum of one hundred million galaxies, one hundred million stars, and one million quasars, with magnitudes, profiles, and observational information recorded in the archive. The anticipated size of this product is about 250 GB. Each detected object will also have an associated image cutout ("atlas image") for each of the five filters, adding 700 GB. The spectroscopic catalog will contain identified emission and absorption lines, and one dimensional spectra for one million galaxies, one hundred thousand stars, one hundred thousand quasars, and about ten thousand clusters, totaling about 50 GB. In addition, derived custom catalogs may be included, such as a photometric cluster catalog, or QSO absorption line catalog. Thus the total amount of tracked information in these products will exceed 1 Terabyte.[4]

Typical Queries

We expect that most of the queries will be of an exploratory nature; initially, no two queries will be exactly alike. Generally, scientists will try to explore the multicolor properties of the objects in the SDSS catalog, starting with small queries of limited

---

[4]All of these numbers are raw values and include no estimates for any system overhead.

scope, then gradually making their queries more complex, utilizing a hit-and-miss search pattern. Thus, several typical types of activities need to be supported: (1) manual browsing, where one would look at objects in the same general area of the sky, and manually/interactively explore their individual properties; (2) the creation of sweeping searches, which extend to a major part of the sky; (3) proximity searches based upon angular separations between objects on the sky; (4) cross-identifications with external catalogs; (5) creating personal subsets, a persistent select; and (6) creating new "official" data products.

Complicating matters are the different spherical coordinate systems astronomers use to describe the location of an object on the sky. These coordinate systems are singular at the poles and may be a function of time, due to the complex motion of the Earth around the Sun. To store all these attributes is simply not practical, if not impossible, not to mention building indices on them all. Instead, we have devised another technique to deal with this problem: we represent all objects as their Cartesian projection onto a unit sphere, storing the three components of the unit vector pointing to the object. Constraints on the different coordinates are converted by the front end into this Cartesian coordinate system, indices are built in this system, and queries are submitted in this form to the database. The different spherical coordinates are computed by methods and returned to the user dynamically.

These functional goals have clearly affected our architecture and design. We defined a set of minimum requirements and enhanced goals before committing to our formal design. We also built a "quick-and-dirty" prototype to test many of our new ideas. This turned out to be a very useful exercise, providing valuable insight into the many of the issues that affected our final design.

Archive Architecture

High-level requirements for the archive included (1) the ability to easily transfer the binary database image from one architecture to another, (2) multiplatform availability and interoperability, (3) simple maintenance for migrating to future operating systems and platforms. In order to satisfy these, the science archive employs a distributed, three-tiered architecture: the *user interface*, the *query support component*, and the *data warehouse*. This approach provides maximum flexibility, while maintaining portability, by isolating hardware specific features. It is illustrated in Figure 11–2.

The data warehouse, where most of the low-level I/O access occurs is based upon an OODBS (Objectivity/DB), which is then responsible for the operating system support. Objectivity/DB is especially powerful in this respect, providing updates on an unusually large number of platforms almost simultaneously. Also, Objectivity/DB's database image is binary compatible and can be copied between different platforms, since the architecture is encoded on every page in the federation.

The other area where portability becomes a major concern is the user interface, where the software has to interact with different windowing systems. We decided to use Tcl/Tk, since it has been ported to all major platforms: multiple flavors of UNIX, Linux, Windows NT, Windows 95, and the Macintosh. Recently a beta

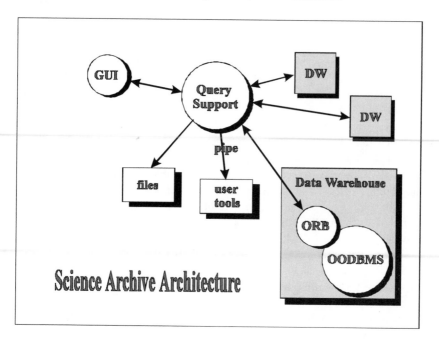

Figure 11–2   A conceptual picture of the three-tiered architecture of the archive. The data warehouse is connected to the query support via a custom Object Request Broker. The query support can send the data to custom user tools directly. It can also connect to multiple data warehouses, both in the case of unavailability of a local server or to connect to different data sets.

plug-in version, safeTcl, became available. The different tiers communicate through TCP/IP sockets using a well-defined ASCII control protocol, while data are transferred in a binary machine-independent format. This communication relies heavily on net.h++, a socket class library developed by Rogue Wave.

- The *user interface* is primarily responsible for aiding in the formulation of queries, and in controlling the flow of the extracted data. A graphical interface is provided that allows the user to construct a query from the attributes retrieved from the archive metadata. Quite complex queries can be built up using a drag-and-drop interface. Queries can be assembled from components. Each component is represented by an icon on the desktop, which can be then connected. The whole desktop can be saved and retrieved for later use. This is a convenient way to built up customized macros, which can also be shared by several users. The graphical object representing the query can be dropped onto an icon, representing the science archive. It is then converted into an ASCII query string (a subset of SQL), and sent to the query support component.
- The *query support layer* then parses, tokenizes, and transforms the ASCII string into a query tree, which encapsulates the geometrical nature of the data. De-

pending on the user's particular request, either the estimated query feedback is returned to the user interface, or the query is optimized and sent to the data warehouse for execution. The feedback mechanism provides a trial-and-error exploratory querying ability that can prevent unintentional queries from wasting system resources. The net result of this process is to aid in the exploration of the data (find the unusual objects) as opposed to the replication of a given query.

- The *data warehouse* contains the actual data as well as the corresponding metadata (data that describes the contents of the archive) for the entire science archive. This data repository is implemented using Objectivity/DB. The interface to the data repository is through a custom object request broker (ORB), which communicates with the query support component. When a query is executed, the ORB opens the appropriate databases and extracts the desired attributes from all objects that satisfy the optimized query. These queries can be executed using several distinct methods of access: an OQL predicate query, an ODBC interface, and an SQL++ interface, all provided by Objectivity. The extracted data are sent to the query support component where they are routed to the user's desired destination, which can include custom tools or applets that can reside on dedicated processors. This allows the user to query the archive via a modem connection, whereas the data warehouse, the query support component, and the analysis tools can all reside within a high-speed networked domain.

Platforms, Tools, Libraries

The development of the science archive utilizes Digital UNIX on DEC Alpha workstations. In order to ensure operating system portability, as well as to satisfy project participants, the archival software is ported to the SGI IRIX and Windows NT operating systems. The actual development of the science archive has benefited greatly from the use of external tools, which often arrived just in time. Clearly, if we had to deliver the system a year earlier, we would have had to write a substantially greater amount of code ourselves. We use INSIGHT for error detection in our C++ code base, and YACC++ for our grammar parsing and lexing. We also use several Rogue Wave class libraries, including tools.h++, net.h++, and their version of the Standard C++ Library. The use of these external tools, along with a reliance on software standards,[5,6] [Cat96] has shortened the design and development cycle and simplified portability concerns.

GEOMETRIC CONCEPTS

Large data sets often contain numerical subsets (i.e., spatial coordinates) that are indexed in order to expedite a certain class of queries. Traditional indexing schemes must be restricted to a few parameters; otherwise, they begin to match the actual

---

[5]ISO/ANSI X3J16 C++ Draft Standard.
[6]IEEE Portable Operating Systems Interface.

data in physical size. Moreover, current archive queries are limited to simple ranges of parameter values, while the desired query may be more complicated. For example, "Find all blue ($g' - r' < 0.7$) galaxies fainter than $g = 22^{nd}$ magnitude that are within 3 arcseconds of a quasar brighter than $r = 18^{th}$ magnitude." Using the formalisms of computational geometry, these types of queries can be succinctly modeled. For instance, the previous example can be modeled "Find all specific data points within a given metric distance of a specified simplex." By incorporating these geometrical concepts into our archival design, we have developed a multidimensional geometric indexing strategy that can be used with any multidimensional numeric data set. In addition to the traditional benefits of an index scheme, this technique also provides accurate predictions of query volumes and times, a snapshot of the spatial relationships that exist within the data set, and also a quantization of data on the storage media.

Our geometric index consists of a modified k-d tree [Fri+77], in which a d-dimensional numerical data set is partitioned using k-key attributes in a tree structure. Within the tree, a node conceptually represents a sub-volume within the entire d-dimensional volume occupied by the data. Thus, the root node represents the entire data set, which is then partitioned using one of the k-key attributes into separate sub-volumes, which are represented by the root node's children. This process continues until a predetermined leaf node level is reached, wherein all objects that lie within the leaf node's volume are quantized and stored contiguously on the storage media in an attempt to ensure efficient cache hits. The leaf nodes, or cells, form a coarse grained density map of the actual data.

This technique can be extended to include disjoint subspaces, such as spatial location and flux measurements, since the splitting of any given node is independent of any other node within the tree. Another possibility is to utilize the same subtree below a given level within the index in an effort to reduce the amount of memory required to maintain the index. The resulting data structure is then a modified k-d tree, as *a priori* domain information is used to dictate the partitions. The index is actually implemented using the composite and visitor design patterns [Gam+94]. The visitor object is chosen according to the accuracy required during the querying of the index.

Queries are first executed on the geometric index, producing a feedback to the user on the estimated number of objects satisfying the search and the estimated search time. Because the index is compact enough to fit entirely within the memory of the user's system, any interactions with the index are extremely fast. Using the information contained within the index, queries can be optimized on a cell-by-cell basis by removing extraneous or redundant portions of the query within the given cell. These optimized container queries fit naturally within Objectivity/DB's database hierarchy, which provides a one-to-one mapping from our leaf nodes to containers of objects on the storage media. The quantization of queries provides an additional benefit of optimizing the query server by instituting a queued container query access (i.e., optimizing cache hits across individual queries). One additional benefit of this indexing strategy is that a given leaf node contains the physical location(s) of the corresponding data. This allows the data to be distributed/replicated in various locations, implicitly introducing parallelization into the design process.

The geometrical indexing strategy can naturally incorporate the actual query, resulting in a more powerful search mechanism. Rather than limit a user to parameter cuts, linear combinations of attributes form the query primitive within our system. These linear combinations can then be combined using Boolean algebra to form complex polyhedra that can carve out complicated volumes within the available parameter space. In order to simplify spatial queries, we work with a Cartesian projection of the spherical astrometric coordinates. This simplifies coordinate conversions, and reduces spherical proximities, and the customary great- and small-circle constraints to linear combinations of the Cartesian coordinates. These techniques are also applicable to GIS systems, where objects are located on the sphere defined by the Earth's surface.

EXPERIENCES AND SUMMARY

We are in the middle of designing and constructing an extremely ambitious archival system, aiming to provide a useful tool for almost all astronomers in the world. We hope that our efforts will be successful, and that the resulting system will substantially change the nature of astronomical research. The day when we have a "Digital Sky" at our desktop may be nearer than most astronomers think. Given the enormous public interest in astronomy, we also hope that the resulting archive will provide a challenge and inspiration to thousands of interested high-school students and a lot of fun for the web-surfing public. To serve a TB archive even to the scientific community is quite a challenge today, to offer it to the wide public will be a task that we have not even started to appreciate. We hope that the pace of current hardware and software technologies in the area of large object databases will accelerate even further, and that the integration of applets into the standard set of scientific data analysis tools will soon commence. We are convinced that this effort would have been orders of magnitude more difficult, if not impossible, without our reliance on object-oriented databases and object technology in general. We feel that this technology has matured to the point where it provides real solutions to real problems.

REFERENCES

[Bec+95] R. H. Becker, R. L. White, D. J. Helfand: *Astrophysical Journal,* 450, 559.

[Cat96] R. G. G. Cattell (ed.): *The Object Database Standard: ODMG-93,* Morgan- Kaufmann Publishers, 1996.

[Djo+92] S. Djorgovski, B. M. Lasker, W. N. Weir, M. Postman, I. N. Reid, V. G. Laidler: *Bulletin of the American Astronomical Society,* 180, #13.07.

[Frit77] J. H. Friedman, J. L. Bentley, R. A. Finkel: *ACM Transactions on Mathematical Software,* 3, 209, 1977.

[Gam+94] E. Gamma, R. Helm, R. Johnson, J. Vlissides: *Design Patterns Elements of Reusable Object-Oriented Software,* Addison-Wesley, 1994.

[GK93] J. Gunn, G. R. Knapp: *Sky Surveys: Protostars to Protogalaxies* in B. T. Soifer (ed.), ASP Conference Series, 43, 1993.

[Kle+94] S. G. Kleinmann, M. G. Lysaght, W. L. Pughe, S. E. Schneider, M. D. Weinberg, S. D. Price, K. Matthews, B. T. Soifer, J. P. Huchra: *Astrophysics and Space Science,* 217, 11.

[Rum+91] J. Rumbaugh, M. Blaha, W. Premerlani, F. Eddy, W. Lorenson: *Object Oriented Modeling and Design,* Prentice Hall, 1991.

III

Object Database Selection and Migration

INTRODUCTION

Object database products have been evolving quite rapidly; the vendors typically have a major software release at least once a year, with possibly several minor releases during the year as well. It can be difficult to keep up with the capabilities of the various products. Chapter 12 presents a comparison of Objectivity/DB and VERSANT by Dietrich, Reghabi, Krahling, and Urban. The chapter begins with a discussion of the authors' experience with a procedure for selecting an object database product to support a commercial telecoms application. The second part of the paper describes Objectivity/DB and VERSANT in more detail, presents a feature comparison and uses a small application built on both systems to demonstrate the support provided by each product for the ODMG standard.

An issue that may face organizations is whether to use a relational database system with an object-oriented programming language or to move to a full object database. As discussed in Chapter 9, an object database provides a seamless language interface and there are no translation costs between language and database objects. In Chapter 13, Woyna, Christiansen, Hield, and Simunich describe their experiences in choosing between using a relational or object database. They describe the problems with the former approach and the benefits of the latter and conclude that object databases can provide support for large and complex data sets more easily than relational databases can.

New technology should be used if it helps to solve business problems, rather than for its own sake. In Chapter 14, Rudge and Moorley pose questions, such as "what are the requirements and drivers in the financial markets?" and "how can new technology help?". They conclude that new technologies, such as object databases and object request brokers, are needed by their company to meet new demands and to remain competitive. They describe their experiences evaluating three object database products: GemStone, ObjectStore for Smalltalk (OSST) and Objectivity/Smalltalk. Their system design requires good integration between an object database and object request broker. This is an area that requires vendor support. Their experiences demonstrate the importance of developing prototype applications, which they feel can be a lengthy proposition, but very worthwhile.

Geographical Information Systems (GIS) are a natural choice for object databases. GIS data are of a complex nature and are not easily represented in a tabular manner without incurring performance penalties. Chapter 15 by Shaw, Chung and Cobb describes their experiences using ObjectStore to solve some of these problems. Detailed descriptions of class definitions and implementation issues are presented. The chapter discusses how ObjectStore was used to (almost) seamlessly integrate an OO model (called OVPF) for GIS data.

12

On Acquiring OODBMS Technology:

A Industry Perspective
and a Case Study Comparison
of Objectivity/DB and VERSANT

Suzanne W. Dietrich, Arizona State University
Saeed Reghabi, AG Communication Systems
Deborah Krahling, Arizona State University
Susan D. Urban, Arizona State University

ABSTRACT

Object-oriented database management systems (OODBMSs) provide data modeling capabilities beyond those offered by relational systems through the use of complex objects, encapsulation, and inheritance. For those application domains that can benefit from the power of object modeling capabilities, object-oriented databases promise reduced development time and increased performance. Industry recognizes the need for positioning itself to utilize this promising technology in future business plans. This chapter provides an industry perspective on acquiring OODBMS technology and uses a case study of a prototypical employee training database application to compare the features (not performance) of two OODBMS products, Objectivity/ DB and VERSANT.

Thanks are due the team members who contributed their time and effort to the collection and review of the detailed information for each product. The authors also wish to acknowledge the representatives of Objectivity (Steve Fox and John Myser) and Versant Object Technology (Sunil Nagdev) who provided a technical review of the paper. We would also like to thank Jeff Garland, a Principal Software Engineer on the Motorola Iridium project, for his industry perspective on the selection process of an OODBMS for a particular application.

INTRODUCTION

Object-oriented database management systems (OODBMSs) have become a serious competitor in the database systems market, offering modeling capabilities beyond those of relational systems. For those application domains that can benefit from the power of object modeling, object-oriented databases promise reduced development time and increased performance. Selecting an OODBMS product, however, can be a confusing assignment. Unlike relational database technology, OODBMSs were developed before the establishment of any theoretical foundations or modeling and access standards. As a result, most OODBMS products provide similar concepts but different approaches to the modeling and creation of object schemas, to the navigational and associative retrieval of objects, and to system implementation details that affect performance.

Fortunately, the development of the ODMG-93 *de facto* standard [Cat96] has helped to provide a common ground for the way in which we view OODBMS modeling and access concepts, providing for the portability of OODBMS applications. Most OODBMS products are committed to conformance to the standard. Current systems, however, still have progress to make with respect to conformance. The ODMG-93 standard combined with additional evaluation criteria, however, can provide a useful basis for the evaluation of OODBMS products.

One purpose of this chapter is to present an industry perspective on the acquisition of OODBMS technology, describing a selection process that provides guidelines for the establishment of evaluation criteria. The intent is that others interested in OODBMS acquisition can make use of a similar process, modifying the evaluation criteria to meet their own specific needs.

In addition to presenting an industry perspective on the evaluation process, this paper also provides an examination of two different OODBMS products, Objectivity/DB (Version 3.5) [Obj95] and VERSANT (Release 4.0.7) [Ver95]. These products were chosen for this study based on their acquisition and use by industry in the Phoenix metropolitan area. Objectivity/DB was recently acquired by Motorola Satellite Communications for the Iridium project, and VERSANT was recently acquired by AG Communication Systems. The computer science and engineering department at Arizona State University also acquired Objectivity/DB to use as a graduate-level teaching tool within an advanced database management course. The primary purpose of this comparison is to illustrate the modeling and access features of each system with respect to the ODMG-93 standard in the context of a prototypical employee training application that was implemented in both Objectivity/DB and VERSANT. A graduate student's project provided the opportunity to prototype the application in Objectivity/DB. A sabbatical opportunity provided the academia-industry technology transfer to prototype the same application in VERSANT. The case study comparison is not intended to be a complete examination of all features of each product and uses the ODMG-93 standard to help illustrate the modeling and access capabilities of the products. Performance issues as well as specialized features such as versioning are not addressed in the comparison.

The focus of this paper is on the acquisition of OODBMS technology and the knowledge gained by the implementation of a prototypical application in two different OODBMS products. The next section provides a telecommunications industry perspective on the acquisition of OODBMS technology. We also briefly describe the employee training database application used in the case study and provide an overview of the ODMG-93 standard and describe the specification of the employee training application utilizing the object definition language. The next two sections provide an overview of the OODBMS products, including a description of the design of the application within each object model as it was implemented. A case study comparison of the products is detailed in the last section. The paper concludes with a summary and a discussion of issues for the utilization of OODBMS.

INDUSTRY PERSPECTIVE

Technology acquisition is the first step in achieving the goal of utilizing a new technology. This section presents an industry perspective on the acquisition of OODBMS technology. This perspective is primarily presented from the point of view of a telecommunications company, AG Communication Systems. Specifically, the process that AG Communication Systems used to select an OODBMS product for acquisition and installation within the company's distributed, heterogeneous computing environment is described. A similar evaluation process was also conducted by the Motorola Iridium project in selecting an OODBMS for a specific application. The additional evaluation criteria considered by the Motorola evaluation team are also presented.

AG Communication Systems is a telecommunications pioneer with more than 100 years of industry experience. The company develops, manufactures, installs, and maintains computerized switching systems for telephone companies' central offices. This core product is the GTD-5® EAX family of digital switching systems. Nearly 17 million telephone subscribers worldwide receive their phone service through connections to a GTD-5 switch. In addition to the core business, a range of new products position AG Communication Systems as a leading supplier of intelligent telecommunications solutions.

AG Communication Systems utilizes database technology, such as VSAM/ISAM and relational database systems, in their application development environment. Their main product, the GTD-5 telephone switch, has its own proprietary database management system.

Most applications for Intelligent Networks are not well served by conventional systems due to the complexity of data, the need for new data types (such as bit maps), and the need to capture complex semantics of interpreting and updating data. Most conventional database applications involve two languages, the Data Manipulation Language (DML) of the database system and a general purpose programming language. These languages are almost always mismatched in their type systems and their programming style. Object-oriented database management systems provide a more powerful data language, so that more of an application can be coded in one language.

Considering the above shortcomings of conventional database systems, AG Communication Systems decided to initiate a project for the acquisition and installation of OODBMS technology within the AG Communication Systems computing environment, thereby allowing the future utilization of OODBMS technology. To achieve the project objective, a strategy was developed for vendor evaluation and recommendation. Obviously, choosing an OODBMS vendor was a difficult and challenging task. There were numerous vendors to evaluate. The OODBMS products were complex and appeared on the surface to be very similar to each other.

The first step in the evaluation process was to understand the functionality promised by object-oriented database technology. This understanding was used as a basis to evaluate the features of current object-oriented database products.

The team that was chartered to identify, evaluate, and recommend OODBMS products, initially defined three essential criteria for the products to meet. This led the team to a narrowing of OODBMS products for more detailed evaluation by the OODBMS team in concert with AG Communication Systems project/application development needs.

The first criteria addressed the architecture of the object-oriented database. The team considered the three architectures; OODB, Server, and Layer. The OODB architecture is a system that uses a single language for both the database and application, where the object semantics execute on the client. The Server architecture also uses a single language for both the database and application, but the object semantics execute on the server. The Layer architecture utilizes a relational database to store information with a layer to manage object-oriented concepts between the application written in an object-oriented programming language (OOPL) and the relational storage level. The team chose the OODB architecture due to the integration of the database and its applications and the improved performance that the integration allows through the utilization of the client.

The second criteria addressed a commitment to be compliant with the ODMG standard, the common object models and language bindings that allow application developers to write portable applications utilizing OODBMS. The compliance with the standard provided us with the confidence to invest in this technology.

The third criteria addressed the object-oriented programming language that was available for use within an OODBMS product. Most OODBMSs provide either C++ or Smalltalk. The preferred language was C++, since it is utilized in the AG Communication Systems development environment.

The initial examination of the OODBMS products with respect to the initial requirements of OODB architecture, commitment to be compliant with the ODMG standard and the availability of the C++ programming language narrowed the field of products to be further examined to ONTOS, Poet, O2, VERSANT, Objectivity/DB, and ObjectStore.

The team utilized the acceptable industry evaluation instruments, such as sources of unbiased data about object databases [BC96] and the results of performance benchmarks [Car+93]), to define a list of criteria for each vendor, including compiler heterogeneity, client/server heterogeneity, backup (batch, online, incremental, distributed), multi-volume support, client cache management, locking granularity, database references, reference counting, collections (list, set, bag, dictionary, array), date and time types, query language, server query execution, tools, nested transactions, security, and versioning. These criteria provide one basis for the case study comparison later in this chapter.

After the team collected the detailed information for each criterion for each vendor, for more accuracy the team solicited input from the narrow list of vendors based on the list of criteria.

In addition to the product features evaluation, other factors such as marketing position, product direction, support, and licensing were also reviewed and taken into consideration for final recommendation. The marketing position of the vendor, including its strength within the OODBMS market, the stability of the company (revenues, growth, number of employees) was especially important to the team. The type of technical support, the quality and cost of online support, and the number of engineers assigned to supporting customers were also important factors.

After reviewing all collected data, the team recommended acquisition of the VERSANT OODBMS product for the distributed, heterogeneous telecommunication environment. VERSANT offered object-level locking and concurrency, online schema facilities to launch new services, database replication, object transparency to effect network-wide changes, as well as many other features. In addition, VERSANT's support of 24x7 (24 hours a day, 7 days a week) operation is a fundamental requirement in the telecommunications industry.

The above selection process represents an evaluation of the various products based on the needs of the computing environment and requirements of generic applications within the industry. A company, however, may use a similar process to choose a product for use on a specific application. Recently, Motorola Satellite Communications evaluated OODBMS products for a particular application within the Iridium project, which will use satellites in low earth orbit to provide a global wireless telephone service. The evaluation criteria used in the Motorola selection process were those features that their application required. The evaluation criteria were also prioritized based on their importance for that application. The evaluation process also included visiting companies that had already deployed commercial OODBMS products and implementing a prototype to become familiar with the characteristics of the OODBMS product. Motorola's team recommended the acquisition of Objectivity/DB for its application within the Iridium project.

THE APPLICATION

The application that we chose for the case study is a somewhat simplified database for maintaining training courses for employees in a fictitious company. The Enhanced Entity-Relationship (EER) diagram [EN94] in Figure 12–1 provides a con-

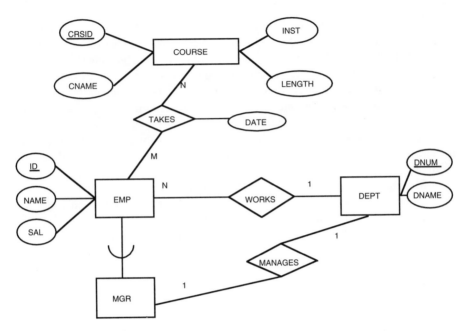

Figure 12–1   Enhanced ER diagram of employee training application.

ceptual view of the schema. The boxes represent entities of interest in the enterprise: Employees (EMP), Managers (MGR), Departments (DEPT), and Courses (COURSE). The MGR entity is a subclass of the EMP entity, indicating that a manager inherits the properties of an employee. The diamonds represent relationships between entities—for example, WORKS, MANAGES, and TAKES—which are linked by edges. The numbers on the edges linking entities to relationships indicate cardinality ratios of the relationship. For example, the WORKS relationship is one-to-many (1:n) since an employee works in one department but a department has many employees working in it.

ODMG STANDARD

The Object Database Management Group (ODMG) was established in late 1991 to expedite the development of standards for OODBMS, providing the common object models and language bindings that allow application developers to write portable OODBMS code. The ODMG-93 standard [Cat96] is currently a *de facto* industry standard that includes an object model, an object definition language (ODL), an object query language (OQL), and programming language bindings for C++ and Smalltalk.

The ODMG-93 object model uses objects and literals as the basic modeling primitives. An object has a unique (immutable) identifier that doesn't change when the value of its properties change. An object has both a state, which is the value of its properties, and behavior, which is the set of operations executed on or by the object. An object's type interface defines its external characteristics and its implementation defines its internal characteristics through the representation of its data structure and methods. The interface allows for the specification of supertype-subtype relationships, providing inheritance of the supertype interface by the subtype and allowing specialization of the subtype interface. Multiple inheritance is also permitted. A literal does not have a unique identifier. Literals can be atomic (short, long), a collection (set, bag, or list), or structured (having a fixed number of elements each having a name and a value).

The Object Definition Language (ODL) specifies the interface of object types. Figure 12–2 provides an ODL definition for the employee training enterprise where method definitions are omitted for brevity of presentation. The interface definition for each entity from the EER diagram includes the specification of extents, which are the set of all instances of a type, and keys, which are a set of properties that uniquely identify the individual instances of a type. For example, emps is specified as the extent of Emp and id as the key that uniquely identifies instances of Emp. Attributes describe the characteristics of entities, and inverse relationships describe the WORKS and MANAGES relationships. The TAKES relationship from the EER diagram is represented by collection literals in Emp and Course. In Emp, the attribute courses_taken is a list of course-date pairs. In Course, the attribute offerings is a list of date-attendance pairs, where attendance is a set of employees that took that course offering.

```
structNametype                              interface Dept
{ String      lastname;                      (extentdepts
  String      midinit;                        keydnum )
  String      firstname;};                    { attribute    String        dnum;
                                                attribute    String        dname;
structcourse-date                              relationship Set<Emp>      emps_of
{ Course      tcourse;                              inverse Emp::dept_of;
  Date        tdate; };                        relationship Mgr            mgr_of
                                                    inverse Mgr::manages_dept
interface Emp                                 // Methods };
( extent emps
  key id)                                     structtakes
{ attribute    String           id;          { Date         odate;
  attribute    Nametype         name;          Set<Emp>     attendance;}
  attribute    Float            salary;
  attribute    List<course-date> courses_taken; interface Course
  relationship Dept             dept_of       ( extent courses
      inverse Dept::emps_of;                    keycrsid)
// Methods};                                   { attribute    String        crsid;
                                                attribute    String        cname;
interface Mgr:Emp                              attribute    Nametype      inst;
{ relationship Dept            manages_dept    attribute    Float         length;
      inverseDept::mgr_of;                     attribute    List<takes>   offerings;
// Methods    };                              // Methods    };
```

Figure 12–2   ODL specification of the employee training schema.

The Object Query Language (OQL) provides a declarative specification for retrieving objects from the database based on the familiar SELECT-FROM-WHERE format of the industry-standard relational query language SQL. Whereas the FROM clause in SQL specifies the relations participating in the query, the FROM clause in OQL specifies the collections that participate in the query where collections can be extents or collections embedded in objects. For example, the following query retrieves the names of employees who have taken the "OODB" course:

```
SELECT e.name
FROM courses c, c.offerings o, o.attendance e
WHERE c.crsid = "OODB"
```

The programming language bindings provide the implementation of a type. The binding maps the ODMG object model into a language such as C++ or Smalltalk by providing a library of classes and functions that implement the concepts defined in the model.

VERSANT

VERSANT Object Technology was founded in 1988. The VERSANT object database management system has an integrated architecture (pure OODB), is committed to ODMG-compliance, and has language-specific interfaces for C++ and Smalltalk (with a Java interface on the way). VERSANT uses a client-server computing model supporting compiler heterogeneity and client-server heterogeneity. The basic architecture of VERSANT is that of a centralized object server. VERSANT's caching approach combines an object cache per application in virtual memory on the client and a page cache per operating database in shared memory on the server. VERSANT queries are executed on the server, returning only desired objects over the network to the client. VERSANT databases are scalable, allowing multiple volumes per database and the unique identification of up to 2^{48} objects. VERSANT provides support for distributed databases, including synchronous and asynchronous replication of objects, two-phase commits, and physical object migration across databases. Other database features supported by VERSANT include flexible backup capabilities, online schema modification, versioning, event notification, multiple processes and threads, short and long transaction models, sophisticated locking models, security, memory and space management, attribute indexing, database administration tools, and tools for schema and object browsing.

Design

The C++/VERSANT interface implements the VERSANT object model using three fundamental classes: PDOM, PObject, and PClass. PDOM contains the database management methods for database connections, sessions, and transaction management. PObject is the root of the persistent class hierarchy and provides behavior common to all persistent classes. The class PVirtual, which inherits from PObject, provides the ability to compare objects by value in addition to identity by defining two virtual methods, hash and compare, which must be redefined by derived classes. The PClass struct provides methods that work against all instances of a class, such as providing a select method for selectively retrieving objects of a class.

VERSANT predefines additional class types for strings, dates, time, links to persistent objects, variable-length storage, collections (list, set, array, dictionary), iterators to iterate over members of a collection class, and containers for collections of heterogeneous (persistent) objects.

Figure 12–3 provides a graphical abstraction using ODMG-like notation of the VERSANT employee training schema definition given in Figure 12–4. Since VERSANT's object model does not include collections of literals (only collections of objects), this schema differs from the ODMG schema by the introduction of a course Offering class type. An Offering represents a course offering on a specific date with the attendance roster for that offering. The MANAGES and WORKS relationships from the EER diagram are modeled using bidirectional links in VERSANT, which automatically manage the inverse relationship. Instead of using bidirectional links to model the TAKES relationship, which now involves the Emp, Offering, and Course classes, the schema uses links and collections to illustrate more of the features of VERSANT.

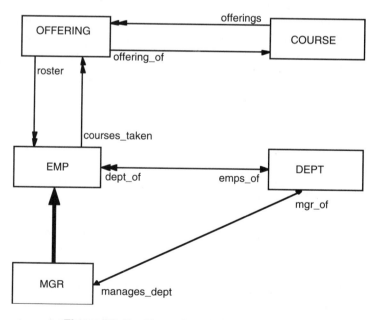

Figure 12–3   Abstraction of VERSANT schema.

```
struct Nametype                              class Dept:public Pobject
{PString            lastname;               {private:
 PString            midinit;                  PString            dnum;
 PString            firstname;};              PString            dname;
                                             public:
class Emp: public PObject                     BiLinkVstr<Emp>    emps_of;
{protected:                                      //Inverse of    Emp::dept_of
  PString            id;                       BiLink<Mgr>        mgr_of;
  Nametype           name;                        //Inverse of    Mgr::manages_dept
  o_float            salary;                  //Methods }
  VIList<Offering>   courses_taken;
 public:                                     class Course:public Pobject
  BiLink<Dept>       dept_of;                {private:
     //Inverse of    Dept::emps_of             PString            crsid;
//Methods }                                    PString            cname;
                                               Nametype           instructor;
class Mgr: public Emp                          o_float            length;
{public:                                       VIList<Offering>   offerings;
  BiLink<Dept>       manages_dept;            public:
     //Inverse of    Dept::mgr_of             //Methods}
//Methods}
                                             class Offering:public PObject
                                             {private:
                                               VDate              odate;
                                               Link<Course>       offering_of;
                                               VISet<Emp>         roster;
                                              public:
                                              //Methods}
```

Figure 12–4   VERSANT employee training schema.

A VERSANT schema is specified in a C++ include file (e.g., training.h), which is then included in the C++ file that implements the methods for the classes (e.g., training.cxx). The include file is input to a schema compiler that generates both a C++ file, which is compiled and linked with the application executable, and a schema file, which is used to update the meta-data for the database.

Figure 12–4 provides the VERSANT employee training schema definition without method prototypes for brevity of presentation. The PString is a VERSANT predefined class type for strings used as attributes in user-defined persistent classes. The Link template class defines an object reference. The LinkVStr template class defines a variable number of object references. The BiLink and BiLinkVStr template classes define bidirectional object references for specifying inverse relationships, such as the WORKS relationship between Emp::dept_of and Dept::emps_of. Note that the inverse is a comment in the schema. The inverse relationship is specified in VERSANT by the initialization of a static dummy variable in the class implementation file. For example,

```
static init_bilink_Emp_Dept =
    BiLink_to_BiLinkVstr<Emp,Dept>::add(&Emp::dept_of,&Dept::emps_of);
```

establishes the inverse relationship between Emp::dept_of and Dept::emps_of with a many-to-one cardinality ratio. The bidirectional links are defined as public since maintaining the inverse relationship requires direct access to attribute names. Collection classes in VERSANT are named `V?List`, `V?Set`, `V?Array`, and `V?Dictionary`, where the `?` indicates the contents of the collection class (E = elemental data type, I = links to objects compared by identity, V = links to objects compared by value). A `VIList<Offering>` template class represents the courses taken by an employee (`Emp::courses_taken`) and the offerings of a course (`Course::offerings`). A `VISet<Emp>` template class represents the set of employees that took a course offering (`Offering::roster`).

Query Capability

VERSANT does not yet provide an object query language, such as the ODMG OQL, or an ANSI SQL interface, although an ODBC-compliant ANSI SQL interface product is forthcoming. Programmatically, VERSANT provides a select method for retrieving objects based on a selection condition. Since VERSANT does not maintain a named extent of a class type, the extent can be derived by the select method call, illustrated for the Course class type: `PClassObject<Course>::Object().select(NULL, TRUE, NULL_PREDICATE)`, which returns an object of type `LinkVStr<Course>`. The parameters of the select method are:

1. The name of the database, where NULL is the default database
2. A boolean value representing whether subclasses should be included in the selection
3. The selection predicate where NULL_PREDICATE represents the retrieval of all objects

For a more complicated example, recall the query to retrieve the names of all employees that have taken the "OODB" course. The application programmer writes a program segment that finds the "OODB" course and then displays the roster for each offering of the course. The code for the VERSANT query is given in Figure 12–5. The left column provides the definition of a static function to find a course object given the `crsid`, which is unique. Since VERSANT does not support the definition of keys, the uniqueness of `crsid` must be maintained by methods for the course object. Note that VERSANT provides for transparent conversion between database links and C++ pointers. The right column illustrates the use of the

```
Course* Course::Find_Course_by_crsid(char* find_crsid);
{
  LinkVStr<Course> courses =
    PClassObject<Course>::Object().select
      (NULL, TRUE, PAttribute("Course::crsid") == find_crsid);
  Course* c;
  if (courses.is_empty())
    c = NULL;
  else
    c = courses[0];      // since crsid is a key
  courses.release();     // release LinkVStr space
  return c;
}
```

```
Course* oodbcrs = Course::Find_Course_by_crsid("OODB");
if (oodbcrs != NULL)
{
  VIList<Offering> oodbofferings = oodbcrs->get_offerings();
  VIListIterator<Offering> offering_iterator(oodbofferings);
  while (!!iterator)
  {
    Offering o = *offering_iterator;
    o.display_roster();
    offering_iterator++;
  }
}
```

Figure 12–5 VERSANT query specification.

predefined template classes for iterating over members of a collection. The use of the iterator template classes is not required for the query specification. The elements of the `oodbofferings` list can be accessed using the (square) brackets operator inside a C++ for loop.

OBJECTIVITY/DB

Objectivity, Inc. was founded in 1988, with the first version of Objectivity/DB available in 1990. Objectivity/DB is considered to be a pure OODB product with language-specific interfaces for C++ and Smalltalk (with a Java binding forthcoming). Objectivity/DB is committed to compliance with the ODMG-93 standard. Objectivity/DB provides a distributed client/server computing model, supporting access to heterogeneous platforms in a transparent manner. The basic architecture of Objectivity/DB is that of a distributed page server. The system provides both client-side and server-side, page-level caching, where the size of a page is configurable. Applications in Objectivity/DB can access multiple, distributed databases transparently to the application. New servers can be added and databases can be relocated to different servers online. Applications can take advantage of the new configuration without requiring code changes, recompilations, or restarting the application. Persistent objects can be shared among applications through the use of locking. Objectivity/DB also provides a fault tolerant option, which extends C++ interfaces to provide distributed database support for wide-area networks, with support for replicated objects and performance enhancements for local object access. Other database features supported by Objectivity/DB include long-duration transactions, object and class versioning, an ANSI SQL query language interface, special indexing for large object retrieval, and development tools for schema and object browsing.

DESIGN

Objectivity/DB is built on the concept of a federated database, which is a logical collection of databases. Each database consists of a collection of locking and clustering units called containers. A container object is a collection of basic objects, which are the application-defined objects requiring persistence. Containers allow the experienced application programmer to place logically related objects together for high performance locking and retrieval. Containers can also be distributed to different sites, providing for the distribution of part of a database.

Through the use of a preprocessor and library files, Objectivity/DB provides seamless integration with C++. The preprocessor translates the schema file into C++ syntax and the library files extend the power of C++ to accommodate database functionality. In Objectivity/DB, `ooObj` is the root of the persistent class hierarchy.

Objectivity/DB predefines class types for strings, references and handles to persistent objects, and iterators that traverse a list of related objects.

Figure 12–6 provides the Objectivity/DB employee training schema definition without method definitions for brevity of presentation. The schema is similar to the abstraction (of the VERSANT) schema given in Figure 12–3 since Objectivity/DB does not support collections of literals (although support for Standard Template Library collections is forthcoming). The type ooVString is a predefined class type for variable-length strings. The class Date is specified as part of the schema since Objectivity/DB does not predefine a built-in date type, although predefined classes for date and time are forthcoming in Version 4.0 of Objectivity/DB. Access to persistent objects are provided through object references (ooRef) and handles (ooHandle). Association links between persistent objects are specified using the predefined class ooRef. The predefined class ooHandle is used for the declaration of variables that wiil reference an object. The WORKS relationship from the EER is modeled using a bidirectional relationship between Emp::dept_of and Dept::emps_of, as indicated by dept_of <-> emps_of[], where one department is associated with many employees. The square brackets denote the to-many association link. The bidirectional links are also used to define the MANAGES relationship and the TAKES relationship. Since Objectivity/DB does not provide built-in collection classes, such as sets and lists, the TAKES relationship is modeled by creating an Offering class, with objects that

```
struct Nametype                        class Dept: public ooObj
{ ooVString       lastname;            {private:
  ooVString       midinit;               ooVString       dnum;
  ooVString       firstname; };          ooVString       dname;
                                         public:
class Date: publiooObj                    ooRef(Emp)      emps_of[k-> dept_of;
{protected:                               ooRef(Mgr)      mgr_of<-> manages_dept;
  Uint            month;               //Methods}
  Uint            day;
  Uint            year;               class Course: publicooObj
//Methods}                            {private:
                                        ooVString        crsid;
class Emp: publicooObj                   ooVString        cname;
{protected:                              Nametype         instructor;
  ooVString       id;                    float32          length;
  Nametype        name;                 public:
  float32         salary;                ooRef(Offering)  offerings[]<->offering_of;
public:                               //Methods }
  ooRef(Dept)     dept_of<-> emps_of[];
  ooRef(Offering) courses_taken[]<-   class Offering:public ooObj
>roster[];                            {public:
//Methods}                              ooRef(Course)    offering_of<->offerings[];
                                        ooRef(Emp)       roster[]<->courses_taken[];
class Mgr:public Emp                     ooRef(Date)      taken_on: copy(delete);
{public:                              //Methods}
  ooRef(Dept)     manages_dept<->mgr_of;
//Methods}
```

Figure 12–6   Objectivity/DB employee training schema.

have information about the course offered, employees enrolled, and date of the course.

A unidirectional association link is used to represent the relationship between an offering and a user-created date object. The copy(delete) clause is a behavior specifier that can be included on any unidirectional or bidirectional link, indicating, for example, that if a copy is made of an offering object, the new object will not be associated to the date of the old offering object. Other options are to copy or to move the association to the new object. A behavior specifier is required on unidirectional links purely for syntactic reasons. Other behavior specifiers can be associated with delete, lock, and versioning operations on objects as well.

Query Capability

Objectivity/DB does not yet provide an object query language, such as the ODMG OQL, but does provide an ODBC-compliant ANSI SQL interface product, called SQL++, that allows querying an Objectivity database using SQL. Programmatically, Objectivity/DB provides a nonpersistent programming construct, called iterators, to allow the traversal of a collection of objects. For example, iterators can be used to traverse the extent of a class or subclass and to traverse a to-many association. An iterator can also include a conditional predicate to select objects that satisfy the condition specified.

As an example of programmatic access to objects using iterators, the query to find those employees who have taken the "OODB" course is given in Figure 12–7. Initially, the `Course::Find_Course_by_crsid` method returns a handle to a course object that has "OODB" as its `crsid`. The `Course::Find_Course_by_crsid` method uses the conditional predicate on an iterator to find those Course objects in the default training database whose `crsid` matches the search `crsid`. The iterator `offeringI` then iterates over all offerings of the OODB course

```
ooHandle(Course)                                      ooHandle(Course)   oodbcrs =
   Course::Find_Course_by_crsid(char* find_crsid)        Course::Find_Course_by_crsid("OODB");
{                                                     if(oodbcrs != NULL)
  ooItr(Course) courseI;                              {
  ooHandle(Course)   c;                                 ooItr(Offering) offeringI;
  char find_pred[32];                                   oodbcrs->offerings(offeringI);
                                                        while (offeringI.next())
  (void) sprint(find_pred,"crsid == \"%s\"", find_crsid);  {
  courseI.scan(default_db,oocRead,oocPublic,find          offeringI.display_roster();
_pred);                                                 }
   if(courseI.next())                                 }
     c = courseI;
   else
     c=NULL;
  return(c);
  }
```

Figure 12–7   Objectivity/DB query specification.

and the `display_roster` method displays the employees that attended that course offering.

COMPARISON

An exhaustive comparison of the Objectivity/DB and VERSANT products is outside the scope of this chapter. In this section, we provide a comparison of the products on (most of) the features used in the industry perspective section of this paper and on the design and query capability issues that the implementation of the employee training database application illustrated.

Both Objectivity/DB and VERSANT satisfied the initial requirements of an OODBMS product specified in the industry perspective, both products having a pure OODB architecture, goal of ODMG compliance, and a language binding for C++. The additional selection criteria collected are summarized in Table 12–1. Both OODBMS products provide heterogeneous support for compilers and client/server platforms. Database capabilities such as backup and multi-volume are also comparable. The locking granularity differs because Objectivity/DB utilizes a page cache, whereas VERSANT uses an object cache. Both products provide logical database references. The products differ in the predefined classes that are offered for schema design, such as collections, date and time types, which will be discussed in more detail later in this section. Both products support short and long duration transaction models, but VERSANT also supports nested transactions. Objectivity/DB provides an ANSI SQL interface product (SQL++) whereas VERSANT's comparable prod-

Table 12–1   Features Summary

Features	Objectivity/DB (Version 3.5)	Versant (Release 4.0.7)
Compiler Heterogeneity	√	√
Client/Server Heterogeneity	√	√
Backup (Batch, Online, Incremental, Distributed)	B,O,I,D	B,O,I,D
Multi-volume Support	√	√
Locking granularity (Page, Object)	Page	Object
Database references (Logical, Physical)	L	L
Collections (List, Set, Bag, Array, Dictionary)	A,D	L,S,A,D
Date and Time types	X^1	√
Transactions (Short, Long, Nested)	S,L	S,L,N
ANSI SQL Interface (ODBC-compliant)	√	X^2

[1]Objectivity/DB Version 4.0 provides date and time types.

[2]Versant Release 5.0 provides an ANSI SQL interface.

uct (SQL Suite) was not available at the time of the case study. The design of the
employee training application illustrated various features of the two products, such
as built-in types and the specification of inverse relationships.

Both Objectivity/DB and VERSANT deviate from the ODMG object model
by not providing collections of literals. Objectivity/DB does not provide predefined
classes for lists, sets, and bags, but does provide predefined classes for arrays and
dictionaries. The version of Objectivity/DB used in the case study implementation
(Version 3.5) did not provide predefined classes for date and time types, although
Version 4.0 of Objectivity/DB will provide these classes. VERSANT's object
model includes collections of persistent objects through the predefined classes for
list, set, array, and dictionary. VERSANT does not provide a predefined class for
bags, which are an unordered collection of possibly duplicate elements. VERSANT
also provides predefined class types for date and time, which was utilized in the
case study implementation.

Both Objectivity/DB and VERSANT provide for the specification of bidirectional relationships in the schema where the referential integrity of the inverse relationship is automatically maintained by the database system. Objectivity/DB's definition of inverse relationships is explicitly declared in the schema and does not
require the bidirectional relationship to be public. Since Objectivity/DB specifies its
schema in its own syntax that is converted to C++ using a preprocessor, Objectivity's approach to defining inverse relationships is closer to that supported by
ODMG-93. In VERSANT, each half of a bidirectional link is declared using a
BiLink or BiLinkVStr depending on the cardinality ratio of the relationship. The
bidirectional links are defined as public, since maintaining the inverse relationship
requires direct access to attribute names. The inverse relationship, however, is not
identified in the schema but through the initialization of a static dummy variable.

To the best of our knowledge, neither OODBMS product provides an object
query language such as the ODMG OQL. Since both products are committed to
ODMG compliance, this feature is probably planned for future releases. Objectiv-
ity/DB has an ANSI SQL interface product (SQL++), whereas VERSANT's comparable product (SQL Suite) is forthcoming. Both Objectivity/DB and VERSANT
provide a tool for browsing a database where objects can be selected and viewed. In
the case study implementation, we described the query capability for programmatically selecting objects within the application program for each product. These programmatic query capabilities appear to be comparable.

Both OODBMS products provide powerful object-oriented database capabilities. As illustrated by the case study comparison, however, both products are not yet
fully compliant with the ODMG-93 standard, although both are committed to conformance to the standard. As indicated by the comparison section, each version/re-
lease of the products provides additional capabilities to each product. This case
study was not an exhaustive comparison, and others interested in OODBMS acquisition are encouraged to modify the evaluation criteria for acquiring OODBMS
technology to meet their own specific needs and to evaluate the latest commercially
available versions of the products.

EXPERIENCES AND SUMMARY

Object-oriented database technology is an interesting and promising area of computer science. The technology allows industry to reap the benefits of object-oriented programming such as code reuse and better code structuring, as well as organizing complex data according to the needs of an application. This chapter provided an industry perspective on evaluating and acquiring OODBMS technology and compared the results of experimenting with the new technology by prototyping an employee training database application in both Objectivity/DB and VERSANT. This process illustrated the modeling and access features of each system with respect to the ODMG-93 standard in the context of the example application.

Evaluation, acquisition, and experimentation are the first steps of a process towards incorporating OODBMS technology into the set of tools that a company has to choose from for future application needs. Another step in this process is the development of a plan for deciding when to choose the OODBMS tool for the implementation of a new application or for the migration of an existing application. Ultimately, the business needs of a company are the driving force for the utilization of new technologies, which help to reduce cycle-time, increase quality, and maintain a competitive edge. Applications that are mission-critical, database-oriented, and object-oriented dictate the utilization of OODBMS technology.

REFERENCES

[BC96] D. Barry, R. G. G. Cattell: *DBMS Needs Assessment for Objects (Release 3.1)*, Barry and Associates, Inc., 1996.

[Car+93] M. Carey, D. DeWitt, J. Naughton: *The 007 Benchmark*. Proceedings of the ACM SIGMOD International Conference on Management of Data. 1993, Washington, DC, 1993.

[Cat96] R. G. G. Cattell, ed.: *The Object Database Standard: ODMG-93*. Morgan-Kaufmann Publishers, 1996.

[EN94] R. Elmasri, S. B. Navathe: *Fundamentals of Database Systems* (2nd Ed.), Benjamin/Cummings, 1994.

[Obj95] Objectivity/DB Version 3 C++ Developer: Objectivity, Inc., 1995.

[Ver95] Versant, Versant ODBMS C++/Versant reference manual. Versant Object Technology, Mento Park, California, 1995.

13

Modeling Battlefield
Sensor Environments:

An Object Database Management System Case Study

Mark A. Woyna, Argonne National Laboratory
John H. Christiansen, Argonne National Laboratory
Christopher W. Hield, Argonne National Laboratory
Kathy Lee Simunich, Argonne National Laboratory

ABSTRACT

The Visual Intelligence and Electronic Warfare Simulation (VIEWS) Workbench software system has been developed by Argonne National Laboratory (ANL) to enable Army intelligence and electronic warfare (IEW) analysts at UNIX workstations to conveniently build detailed IEW battlefield scenarios, or "sensor environments," to drive the Army's high-resolution IEW sensor performance models. VIEWS is fully object-oriented, including the underlying database.

INTRODUCTION

The VIEWS Workbench was designed to allow an intelligence and electronic warfare (IEW) analyst access to a reference database via a convenient graphical user interface in order to build, display, and modify the detailed scenario specifications and ancillary data necessary to exercise a suite of IEW sensor performance models.

This work was supported by the United States Army Training and Doctrine Analysis Command (TRADOC), Fort Leavenworth, Kansas, through interagency agreement P86112 with the U.S. Department of Energy.

IEW battlefield scenarios must include all entities in a friendly and/or a hostile force that could be detected by Army sensor systems. Every vehicle, aircraft, fixed site, radio, radar, jammer, and weapon on one or both sides of a simulated conflict must be represented. Once these myriad entities are deployed geographically on a high-resolution terrain grid and transportation network, their movement and behavior must be tracked and updated very frequently (e.g., once per simulation second) to build a realistic sensor environment.

The VIEWS Workbench is a fully object-oriented representation of the battlefield, supported by a VERSANT object database [Ver94a]. It includes an embedded Combined Arms Army Movement Model (CAAMM) [PAR86], which simulates vehicle-level movement. The user interface is also an object-oriented windowing system, based around the XView toolkit and OPEN LOOK.

The VIEWS Workbench provides the following general capabilities:

- Interactive construction and maintenance of an IEW reference database
- Interactive/automatic construction of Tables of Organization and Equipment (TO&Es) for military forces to be simulated
- Interactive/automatic dynamic scenario simulation, aided by an embedded Combined Arms Army Movement Model
- Automatic generation of mutually consistent inputs for multiple sensor performance models

The VIEWS Workbench's operating environment is characterized as follows:

- Hardware Platform: Sun SPARCStation, portable to any UNIX workstation that can support the XView toolkit and the VERSANT ODBMS.
- Operating System: UNIX.
- Database Management System: VERSANT Object Database Management System Version 3.14.
- User Interface Standard: Open Look.
- Source Language: C++ (230,000 lines)
- Operating Mode: Multi-user operation with each Scenario Library lockable by one user at a time.

DATA MODEL

The VIEWS Data Library is the repository for all data generated through the VIEWS user interface. The Data Library is partitioned into a Global Library and a set of user-defined Scenario Libraries. Each Scenario Library contains a set of user-defined Scenario Version Libraries. Each Library contains all the data necessary to support the IEW sensor performance models, including:

- TO&E data sets containing nations, military branches, military echelons, combat postures, military unit types and deployment templates, platform types, payload types, and communication net types.
- Force Rosters containing multiple instances of various unit types, platform types, payload types, and communication net types.
- Sensor Performance Model data sets containing sensor types, sensors, antennas, emitter types, emitters, communication nets, weather data, smoke data, cloud data, and vehicle detection signatures.
- Data sets containing technical specifications for telecommunication equipment.

All data are modeled as objects and are stored persistently in the object database management system. The current schema represents over 250 persistent classes containing over 1000 attributes and 4000 methods.

USER INTERFACE

The VIEWS Workbench user interface communicates with the user via an object-oriented UNIX graphical user interface toolkit. The User Interface Manager (UIM) and the Graphics and Imagery Manager (GIM) toolkits were written by ANL [FW91]. The toolkits are written in C++ and package the C interface of the XView and Xlib libraries used by OPEN LOOK into objects.

Each VIEWS window is itself an object in which toolkit objects are embedded, thereby capturing the functional behavior of the window. The methods of the VIEWS window objects communicate with the rest of the system by sending messages to other inline data objects, including persistent objects stored in the object database.

All actions are driven by user-initiated events such as a mouse click or a key press. The current system (version 1.1) has 250 window objects.

DATABASE MANAGEMENT SYSTEM

Although the VIEWS Workbench itself is fully object-oriented, it was originally designed and partially implemented with a relational database management system as the object store. Persistent classes were to be mapped to the relational database by embedding the necessary SQL code within persistent class methods. This approach allowed the programmer to treat the real-world entities as objects within VIEWS while encapsulating the interface to the relational database within the objects. While this approach worked, several problems areas were identified:

Schema Support

- The database schema language was the not same as the programming language, requiring that the C++ classes be normalized to produce a set of SQL create table statements. This required that someone on the VIEWS development team be proficient in relational database design.

- Complex structures had to be converted to an artificially "flattened" representation in a relational system.
- Programmers had to learn an additional language (SQL) to define the schema.

Additional Input/Output Code

- The need to maintain two representations of data (database and application) was burdensome. Extensive code was needed to keep both representations of the object in agreement.
- Input/output code was needed to translate data from the database to the internal representation. This code was a significant fraction of the overall system code.

Application Language Interface

- A loose binding existed between the application language (C++) and the database manipulation language (SQL).
- Programmers had to be proficient in two languages (i.e., C++ and SQL).
- SQL and C++ are not based on a common data model and data type set.

Performance

- Reconstituting complex, normalized objects required joining many tables, a relatively expensive operation.
- Since all relational objects were cached on the database server, repeated reference to the same object required repeated fetching of the object from the database server.

An excellent solution to these problems was to convert the system to an Object Database Management System (ODBMS). While most ODBMSs are proprietary, the benefits from moving to an object-oriented system outweigh this limitation. These benefits include:

Schema Support

- The database schema "language" is the same as the programming language (C++), and the schema is automatically captured from the application code.
- Object structures do NOT have to be "flattened" into another representation.
- No need for additional Input/Output or synchronization code. Objects are referenced as if they are in memory at all times.

Performance

- Client-side object caching makes accessing the objects efficient (most recently referenced objects remain within the cache).
- Improvements range from 10 to 100 times faster than the relational approach.

Unique Features

- Support for design transactions allows transactions that can span multiple database session that can last several days with full commit or rollback capability.
- Support for versioning of objects.

After a review of several commercial and prototype object database management systems, we selected the VERSANT Object Database Management System, by Versant Object Technology, Menlo Park, California.

Converting to VERSANT required approximately ten person-days of effort to convert the approximately 30,000 lines of C++ code completed. The conversion process required the following steps [Ver94b]:

- Derive all persistent classes from the Versant PObject class to inherit persistent behavior.
- Convert standard C pointers to Versant Links, the persistent database equivalent of a transient pointer.
- Add the Versant dirty() method to all methods that update a persistent object.
- Convert our transient version of a linked list to the persistent Versant VIList linked list class.
- Remove the methods that implemented persistence in the persistent classes that were no longer needed.

CONCLUSIONS

This chapter described the current implementation of the VIEWS Workbench. In developing VIEWS, we have demonstrated the feasibility of using a commercially available object data management system in support of a complex, large-scale application. While there were a few limitations in using the ODBMS, it proved to be a far better approach in managing large, complex data sets than relational systems.

REFERENCES

[FW91] R. Fuja, M. A. Widing: *Application Interface Engine Language and Object Reference Manual*. Argonne National Laboratory Technical Memorandum ANL/EAIS/TM-72, Argonne National Laboratory, Argonne, Illinois, 1991.

[PAR86] PAR Government Systems Corporation: *Intelligence and Electronic Warfare Movement Simulation*, Vols. 1–10. Technical Report TRANSANA-TR-2-86, U.S. Army TRADOC Systems Analysis Activity, White Sands Missile Range, White Sands, New Mexico, 1986.

[Ver94a] Versant Object Technology, Inc: *Versant DBMS*, 1994.

[Ver94b] Versant Object Technology, Inc: *C++/Versant Reference Manual*. Version 1.7, Menlo Park, California, April 1994.

14

Transaction Processing
in the Capital Markets

Jeremy F. Rudge, Cumulus Systems Ltd.
Andy J. Moorley, Cumulus Systems Ltd.

ABSTRACT

The requirements of transaction processing in the increasingly global capital markets coupled with the desire to satisfy all processing requirements in a single system has lead to a unique set of technical challenges. Object technology appears to offer significant advantages when applied to this problem, especially when all aspects of the system are object-oriented. However, object database management systems are yet to gain acceptance in mission critical transaction processing systems. This chapter details one such system that proposes to use an ODBMS and presents an account of the reasons behind the choice and the experiences with various ODBMSs.

INTRODUCTION

Cumulus Systems Ltd. is a UK software house of sixty people that was founded in 1973. It is fundamentally a company that develops vertical market products with wide applicability in various sectors of the capital markets. These products have focused upon the international and certain domestic bond markets and for this sector have provided, within the context of a single integrated system, a full range of functionality from dealer support, through transaction processing and settlement, to accounting and general ledgers.

The current mainstream Cumulus product is a traditional client-server application with UNIX-based dealer facilities linking into a VMS-based core transaction processing system. In 1992 Cumulus commenced a strategic review of product strategy in order to meet the needs of the industry for the mid-late 1990s and into the next millennium. This review started by analyzing the key market drivers; what support do banks and other organizations involved in capital markets trading activities need from their computer systems? Some of the most important of these market drivers are that systems should be:

- Responsive to growth in the organization
- Responsive to change in the organization
- Able to integrate data across a wide variety of activities
- Able to operate across multiple locations and time zones

Many very large organizations have spent hundreds of millions of dollars attempting to write comprehensive integrated systems that would provide for all their needs; Cumulus analyzed in depth the relative success or failure of a number of such projects. It is generally recognized in the banking industry that these developments often did not meet with the level of success expected, many projects being abandoned or significantly scaled down. These projects typically used a conventional approach to systems development, namely the use of a relational database (RDBMS) running on a UNIX platform and a Rapid Application Development (RAD) environment to generate the user screens and to provide access to the database. The general conclusion of most importance was that with the technologies employed, the level of complexity inherent in the requirements of the more ambitious projects exceeded expectations and could not be managed by the system designers and implementers.

One key characteristic of the capital markets is that they contain many activities that are quite individual in nature but which nevertheless interact in some critical aspects. Hence system designers have traditionally been torn between focusing on the specific needs of each activity and the more general needs resulting from interactions between these activities and requirements for company-wide consolidation. The problems are compounded by the sheer size of the requirements in relationship to the time-scale for delivery. For each of the major activities, it has typically taken well in excess of 100 man-years to produce a fully functional system.

Cumulus evolved a vision for a system that would meet the market requirements, and decided that the whole-hearted adoption of emerging object-oriented technologies would enable such a system to be built. This vision can be summarized by just four key descriptive features, which are that the system must:

- Be responsive to change and capable of natural growth, that is, an organic system
- Provide a unified, strategic infrastructure for all relevant IT needs

- Be business-centered and user-controlled, where the term "user" is taken to mean the using organization
- Have mechanisms to capture business knowledge in ways that are essentially technology independent

A project, code-named Aurora, was instigated in 1993 to realize this vision. Aurora had the following goals:

1. The system would contain software structures that directly reflected the business. Generic business processes and structures would be separately modeled by the software. These structures should mold to business patterns rather than providing fixed templates for the business to fit in.
2. Wherever possible, control of the system would be transferred from the vendor to the users. User empowerment at all levels of the organization would be enabled, implying that users have a clear understanding of system behavior and an appropriately personalized perspective of the system. User control should be enhanced by a "WYDIWID" paradigm, that is, "What you define is what it does."
3. The system would be specifically engineered from the outset to facilitate future extension and to accommodate ongoing change smoothly. System design should recognize that different rates and scales of change apply to different aspects of the business.
4. All available mechanisms to limit and manage system complexity would be employed. This was felt to be a key goal that clearly facilitated some of the other goals such as simplifying future extension. Some of the more specific objectives here were to migrate complexity to managed partitions in the software, to separate process from context (the "what" from the "how"), to simplify the capture of business logic and to execute such logic by standard mechanisms.
5. The system would provide pervasive access to all its information. That is, information should be universally available to all users authorized to see it, it should be dynamically updated where relevant, and there should be a minimal "window of non-availability."

The major tools sets were determined during 1993 and coding commenced in the second quarter of 1994. The use of object databases will be described in more detail below.

TECHNOLOGY PRODUCT SET

It was taken as a prerequisite that OO techniques should be applied in a relatively pure way to all analysis, design, and implementation. A major decision was, of course, the choice of implementation language. Some of the less common languages, principally Eiffel, were considered, but it was felt that there was insufficient industry acceptance to warrant their use in this project. Thus the decision was between C++ and Smalltalk (at that point, Java had not yet been developed). The decision criteria used included a perception of lifetime "cost of use," performance, compatibility with the objective of keeping to a pure OO implementation, user acceptance, expertise required for effective use, availability of experienced staff, technical differences between the languages, and the training time required to become proficient. Under the first criterion, cost of use, come a number of subheadings, such as what proportion of a developer's time is spent on business issues as opposed to purely technical programming issues, and which is the better language from an ongoing maintenance perspective. It was decided that Smalltalk came out significantly ahead of C++ on the key criteria, and hence that this should be the primary implementation language. The use of C++ for specific parts of the development was not ruled out. Since this time, Java has been released and is the subject of a great deal of interest. We feel that Java has many of the same advantages over C++ that Smalltalk already possesses. We also feel that since both languages share common Virtual Machine technology, it is likely that choice between these two languages will not be an issue in the future.

The required platforms for target users include UNIX as well as Windows on PC and so the natural selection was VisualWorks from ParcPlace Systems (now ParcPlace-Digitalk, "PPD"). IBM's Visual Age was not available at the time of selection and, we consider, still trails VisualWorks in some key aspects. The development is being supported by the use of ENVY Developer, a team programming environment for Smalltalk users now also supplied by PPD.

Almost from the start of the project the use of an object request broker (ORB) was seen as mandatory, for a number of reasons. Principally, the common object request broker architecture (CORBA) was deemed a fundamental part of the architecture for any distributed object system by the Object Management Group [OMG92]. Systems evolved from the Aurora project will often be distributed both across multiple platforms and geographically. Second, in most environments these systems will interact with other systems and this interaction is dramatically simplified if the industry standard mechanisms for communication and distribution are used. With the advent of CORBA 2 [OMG95], the prospect of multiple systems exchanging information about objects of joint interest, even though different ORBs are being used for these systems, becomes a reality. A number of ORBs were investigated for use in the Aurora project and it was decided that although ORBs without a Smalltalk interface could be used, this would introduce unnecessary complexities. Hence Distributed Smalltalk from Hewlett Packard (DST) was selected. This product has since been taken over by PPD.

The selection of an appropriate database was one of the most difficult decisions in the project. At the outset it was provisionally assumed that object databases were not at a sufficient stage of maturity to be viable. However, an investigation into the advantages and disadvantages of both an ODBMS and a relational database was undertaken. The results of this investigation are summarized in the next section.

RELATIONAL OR OBJECT DATABASE?

There have been numerous articles written on this subject [Bar94, Bur94, DG94]. Traditionally, when deciding upon the most appropriate database for any particular project, the major features of importance are selected and then alternative databases are assessed against this list of features. A typical list might include how the DBMS represents the data model and the links that can be established between data items, data consistency rules, ease of access to data, data security, administration and control, performance, and so on. We felt it more appropriate to consider initially the high-level project goals, and how the use of either relational or object databases fitted against these goals. Thus we review these goals, as stated above, in the specific context of the database.

1. *Software structures that directly reflect the business.* The characteristics of the database must not impose restrictions or limitations on the types of structure that can be represented in them.

2. *User empowerment.* Understanding of system behavior is facilitated if the software structure directly reflect the business. The database must not hinder the mechanisms by which user-definable procedures are implemented.

3. *Engineered for future extension.* The database must facilitate the design and implementation of changes to the system, which will often involve the modification and extension of existing data structures as well as the addition of new ones. This should not necessitate changes to existing application code and it should be possible to migrate one set of structures to another in a seamless manner.

4. *Management of complexity.* The use of any database will add a necessary extra dimension to the complexity of a system. However, its impact on system development should be minimized wherever possible.

5. *Pervasive access to information.* The database should provide, or at least not inhibit, controlled access to data and the maintenance of up-to-date data in user facilities.

In addition to these criteria, there are also a number of other factors that must be taken into account. These impact on issues such as development costs and commercial viability, and include:

- *Vendor independence.* As a commercial prerequisite, Cumulus did not wish to produce a system that by design would only operate with the database from a single vendor. Hence, if a particular type of database can only meet the requirements with many proprietary features from such a vendor, this would be a significant disadvantage.

- *Compatibility with the overall development process.* The database should ideally form a natural part of this process. Time spent on database-specific issues that could be spent instead on business issues is effectively a cost drain to the project, and is likely to continue to be so in respect of future modifications.

- *Vendor stability.* It is important that the database vendor is a stable supplier committed to the product, including a commitment to future product enhancement.

- *Standards.* Overlapping with these issues, the database should be designed according to industry standards. If the vendor is committed to such standards, then the issues of vendor independence and stability are somewhat less critical.

There are clearly many requirements that databases have to meet to a greater or lesser extent, and these will undoubtedly conflict to some degree. Moreover the ability of various databases to meet such requirements will change quite rapidly over time. We were concerned with making the correct strategic choice for the Aurora project. Some of the relevant characteristics of both relational and object database systems are now reviewed.

Relational Databases

Relational databases have many advantages over earlier database management systems. These include the good theoretical basis, a high degree of data independence and the provision of high-level manipulation languages such as SQL. Because of their success huge amounts of investment have been made by the major RDBMS vendors into improving their products. They represent proven technology in large-scale MIS applications. In terms of the initial list of features mentioned in the previous section, they generally score well. Possible exceptions are "links between data" and "performance." In spite of all the efforts of the vendors to improve performance, this can be a real concern in practice. Moreover, in order to maximize the performance of a system, it is often necessary to use proprietary features, thus increasing dependence on a single database/supplier. The issue of links between data is part of a general point concerning the data model that is now discussed in more detail.

The major disadvantage of the relational model is that data are restricted to tables and simple attributes. One important aspect of this is that hierarchical data structures cannot easily be directly represented. Hierarchies are typically compressed into compound keys. Integrity constraints must be imposed to prevent foreign keys (attributes in one relation that are a key of another relation) having values that do not exist in the related table. The semantics of the data are split between the relations and thus maintaining the integrity of the schema is difficult. In general, it is often not possible to capture completely the semantics of the data in the database.

At a more general level, it is unrealistic to expect this restrictive model to represent adequately the complexities of the real world that the software must reflect. For simple applications, the notion of tables of data is sometimes quite natural, a fact that is supported by the popularity of spreadsheets. However, within the capital markets there are very many complex structures and associations between the elements of these structures. While some of these structures can be fitted into a relational model, the impact of so doing is:

1. It can be difficult and time consuming.
2. The data model becomes inherently different from the real world, a feature that inhibits understanding and complicates development generally.
3. There is a tendency to restrict the business functionality when this process becomes too difficult to implement effectively.
4. The details of the implementation are determined by the initial requirements, making it more difficult to modify or enhance subsequently.
5. The performance of the system ultimately suffers.

Object Databases

The distinguishing feature of an object database is its ability to handle objects rather than data. This involves the provision of features such as object identification, data abstraction, class structure, encapsulation, inheritance, polymorphism, extensibility, and integration of a database manipulation language (DML). The DML of an RDBMS, typically SQL, does not allow an application to be programmed in its entirety and hence it has to be integrated into other general programming languages. The programmer must handle two different paradigms at the same time. For an ODBMS, the DML is provided essentially by extensions to the general programming languages.

In terms of the project requirements stated above, there are today some very clear advantages and disadvantages of object databases. In regard to the basic list of features required, an object database will generally provide all such capabilities, but in some cases the facilities provided will not currently match those of the more mature RDBMSs available. This is likely to be the case with "ease of access to data" except where the ODBMS provides the object query language (OQL), and also with data consistency under certain failure conditions. Administration and control facilities will typically not be as sophisticated with the newer products.

Performance is an issue upon which it is difficult to draw definitive conclusions (see for example [Vät+96]). Undoubtedly, certain types of operation (such as data retrieval requiring information from many tables) will perform much faster on an ODBMS. There is also the general point that in an system written in an OO programming language, with an RDBMS there is always an overhead of translation between the object and relational forms. Object systems refer to objects via object identifiers. These must be translated to and from appropriate relational keys and then the attribute values must be separately loaded or unloaded. When one object is related to many other objects, the object identity to key translation must be performed for each such relationship.

With respect to the primary goals of the project, an ODBMS appeared to fit very well. The system must be focused around the user and the business and must facilitate change and extension. Ideally, the database should be a "non-issue"; it is simply a mechanism for maintaining data persistently subject to a number of minimum conditions. Clearly, in principle at least, an ODBMS meets this requirement.

The fact that there appears to be a variety of different architectures for an ODBMS itself adds additional complexity when comparing ODBMSs. We choose to divide the main database offerings into three groupings, which we refer to as client-centric, server-centric, and three-tier. In a client-centric database, the server is generally only responsible for such things as locking and each client process performs its own disk and network I/O. Queries are all to be performed within the client's address space. This sort of architecture relies heavily on a client-side cache that can provide very fast access to all objects in the cache. Where the working set of objects can be kept within the cache and the cache does not become stale too quickly, then the performance can be impressive. Within this first grouping there also seems to be distinction between those databases that extend Virtual Memory (e.g., ObjectStore) and those that use something akin to a Proxy Pattern [Gam+95]. The server-centric databases will have an architecture much closer to that of RDBMSs (and object-relational databases). These databases tend to provide very efficient query mechanisms using indexes, query optimizations, and so on. However, as with an RDBMS, the single server can become a bottleneck, so techniques such as replication are required to overcome this. The last grouping is exemplified by the GemStone ODBMS. This product provides a middle tier that allows behavior to be provided "in the database." This is achieved by the use of a persistent Smalltalk environment. This environment becomes the server to the user-written database client process. In this approach the business logic would typically be encapsulated in the persistent middle layer, with the client often being a GUI written in, say, VisualWorks. We feel that it is therefore important to understand which of the architectures will best match both the data access patterns and the architecture of the proposed software solution.

Vendor independence is only achievable by a combination of the use of the standards together with explicit system design. The standards body for object databases is the Object Database Management Group (ODMG). This was established in 1991 by the major ODBMS vendors and other interested parties. Their objective is to allow portability of customer software across ODBMS products. The Object Database Standard, ODMG-93 [Cat96] was first published in 1993 and is being followed up by another release in the near future. [Bar95] provides more information about the ODMG. At present the ODMG standard only focuses on harmonization of the various APIs to a database. It does not as yet provide interoperability between the databases. Thus, any investment in software can be protected since porting software between ODMG-compliant ODBMSs should be trivial. However, both the metadata (schema) and the data stored in the database cannot easily be transferred between ODMG-compliant databases. We are aware of work being carried out by both the ODMG and the individual vendors to overcome these problems—for example, HTML is being looked at as a possible way to transfer objects between different ODMG databases. Thus we believe that although this standard is a useful step in the right direction, there is still some way to go before true portability will be provided.

Vendor stability is an issue that must be taken seriously. Since some of the vendors are quite small companies, their background and future prospects have to be investigated in detail before committing to use of their products. Naturally, this is somewhat less important if it easy to switch between standards-compliant databases.

Object-Relational Database Management Systems

These systems are an attempt to provide the best of both worlds from the relational and object environments. They build upon the relational foundation of good security, integrity, reliability, and SQL support while adding object-oriented extensibility to handle complex data. However, as far as the Aurora project is concerned, we feel that the products currently available fall between two stools. The main point is that the DMLs are typically not as close to the implementation programming language as most of the pure ODBMSs. In addition they are not as mature as the major relational databases. Nevertheless, this is a market that we will watch with interest.

The Selection for Aurora

Because of the major differences between the two types of database, it is not surprising that we concluded that the most appropriate choice for any particular project depends on the particular characteristics of that project. For example, where the project is to provide new facilities based on the information currently maintained in an RDBMS, and where this information is also used or updated by other systems, it would almost be a prerequisite to continue using this database as the primary persistence mechanism.

The Aurora project has a number of particular characteristics as implied by the goals that have been described earlier in this chapter. In addition, it is planned that strategic systems will be built upon the infrastructure created by the project and that these systems will be operational well into the next decade. We decided that for this reason and in order to effectively meet the goals, an object database was the natural choice for Aurora. Having carried out several investigations into the ODBMS market, we also believed that within the project time scales, there would be a number of such databases that would be of suitable "industrial strength" from companies committed to the market. We therefore concluded that the most appropriate strategy in respect of database deployment will have the following elements:

1. An architecture designed as far as possible to be database independent.
2. An ODBMS from one of the leading vendors as the core persistence mechanism.
3. The ability to interact with data from other databases, including relational databases, where relevant.

ODBMS SELECTION

As indicated previously, the Aurora project had a very clear set of goals. These could be applied both to the database and to the architecture of the project as a whole. Since the success of the project was largely dependent on a successful architecture, the architecture was designed independently of the database choice. Therefore, when selecting a database we had to ensure that it fitted well with the architecture. The architecture we employed is explained in the next section. Also, a prerequisite for selecting a database was that it appeared to be able to support the scale and performance of the systems we will deploy. It was also necessary to ensure that we forged a successful commercial relationship with the vendor of the chosen ODBMS.

Architectural Overview

The Aurora architecture has been designed with a key goal of scalablity. We believe that the key to achieving this is to have a distributed system. The first model of distribution included in the architecture is a client-server one, shown in Figure 14–1.

The intention of the architecture is to separate external components from the core of the Aurora business model. From the point of view of distribution, those elements of the system lying inside the generic external interface layer marked SI appear as a logical server to all external components, as illustrated below.These external components will typically be instances of various interface domains, such as a GUI or maybe an interface to a Stock Exchange.

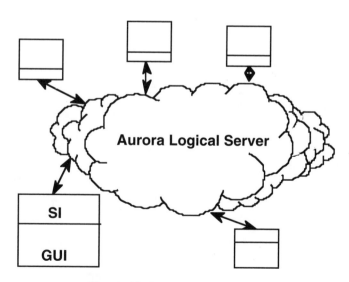

Figure 14–1   Aurora architecture.

In our implementation of this model, the communication between the client and the server is achieved via an ORB. In fact, all of our business objects are CORBA objects (i.e., they conform to the protocols defined by CORBA) and can thus be directly accessed by the client processes. These business objects are always accessed remotely and are never copied into the client, since this allows the clients to be "thin" and they are not required to contain business model code. In addition to being CORBA objects, the business objects are also made persistent by the database. This calls for special coordination between the ORB and ODBMS. This will be discussed in the section entitled "Building an Object Database Adapter."

The Aurora logical server itself is also a distributed system, thus making the architecture a multitier one. It will be realized in terms of a number of "application servers" that will typically be replicas of each other. Clients with similar working sets will be allocated to the same server to make optimal use of database caching; however, many frequently accessed objects will be replicated in many of the servers. Thus, generally data will distributed (i.e., copied) between application servers by the database, but data will be distributed (i.e., accessed remotely) between clients and servers by the ORB. There is, however, a case where this is not appropriate. If a business object is frequently updated as the result of the actions of many different application servers (e.g., some object representing a global portfolio), then the overhead of keeping the many copies of the object in the different application servers will become prohibitive. In this case, the object will only be instantiated in one application server. When a message needs to be sent to this object, the ORB will be used to deliver this message remotely and thus the object will be update in situ.

Thus we could draw an example configuration for the Aurora architecture as shown in Figure 14–2. Application servers A_1 and A_2 are replica servers, whereas A' contains the business model associated with frequently updated objects.

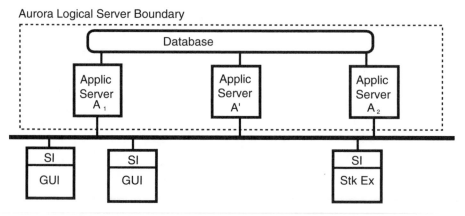

Figure 14–2   Example configuration for Aurora architecture.

Language Binding

Given the selection of Smalltalk as the primary development language, the choice for object databases is more severely limited than would be the case for a C++ project. In order to ensure productivity of developers coding business logic, it was felt that the impact of the database should be minimal on their code. We therefore had looked very carefully at how naturally the ODBMS language binding fitted within the Smalltalk paradigm and practices. For example, we considered that "transitive persistence" [as defined in ODMG-93, section 6.3.1.1] was vital. Even within ODMG compliant interfaces there is sufficient scope for API variations to make the difference between a good and a poor fit. For example, an API that requires that each object that has been updated is marked as "dirty" would add extra complexity to business logic and would place extra burdens on the business developer.

Building an Object Database Adapter

Since the business objects in our system are both CORBA objects and also made persistent via an ODBMS, some special coordination between the ORB and ODBMS is required. Within the CORBA framework there appear to be two main ways to achieve this.

One of these involves using the Persistent Object Service (POS) service of CORBA. This approach allows for a very loose binding between the ORB and ODBMS, but requires that clients of an object are responsible for informing the object when to store and restore its state. The alternate approach is unfortunately much less clearly specified. Both the CORBA specification and the ODMG-93 specification present the concept of an object database adapter for the ORB. This is shown diagrammatically in Figure 14–3.

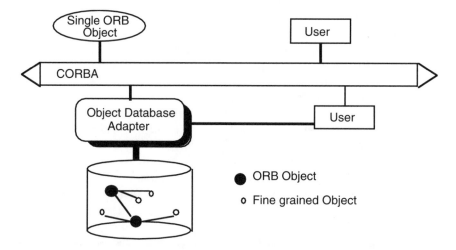

Figure 14–3   Example showing object database adapter.

In most distributed object systems there will be a split of large-grain and fine-grain objects. The objects we describe as large-grain are those for which the millisecond response time of a CORBA environment are satisfactory. There are also fine-grain objects that cannot have the overhead of ORB response times. For these objects, a direct object manager such as an ODBMS is required that can efficiently manage the access to and caching of these objects. Within the Aurora system the large-grain objects will be the business objects (which will be distributed as CORBA objects *and* made persistent by an ODBMS). There will also be many fine-grain objects that will simply be ODBMS objects.

In attempting to integrate an ORB like DST and ODBMS, there are several issues that must be addressed:

Persistence of Object References

The CORBA specification is weak when describing the lifetime of an object reference to a remote CORBA object. In our architecture we require objects that are persistent to be accessed remotely via the ORB. Furthermore, we require that our persistent objects can hold references to other persistent objects via their ORB references rather than via their database references (they might not belong to a database known to the server or even one of the same flavor).

This implies a certain persistence in the behavior of the ORB's object adapter. This is the component that registers ORB identity and uses this to locate objects in response to incoming requests. This mechanism must therefore be extended to ensure that objects that are managed by the object database adapter have their ORB identity also stored persistently in the database.

The Object Transaction Service

One of the advantages of using an ODBMS to make our objects persistent is that we gain ACID transactions. However, we must now ensure that requests to persistent CORBA objects are performed in a transaction-consistent way. Furthermore, we must be able to coordinate many requests to persistent CORBA objects on different remote CPUs into a single "distributed" transaction. Fortunately, the OMG has defined two such standards that facilitate this latter requirement—the Object Transaction Service (OTS) and the Concurrency Service.

The OTS gives us the tools to coordinate distributed transaction, but it is necessary to modify the section of the ORB that handles the "server" side of the message invocation to ensure that the transaction paradigm is enforced. Access to persistent objects outside of an OTS transaction must be disallowed while access inside OTS transactions must be correctly serialized. The registration of persistent objects must also occur within transactions to ensure that ORB identity is correctly maintained for an object.

It should be noted that the OTS requires a database to expose a two-phase commit protocol to its client. At the time of writing, none of the ODBMSs we have examined provide this protocol.

Multithreaded Adapter

In order for a distributed system to scale the processes that contain the persistent CORBA, objects must be capable of simultaneously satisfying many concurrent requests (provided that they can be performed in isolated transactions). This implies that the object database adapter must be multithreaded. To support this, the database client API must also be capable of support multiple concurrent transactions for a single operating system process. This is a feature that few ODBMSs yet attempt to provide.

Approaches to Evaluating an ODBMS

Although an initial opinion of an ODBMS can often be formed by collecting information on the product and considering how it might fit into the project, a much deeper understanding and a higher level of confidence can be gained by a hands-on evaluation of the product. At present, the ODBMS vendors appear very willing for potential customers to evaluate the products for a limited period. However, as we have discovered, *how* to evaluate the product is less straightforward than at first might appear. We have now performed three evaluations and each has taught us more about how the exercise could be done better:

Familiarization and Trial Applications

Our initial evaluations took place when the project was still in its infancy. At that point we had little understanding of ODBMSs and thus a large part of the evaluation was a learning exercise. We are very concerned about the issues of performance and so the key part of the evaluation was to build a simple trial application and measure its performance. This application took the form of a simple accounts system that would accept a series of debit and credit ledger entries, record these against various accounts, update account balances, and produce a simple trial balance. We felt this was the sort of thing a relational database would do very easily and therefore was a good test. We also felt it was a good (if over simplified) example of the kind of work that would be done in our system. This exercise did teach us a lot about ODBMSs, however. With hindsight, the characteristics of our architecture deviated so much from this simple test that any results we obtained were fairly meaningless.

Benchmarks and Metrics

The performance claims of ODBMS have been subject to a great deal of public debate and are presented as differentiating factors between the databases by many of the vendors. However, equally well discussed are the problems relating to the use of benchmarks and collection of performance metrics [Cha96]. We have therefore been somewhat reluctant to place too much weight on existing public benchmarks. For our given project, the existing benchmarks have a number of features, which leads us to believe they are not that helpful. The first of these is that our architecture will lead to significantly different access patterns to those typically used. The most common benchmarks tend to be CAD-based and therefore have data in a "bill of materials" structure. For our application, we will have many large collections containing the objects and the correct object must be quickly located from some of its values. It is for these reasons that we do not really feel it appropriate to publish any performance figures we have. In fact, while raw database performance is clearly an important factor in overall performance, the performance targets for the system will always be set and measured in terms of application specific metrics (e.g., trades per hour). Since the system consists of so many different components, the relationship between raw database performance and system performance is far from clear, and it would therefore not be possible to use performance values to infer much at all about the database performance.

Second, the benchmarks usually perform most of their work in a single transaction with the database. Some benchmarks attempt to simulate multi-user access, but still the metrics recorded do not really give any indication of overheads of starting and committing transactions. This is because the benchmarks tend to assume relatively long transactions, whereas a transaction processing system tends to have many more smaller transactions.

Third, the published metrics usually have been done with a C or C++ API. For our internal use we have redone the 001 benchmark [CS92] for one Smalltalk API. The values are significantly different than for the C++ API of that database. There seem to be a number of different reasons for this, perhaps the most interesting is the time taken to transfer data to and from the cache. Typically, the "in cache" representations of the objects are much closer to a C++ representation of the object than the internal Smalltalk representation. There is therefore an overhead in marshalling one representation to the other and hence database performance may become CPU bound much more quickly with Smalltalk. Another area of interest is various issues related to schema maintenance. Since the Smalltalk schema is much more dynamic, the database has to do much more dynamic checking and mapping than for a C++ interface. The finally issue is with mapping between primitive data types. The database typically has a set of primitives similar to those found in C. Smalltalk, on the other hand, has a much more complex internal implementation (e.g., strings are first-class objects but support "value" semantics). Handling these complexities also requires noticeable CPU resource.

Having stated the above, we are in favor of increased use of benchmarks (both existing and improved ones) within the industry. We feel that such tests will lead to increase overall performance of the ODBMSs and as such can only be good for all ODBMS users.

Prototype Application

We have concluded that the only true evaluation is to build a prototype of the target application using the candidate database. This has proved to be a good approach for us, since the database is isolated within our architecture and can therefore be swapped with relative ease. This approach is most likely to lead to key requirements being identified and tested at a much earlier stage. The prototype should focus on those areas that are most risky to allow those challenges to be better understood. Unfortunately, this approach is still not guaranteed to succeed, especially if some features that are (or become during the evaluation) critical are not currently available. For example, since two-phase commit is still not available in any database we have evaluated, this remains an area we have been unable to prove by a prototype.

EXPERIENCES WITH THREE ODBMSs

Over the past thirty months we have evaluated—and in one case used over an extended period—three ODBMSs. In each case we have only used the Smalltalk API of each product. The three products were GemStone, ObjectStore for Smalltalk, and Objectivity/Smalltalk. We will briefly present our experiences with each of these products.

GemStone

This was the first evaluation we carried out, and it took the form of a trial application. At the time, this was one of two commercial databases we identified that had a Smalltalk API. As indicated previously, this evaluation taught us a lot about ODBMSs and made us aware of various issues we had not considered before. First, the issues relating to transactional overheads. It was important to do as much as possible in a single transaction. This was especially true in GemStone, which had a "no-write-in-place" policy. Therefore, updates to a given object were much less efficient when done in many sequential transactions than when performed in a single transaction. The evaluation also brought to our attention the importance of managing and understanding large collections.

The chief technical reason why GemStone did not seem that suitable for our project was an architectural mismatch. We already have a multitier architecture, but GemStone adds an additional layer with its active GEM processes, which seemed to add unnecessary complication into the design. In addition to this, to gain the maximum from GemStone would have involved having a lot of code written in their variety of Smalltalk (at that time called OPAL, now called SmalltalkDB). In the extreme this would have implied that all our Business Logic was written inside GemStone. This represented too much dependency on a single vendor. Also at that time we found Servio (the name at that time of the manufacturers of GemStone) to be less accessible to us than we would have liked and that their forward strategy and market position appeared to be in a state of flux.

It is interesting to note that GemStone has now changed its marketing model, and now presents itself as environment for building an "object server," that is, they are recommending an approach in which the Business Logic is captured within GemStone. In line with this they will be providing a CORBA interface into the object servers. Also of interest is the ability to write some Object Servers in Java rather than Smalltalk, since once again the VM technology required is common.

ObjectStore for Smalltalk

One of the key attractions of the ObjectStore products was that Object Design was at that time the largest ODBMS vendor by a considerable margin. We also found the company to be very approachable and open towards us. However, at the start of the Aurora project they did not have a Smalltalk binding. During the period we have been looking for an ODBMS, they announced and subsequently released Object-Store for Smalltalk. We first obtained and evaluated a copy of this product in its beta release in the summer of 1994. The architecture of the product was significantly different from GemStone, VERSANT, and so on in that Object Design's approach had been to apply their Virtual Memory Mapping Architecture to Smalltalk. This led to a very clean Smalltalk API and its relative simplicity seemed a very good fit with both our architecture and goals.

Our initial investigation used a similar approach to those for GemStone and delivered good results. However, by now we were very much more aware of the key role to be played by the ORB and the requirement for a close integration between the ORB and ODBMS. Although Object Design recognized the importance of this, they did not feel able to provide this integration within the time frame to which we were working. It was a year later before some joint work between Object Design and ourselves was instigated that allowed us to create an object database adapter for ObjectStore and DST.

Despite the initial promising start, the use of ObjectStore has not been as successful as we had hoped. This is because the planned future releases upon which we were heavily dependent have been cancelled. Object Design has now decided to refocus into other areas based around its C++ strengths and also to support the Java market. The Smalltalk interface has thus been frozen and, at the time of writing, there is not a supported interface for any current release of Smalltalk. Our requirements for two-phase commit and multithreaded, multitransaction APIs now seem unlikely to be met within our project time frame. We have therefore been forced to consider alternative databases.

Objectivity/Smalltalk

By the spring of 1996, the number of database vendors that either had or had announced Smalltalk bindings had increased. One of these newer entrants was Objectivity/Smalltalk. On initial investigation, the API seemed to be good and some work has been done on multiple transaction support. Our initial meetings with both the UK distributor (Pantek Ltd.) and Objectivity, Inc. revealed an open and forward-looking company. On these strengths, in May 1996 we embarked upon another evaluation. The primary goal was to build a prototype demonstration on top of Objectivity by porting our current ObjectStore implementation. We would then look at performance and other related issues. Unfortunately, we would not be able to prototype either two-phase commit or a fully multithreaded adapter, but we would be able to precisely understand the work still required by the various parties to achieve this. At the time of writing, we have completed the evaluation that has shown that Objectivity is a suitable candidate for use within Aurora. Again Objectivity/ Smalltalk is a young product, but being based upon a good C++ product, many of the features required for commercial operation are already available in the core system even if not yet exposed in the Smalltalk API. There has now been a second major release of the Smalltalk binding that has added some important features, but development of the product is occurring at a somewhat slower pace than we would like to see.

EXPERIENCES AND SUMMARY

For a project that is both designed and coded with object-oriented techniques and programming languages, the use of a relational database is not appropriate in many cases.

The ODBMS market is maturing and many of the products appear to be ready to support mission-critical systems. However, choosing the best database is a task that is far from straightforward. Since, in an object system that has distribution as its foundation the role of the database may be much less pervasive than for a traditional system, it pays to ensure that the database is chosen to fit the design of the system not the other way around.

REFERENCES

[Bar94] D. Barry: *Should You Take the Plunge?* Object Magazine, February 1994.

[Bar95] D. Barry: *The ODBMS Industry Is Maturing.* Object Magazine, February 1995.

[Bur94] D. K. Burleson: *Mapping Object-Oriented Applications to Relational Databases.* Object Magazine, January 1994.

[CS92] R. G. G. Cattell, J. Skeen: *Object Operations Benchmark.* ACM Transactions on database systems, 17 (1), March 1992.

[Cha96] A. Chaudhri: *Object DBMSs: To Benchmark or Not to Benchmark?* Object Magazine, July 1996.

[Gam+94] E. Gamma, R. Helm, J. Johnson, J. Vlissides: *Design Patterns—Elements of Reusable Object-Oriented Software.* Addison-Wesley, 1994.

[DG94] M. DeSanti, J. Gomsi: *A Comparison of Object and Relational Database Technologies*, Object Magazine, January 1994.

[OMG92] OMG: *Object Management Architecture Guide.* Revision 2.0, 1992.

[OMG95] OMG: *The Common Object Request Broker: Architecture and Specification,* Revision 2, July 1995.

[Vät+96] K. Vättö, R. Yairi, M. Palkama: *Integration of an ODBMS into Legacy Telecommunication Systems*, Object Expert, March-April 1996.

Migration Process and Consideration for the Object-Oriented Vector Product Format to ObjectStore Database Management System

Kevin Shaw, Naval Research Laboratory
Miyi Chung, Naval Research Laboratory
Maria Cobb, Naval Research Laboratory

ABSTRACT

This chapter presents an object-oriented approach for handling Vector Product Format (VPF) mapping databases as produced by the U.S. Defense Mapping Agency. This approach is implemented in the Object Vector Product Format (OVPF) Smalltalk prototype developed by the U.S. Naval Research Laboratory and the University of Florida. OVPF provides an integrated framework for four VPF products: Digital Nautical Chart, World Vector Shoreline Plus, Urban Vector Smart Map, and Vector Smart Map level 0. Having four VPF products and with the update capability, persistent storage of these spatial data was one of the concerns. This chapter will introduce the changes to the data model to accommodate the ObjectStore implementation and migration process of each of the products to the ObjectStore ODBMS.

We wish to thank our sponsor, DMA, Mr. Jim Kraus, and Mr. Jake Garrison, program managers, for sponsoring this research. We would also like to thank Mr. Mike Harris for performing the technical review of this chapter.

INTRODUCTION

This chapter documents the integration of the commercial object-oriented database management system (ODBMS) ObjectStore (by Object Design, Inc.) with the Object Vector Product Format (OVPF) Smalltalk prototype, including both design and initial implementation. The work documented in this chapter was performed as part of the Object-Oriented Database Exploitation within the Global Geospatial Information & Services (GGI&S) Data Warehouse project conducted by the Naval Research Laboratory and the University of Florida and sponsored by the Defense Mapping Agency (DMA). The purpose of the project was to determine the potential impact of object-oriented (OO) technology on DMA's GGMI&S) initiative. Other reports [Sha+95, Chu+95a, Arc+95a, Arc+95b] have documented the integration of multiple Vector Product Format (VPF) products into OVPF, network investigation results, and evaluation of a hybrid object-relational database management system.

As a brief orientation for the reader, VPF is a military standard for the storage and exchange of digital vector data, which consists of a hierarchical system of ASCII data files organized in third-normal relational form. It emerged in the late 1980s as DMA began converting its paper maps into digital format. The VPF relational data model, however, has problems representing complex spatial data. As a result, in 1991, the U.S. Navy, a DMA database user, began investigating how object technology could improve these digital maps. This research led to the development of the OVPF, an object-oriented approach to viewing and editing digital maps and charts. By combining multiple relational databases into a single OO database, OVPF offers users such key advantages as the ability to immediately update and modify the content of the original data. The initial OVPF prototype consisted of approximately 400 classes (in addition to those provided in the Smalltalk class library) and several thousand methods. Benchmarking and comparisons to VPF are documented in [Arc+95c] and showed roughly an order of magnitude improvement in importing time.

The OVPF prototype application has been designed and implemented with the ParcPlace Systems' VisualWorks version of the Smalltalk programming language. This choice is primarily due to the sophistication and productivity of the Smalltalk development environment for building complex applications. Due to the semantic differences among OO programming languages, the terms and definitions used here may not apply consistently across all such languages. However, the concepts represented by these terms should be general enough to be implemented in other OO languages. The commercial ODBMS has been chosen with this in mind as well—ObjectStore includes interfaces to Smalltalk and C++ so that objects created and stored by a Smalltalk program should be accessible to programs written in C++. This is not yet possible with current products as we write, but industry efforts to develop cross-language compatibility for ODBMSs are underway.

In this chapter, design issues are emphasized with respect to OVPF, as well as the experiences incurred, lessons learned, and potential impact from the actual implementation of ObjectStore, one of the leading commercial ODBMSs. The next section provides an explanation of why ODBMS is used along with an introduction to basic ODBMS concepts. The following section describes background information on object-oriented symbology and terminology, along with a brief description of the OVPF structure, including the design of the class hierarchies for importing and representing multiple VPF products. Implementation design to integrate ObjectStore with OVPF is presented in the next section, and the last section concludes with key findings and summary of the integration effort.

ODBMS INTEGRATION

Why Use an ODBMS?

With support for multiple VPF products now integrated into OVPF's framework, we turn to the issues and tradeoffs of support for commercial ODBMSs. This section presents our current experience and understanding with respect to the issues and effects of alternative ODBMS architectures on OVPF's design. In this regard, we will be distinguishing between internal and external databases. The internal database refers to OVPF's computer-memory-resident object space of metadata and feature objects. The external database refers to the disk-resident database implemented using the commercial vendors' ODBMS products as an alternative to the data storage.

In today's distributed processing environment, each OVPF user is likely to be working on a networked computer workstation that is separate from, but perhaps just as powerful as, the workstation housing the shared external databases. OVPF will be seen as a *client* process making requests for data from a *server* process running on the central host. Commercially available ODBMSs typically fall into one or both of two types of client-server architecture: object-server or page-server. The distinction is based on the unit of data transfer between the server and client processes. In an *object-server* architecture, the server understands the client's concept of an object. In this model, each transfer from the server to a client process is based on groupings of interconnected objects. A *page server,* on the other hand, is unaware of "objects" as such, but transfers data in units of a disk page that is typically 4 KB.

As described above, OVPF can function without a database management system. Relational tables as stored in directories according to the VPF specification [DMA92] are processed and information is brought into memory upon import of one or more coverages. Once in memory, disk resident data are never subsequently accessed. The advantage to this approach, besides its simplicity, is that the memory resident data are quickly accessible for manipulation, eliminating the need to perform costly disk accesses and table joins. The disadvantages are primarily: (1) the amount of data that can be imported for a single session is limited by the capacity of physical memory, and (2) data are not made available for concurrent access by multiple users; thus, changes to the data made through the use of OVPF are not readily apparent to others.

The use of an ODBMS eliminates both of these concerns, as well as providing additional advantages. For example, with this approach, OVPF is no longer limited by memory size for data import and viewing; data are simply stored in the database until needed, then brought into memory for display or editing purposes. Additionally, geographic object level security and auditing can be readily managed.

The function of any DBMS is to provide persistent (maintained from session to session) storage of data, controlled access to the data, and backup and recovery capabilities, among others. Object-oriented DBMSs provide these functions specifically for *objects*—units of data defined and assigned values through the use of an OO programming language such as Smalltalk or C++. While objects are generally considered to consist of both state (data) and behavior (procedures), ODBMSs are typically concerned only with the storage of the state information, as are traditional relational database management systems.

ODBMS Concepts

Following is a list of three significant high-level concepts concerning ODBMSs. Each is elaborated upon in the discussion that follows.

- Persistent versus transient objects
- Transactions and concurrency control
- Security and authorization

The distinction between persistent and transient objects is somewhat less clear for ODBMSs than for RDBMSs, due to the tightly coupled nature of the database with the application. *Transient objects* are defined to be those objects that exist in the computer's memory only during execution of the application, such as the window system objects for displaying the key data. *Persistent objects*, on the other hand, are those representing the key data, whose state is maintained in the database and exist even when there is no application program running.

Transient and persistent objects can coexist within a running process. The distinction becomes blurred because persistent data accessed from the database can be assigned to a transient object. It is important for application programs to manage both transient and persistent data in consistent ways so updates to persistent data are made when needed and so data that should remain transient are not inadvertently made persistent. For example, a web of interconnected transient objects can be made persistent simply by allocating space in the database for the "root object" of the web. Once this transaction is completed, the ODBMS will migrate the transitive closure (entire web) from the root object into the database. It is important, therefore, to be sure that such a transitive closure does *not* include references to objects, such as the window system in which the data are being displayed, as this would "pull" a very large and unnecessary part of the application objects into the database.

All accesses to persistent data are typically made within a *transaction*. A transaction is defined to be a sequence of instructions that access the database and whose execution is guaranteed to be atomic; that is, either all or none of the instructions are executed. *Read* transactions are defined as those that retrieve data only, while *write* (or *read-write*) transactions are those that actually change the data. When a transaction has successfully terminated, it is *committed*, meaning that any changes made to persistent data within the transaction are written to the database and will not be undone. If a transaction is *aborted*, the ODBMS will cause a roll-back of changes made to the objects to return them to their state as existed prior to the beginning of the transaction.

A related issue is that of *concurrency control*. Concurrency control is an issue only for multiuser DBMSs and is concerned with ensuring, usually through the use of locks, that when a user is accessing persistent data within a transaction, other users cannot simultaneously change the data, resulting in the database being left in an inconsistent state. Database inconsistency can easily result from the interleaving of different users' instructions regarding the same persistent data.

It is widely recognized that data are one of the most valuable assets of any organization. With that recognition comes the need to protect such data. As a result, DBMSs typically provide some system of restricting access to data based on a user authorization system. Different sets of privileges may be provided for different classes of users. Privileges may include the right to read or modify data, as well as the ability to modify the database schema itself.

ObjectStore

ObjectStore was selected for integration with OVPF for the following reasons:

- It is a well-established, commercially successful ODBMS.
- It is available with both Smalltalk and C++ language interfaces.

ObjectStore ODBMS functions as a simple repository of data. Three major processes are used in ObjectStore: the server, the client, and the cache manager. These are shown in Figure 15–1. The database and the files consist of the cache, communication segment, and the database. The *ObjectStore server* provides I/O services to databases that reside on local and remote disks.

ObjectStore is based on a page-server architecture in which the server uses a two-phase commit protocol in conjunction with other servers to guarantee consistent transaction completion in a distributed database environment. The *ObjectStore client* allocates and deallocates storage for persistent objects. Communication with the ObjectStore server is managed for fetching and locking pages. Pages are

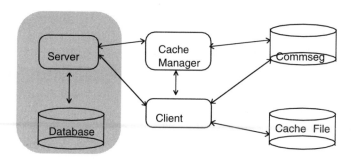

Figure 15–1 ObjectStore configuration.

mapped into the virtual address space of the client processes. Recently referenced pages are maintained and coordinated with the cache manager to hold locks as long as possible for minimizing network I/O traffic with the server. Transaction commits are performed to transmit any modification to the database. The *ObjectStore cache manager* handles asynchronous lock callback requests from the ObjectStore server. This capability provides immediate response to the ObjectStore server, which in turn leaves the ObjectStore client library free to make only synchronous requests.

To reduce network traffic with the server and to provide coordination via shared access to the client commseg file, a "lazy" lock release mechanism is coordinated with the ObjectStore client. The ObjectStore database can be accessed only by the server. However, the client is responsible for database organization and structure. Cache and commseg files are used for controlling encached data. The cache file is used as a swap space for persistent data, and as a backup store for in-memory persistent objects. The commseg file tracks the status of encached pages. This file is used by the client to determine whether a page can be accessed and locked. The cache manager uses this file to check and/or give up locks upon the server's request.

ObjectStore uses a "pessimistic" approach to transaction management that requires every database access to occur within the bounds of a transaction. This guarantees data integrity among all users at the cost of potentially blocking some users while one is accessing a particular page of data. Transaction bounds are explicitly stated by the use of messages to ObjectStore's class OSTransaction. This helps ensure that each transaction will be as short as possible, thus minimizing blocking of other users.

For a more detailed explanation of ObjectStore features, the reader is referred to [Sha+95].

OVPF DESIGN

Introducing Object-Oriented Class Diagrams and Terms

Integration of ObjectStore with OVPF is much desired based on the advantages of using an ODBMS as mentioned. To pave a ground for understanding, OVPF design is provided to determine how OVPF was modeled and also to understand the impact of integration in the design. Some of the syntax and semantics used in the Smalltalk object-oriented environment is provided along with the actual implementation of the OVPF model.

Figure 15–2 presents a partial cross-section of the class hierarchies designed to support multiple products. First, notice that some class names in Figure 15–2 are underlined, while some are not. Classes whose names are underlined are called *abstract superclasses*, meaning that they represent a definitional abstraction (such as definition of instance variables and/or behavior to be shared by their respective subclasses) and that instances would not normally be created from them. Classes whose names are not underlined are called *concrete subclasses*, meaning that they are expected to have instances made from them. These terms are mainly used to aid in

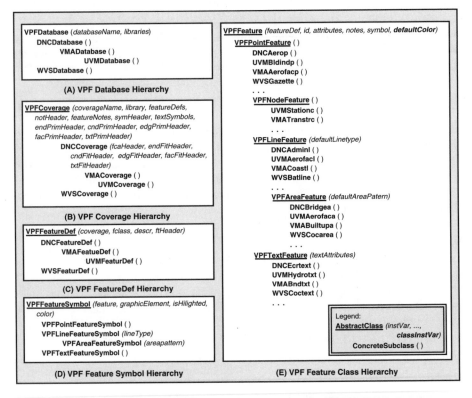

Figure 15–2   Class hierarchy cross-section.

learning about a class hierarchy; to call a class "abstract" implies that it lacks behavior needed for creation of a "useful" instance-object.

Figure 15–3 presents a partial view of the data structures defined for each of the key feature definition hierarchies, while Figure 15–4 presents a partial example of feature data and metadata objects that might be seen after importing Digital Nautical Chart Coastline (DNC COASTL) features. These *object diagrams* have two main sections: (1) the class name and (2) a list of instance variables, class-instance variables, and/or class variables (where applicable). These variables are described briefly below.

Instance variables are data structures for which each instance-object has its own private copy; these begin with a lowercase letter. *Class-instance variables* are data structures for which the class object and each of its subclasses are defined to each have a private copy of the variable. Class-instance variable names are shown ***bold-italicized*** in Figure 15–2 to help distinguish them from instance variables. *Class variables* are data structures for which the defining class has a single copy that can be directly accessed by all instances of itself and its subclasses. Per Smalltalk convention, class variables (and other shared objects including classes) have names that begin with an uppercase letter.

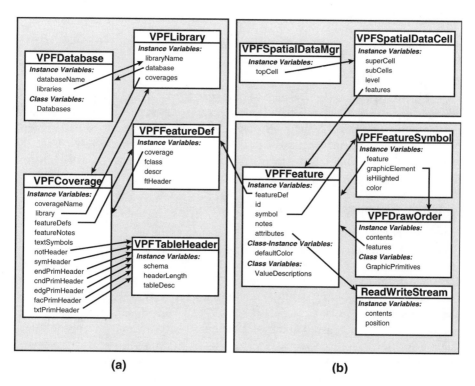

(a)   **(b)**

Figure 15–3   Data structures for key feature definition hierarchies.

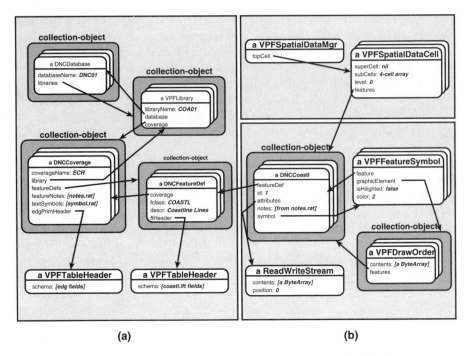

Figure 15–4   Partial feature data and metadata for DNC COASTL features.

Note the use of *collection-objects* in Figure 15–4—these are instances of pre-defined classes in Smalltalk that are used to encapsulate a collection of one or more types of other objects. Collection objects simplify the management of large groups of objects when it is important to be able to sequentially or randomly access the group members. Libraries, coverages, featureDefs, and feature objects are frequently held and accessed from collection objects in OVPF.

Metadata Classes and Instances

It will be helpful now to introduce the metadata (schema definition) classes in OVPF. VPFFeatureDef and its subclasses form an important link between feature objects and their defining schemas. Figures 15–2, 15–3a, and 15–4a show the classes that define the structure of each VPF database product. The classes VPF-Database, VPFCoverage, and VPFFeatureDef all have product-specific subclasses. The need for product-specific subclasses is most concerned with the feature import process and will be discussed in the next section. What is more pertinent for now is that much of the feature metadata is stored in instance variables whose names end in "Header," such as *ftHeader* in VPFFeatureDef class. These variables each hold onto an instance of VPFTableHeader, which in turn holds a schema of information such as the field id, description, data type, and length of each column in the table, as documented in the VPF product specification. Another role of the VPFTableHeader schema is to support the actual conversion of source data bytes into usable numeric values and vice versa, as needed.

Feature Attributes

As shown in Figure 15–2, each subclass of VPFFeature inherits an *attributes* instance variable. The *attributes* variable holds onto the contents of a record from the *.PFT, *.LFT, *.AFT, or *.TFT feature table. Each of these records contains the integer or character values of attributes common to all features of a given class, such as ACC (accuracy code) or SLT (shoreline type).

Figure 15–2e shows that VPFTextFeature also defines a *textAttributes* instance variable. This variable holds onto a set of values from the SYMBOL.RAT file (if present) that defines text font, style (italic, bold, etc.), size, and color for one or more text features.

Both *attributes* and *textAttributes* are stored and processed in the same manner. They use a predefined Smalltalk class called ReadWriteStream that provides an efficient means of storing, reading, and updating an arbitrary sequence of bytes. Since floating-point and integer values are stored somewhat differently among the various computer systems (UNIX, DOS, and Macintosh), we chose to defer translating the bytes into user-understandable values until the user actually requests to examine or modify them. In addition to reducing processing time during feature import, this also greatly reduces the total number of objects we have to handle. Since we are using a single ReadWriteStream object for each set of attributes instead of creating a separate integer or character value object for every attribute, we are greatly reducing the load on the computer system's internal I/O channel and memory.

Since these attributes are normally maintained as an arbitrary sequence of bytes within OVPF, it is necessary for a given feature object to have access to the byte-offset and length of each of its attributes in the ReadWriteStream object. This information is read and stored during metadata initialization of a VPF database, and is held in the *ftHeader* schema defined in VPFFeatureDef (for attributes defined in feature table headers) and in the *symHeader* schema defined in VPFCoverage (for text attributes defined in SYMBOL.RAT).

Integer and Character Value Description Tables

One set of tables all VPF products have in common includes the *integer value description table* (INT.VDT) and the *character value description table* (CHAR.VDT). Each coverage has these VDT files to store the descriptive text associated with each of the valid ranges of feature attribute values. In OVPF, the set of all VDT data is held in a class variable of VPFFeature class called *ValueDescriptions*. This is organized as a nested hierarchy of tables, so that the valid range of integer and textual values for a given attribute is easily found. The *ValueDescriptions* structure is populated during database initialization.

Holding all of these VDTs in a single hierarchical collection structure has proven useful in identifying inconsistencies among values and descriptions across coverages, libraries, and databases. Some of these differences reflect errors in the data, but most are due to design differences in the use of a given feature attribute among different VPF products.

Feature-Related Notes

If a coverage includes a NOTES.RAT file, this is read into the VPFCoverage subclass' *featureNotes* instance variable during database initialization. A NOTES.RAT file normally has many-to-many links with feature objects; that is, any one feature may be linked to many records in the NOTES.RAT file, and any one note in the NOTES.RAT file could be linked to many different feature objects. The purpose of the *notes* instance variable defined in VPFFeature is to hold onto a list of note IDs from the NOTES.RAT file for lookup into the VPFCoverage sub-class' *featureNotes* collection. The *notHeader* schema defined in VPFCoverage is used when reading these notes from disk. So far, DNC appears to be the only VPF product using NOTES.RAT.

Graphical Primitives

Each feature object is associated with a set of latitude-longitude coordinates, referred to as graphical primitives. Point and node features are associated with entity- and connected-node primitives. Line features are associated with edge primitives. Area features are associated with a face primitive consisting of a "ring" of edge primitives, and text features are associated with a "path" of coordinates. Because any one-line feature object may consist of multiple edges, and any single node, edge, or face primitive could be used by more than one feature object, great care must be taken to maintain the correct linkage between the features and primitives. Topological relationships (adjacency and contiguity) among the primitives must also be maintained across all features within a given coverage and tile, according to the VPF specification.

The design of spatial topology within OVPF is documented in [Chu+95b] and it is not an intention in this chapter to elaborate on the intricacies of such. Therefore, for purposes of this chapter, graphical primitives will be treated as if all were instances of the same class and will be called VPFDrawOrder. This approach is sufficient for explaining the manner of encoding each primitive's location coordinates. Also, VPFDrawOrder is the superclass from which all the topological primitive classes are derived in the topology framework.

As seen in Figures 15–3b and 15–4b, VPFDrawOrder objects have a pointer to a collection of feature objects. This is to allow each graphical primitive (draw order) to know and communicate directly with the feature(s) in which it is used. Figure 15–3b also shows a class variable *GraphicalPrimitives* defined for VPFDrawOrders.

This is to hold the set of all VPFDrawOrder instances imported or created in the current work session.

VPFDrawOrder objects hold all location coordinates in a specially encoded array of bytes and work much like the ReadWriteStream used to store and process a feature's attributes. A VPFDrawOrder object has an instance variable that contains the byte array. This byte array has three parts:

- Opcode byte—an 8-bit integer used to define what kind of operation is to be performed; e.g., 199 means "set polyline"
- Length byte—an 8-bit integer containing the number of data bytes to follow
- Data bytes—sequence of bytes representing a color index, location coordinates, and so on.

Instances of VPFDrawOrder are used to represent nodes, edges, the polylines forming each character in a text feature's string, and any other graphical entity associated with a feature object. These VPFDrawOrders can be concatenated into arbitrarily long sequences of bytes for any given purpose. This is a computationally efficient means of managing the storage and processing of the tens and hundreds of thousands of coordinate points that are required to represent a VPF database.

Spatial Tree Indexing Framework

Two classes shown in Figure 15–3 and 15–4, VPFSpatialDataManager and VPFSpatialDataCell, are used to implement and manage a spatial tree indexing framework. This framework presently uses a quadtree organization in which each spatial data cell holds pointers to four subcells and each subcell holds a pointer to its parent or supercell.

This spatial tree design is independent of the VPF database to be imported. All access to the spatial tree from within OVPF is done through a spatial data manager object. Each feature passed to the spatial data manager is inserted into the appropriate spatial tree cell based on the feature's minimum bounding rectangle. The spatial data manager also responds to user requests to obtain or delete the features appearing within a particular region in space.

This design allows us to modify the implementation of the spatial tree at any time without affecting the rest of OVPF or the source data. Thus, in the future, we could easily substitute an R$^+$ tree [Sto+86], PM Random (PMR) quadtree [NS87], spatial splay tree [Cob+95], or special optimizing techniques in place of the present quadtree approach. We could also support the simultaneous implementation of multiple spatial indexing schemes to allow choice of the most efficient spatial tree design for a given source database. This may be important as we provide support for Raster Product Format (RPF) and other non-VPF databases.

DATABASE IMPLEMENTATION

The implementation of the database necessitated the following steps:

1. Making design decisions such as:
   - Deciding which objects should be transient and which objects should be persistent
   - Deciding on physical partitions of the database
   - Deciding on roots of persistent object trees
   - Establishing a security model

2. Modifying the existing implementation of OVPF in the following ways:
   - Reorganizing or creating new classes and methods needed for database use
   - Inserting correct references for persistent objects and ensuring that no persistent object references are permanently held in the application program
   - Placing transaction boundaries in appropriate places

3. Loading the OVPF database with the VPF data, including:
   - Building the initial database file
   - Importing and migrating the metadata
   - Importing and migrating the feature data

The relation of each of these steps to ObjectStore is discussed in detail in the following section.

Persistent Object Webs in OVPF

The first step of the external database design involves the decision regarding which sets of objects to make persistent. This is very different for OO than for relational DBMSs. Any object within OVPF's internal memory can become a persistent object in an ODBMS merely by "asking" it to be. However, this not only copies the requested object into the external database, it also copies the object's transitive closure of every object to which it points. However, it is often undesirable to store some objects in such a transitive closure in the external database. Each of the ODBMS products provides a means to bypass the transitive closure under certain conditions so that only selected links are followed. The implications of this issue within OVPF are discussed below.

In this section, three main groupings of database objects have been presented: the metadata object web, the feature objects, and the *ValueDescriptions* data structures. Each of these object groups is made persistent. Another category of OVPF objects includes the user interface classes. These are the support classes that present the map on the computer screen and allow interaction with the user. Instances of these classes should not be made persistent.

Typically, a complete web of objects is made persistent by reference to some "root" or "parent" object for the group. This also provides a named entry point to the persistent object web for future access by other application programs. In the case of the metadata object web, the root is a collection object containing pointers to all initialized databases, as shown in Figure 15–4a. For example, this collection has a member called DNC01 that points to its libraries, each of which points to its respective coverages, and so on. In the non-database version of OVPF, this root collection of databases is held by the VPFDatabase class variable called *Databases*. However, with the integrated database, this metadata object web is made persistent, thereby alleviating the need for the *Databases* class variable.

For the feature objects, the logical root object is the spatial tree manager that holds a pointer to the linked list of spatial tree cells, each of which holds pointers to the features whose bounding rectangle falls within the cells boundaries. Each feature object (instance of a VPFFeature subclass) holds onto its attributes stream and its symbol (instance of a VPFSymbol subclass).

For the graphic primitives, the logical root object is the collection of all VPF-DrawOrders, presently held by the VPFDrawOrders class variable *GraphicPrimitives*. This root collection object is made persistent in the object database. Therefore, as was the case for the *Databases* class variable, there is no longer a need for the *Graphic-Primitives* class variable. Likewise, the *ValueDescriptions* structure held by the class variable of VPFFeature is handled in a similar manner.

ObjectStore

ObjectStore provides a relatively small set of low-level operations for database accessing and manipulation. Thus, integrating ObjectStore with OVPF was a fairly nonintrusive operation, requiring some restructuring of the OVPF class hierarchy, but few changes in fundamental design or implementation.

Conceptual Database Organization

One of the first changes made was a reorganization of the OVPF class hierarchies to change the usage of class variables. ObjectStore does not allow objects held by these kinds of variables to be made persistent; instead, all persistent states should be held by instance variables. For example, as discussed earlier, OVPF previously used class variables of the graphical primitive classes to hold centralized collections of all primitives organized by coverage. This collection was moved and divided to be held by instance variables of each coverage object so that each coverage now holds a collection of just its own primitives. Another class variable previously held the root of a tree structure of all value description table (VDT) entries in a given database. This collection was also moved and divided so that each features metadata (called its featureDef) object now holds a collection of just the VDT entries for that feature class.

Physical Database Design

ObjectStore facilitates clustering of data through the use of *segments*. A segment is a variable-sized region of storage composed of disk pages. Segments or pages can be specified as the unit of transfer of data from disk to memory, and can range in size from the default of 4 KB to over 128 MB. Unless otherwise directed, all data are automatically stored in a predefined segment called the *default segment*. However, it is usually desirable to create multiple segments, as the appropriate designation of segments for specific groups of objects can dramatically improve database performance by defining which objects are transferred together.

OVPF uses four segments, known as the *default segment*, the *spatial segment*, the *feature segment*, and the *primitive segment*. Each segment stores a group of related objects as given below:

- **Default segment**—the database metadata
- **Spatial segment**—data relating to the spatial index (quadtree)
- **Feature segment**—all feature-level data
- **Primitive segment**—all graphic primitive data; for example, edge, face, node data

This physical partitioning of the data was performed to support an optimal clustering strategy. This helps prevent unnecessary data from being transferred upon access to the database. Very little change was required in OVPF to define and access these segments.

ObjectStore allows multiple entry points to each database to provide efficient access to various logical hierarchies of data. Each entry point is referred to as a *named root* of persistent data. Each object designated as a root object can be accessed directly through the use of its name. All objects in the root objects composition hierarchy can then be accessed by navigating through its instance variables.

Two root objects were created for the OVPF database. These are OSDatabasesRoot, which provides access to the different VPF databases such as WVS+ and DNC, and OSSpatialIndexesRoot, which provides an entry point for the quadtree spatial indexing structure. In OVPF, the spatial indexing organization was modified somewhat so that each coverage has a pointer to its own quadtree in the database. Direct access to each quadtree is essential for fast responses to user queries, and the OSSpatialIndexesRoot provides access to the roots of all quadtrees in the current database. While the term *quadtree* is used in this chapter, OVPF is organized to support any combination of different types of spatial indices among VPF products, with each feature coverage specifying its own spatial index. Figure 15–5 shows the four OVPF database segments and their connections to each other. Database roots are noted through the use of the symbol.

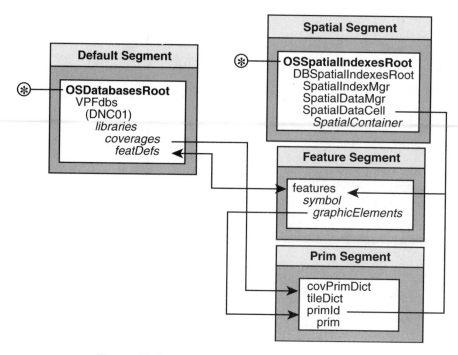

Figure 15–5   OVPF ObjectStore database segments.

Proxies and OSReferences

The class OSReference is provided by ObjectStore to handle inter-object references from transient to persistent objects. An instance of the OSReference class replaces a reference from a transient to a persistent object upon transaction commit. OSReferences provide object identifiers that are valid across transactions. OSReferences forward messages within a transaction to the persistent objects they represent and as such can be used in a manner similar to that of the persistent objects themselves. OSReferences were used in OVPF for instances of the metadata classes VPFDatabase, VPFLibrary, VPFCoverage, and VPFFeatureDef.

Proxies, implemented by the lightweight OSProxy class, are used when a handle to a persistent object is needed, but when references to that object do not necessarily require all of the objects data. A string can be assigned to a proxy object such that references to the persistent object represented by the proxy that occur outside of transactions will return the proxy's string. Any references made to the proxy while inside a transaction will return the persistent object. Figure 15–6 illustrates the use of proxies with OVPF.

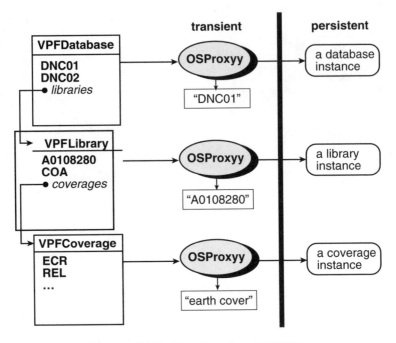

Figure 15–6   Use of proxies with OVPF.

Loading the Database

Once the database file has been created through use of the appropriate Object-Store method, it may be loaded with the VPF data. This is done in two steps. First, the metadata is imported from the VPF tables (metadata includes VPF tables such as the Database Header Table (DHT), Library Attribute Table (LAT), and Library Header Table (LHT), each feature class's schema, and the VDTs). After the metadata have been loaded and migrated to the database, feature data are imported from the VPF database, one coverage at a time, and placed in the memory-based quadtree spatial indexing structure. The features and the quadtree are then migrated to the database in their respective segments upon commit of the feature loading transaction. After the bulk loading of the databases in this manner, the relational tables are not used for subsequent data access—all manipulation of the data involves only the object database.

EXPERIENCES AND SUMMARY

The integration of ObjectStore with OVPF has proven to be promising. One of the major accomplishments in this effort is that an ODBMS was integrated as a layer to the OVPF model. In other words, major changes to the OVPF model were not required for integration with ObjectStore. It is possible that OVPF design and implementation are stable and robust to support add-on modules. However, this needs to be explored more.

With a database management system, our prototype has shown improvements both in performance and in the design. Modifications had to be made to the OVPF model to integrate it with ObjectStore. However, these were minor changes. Eliminating all class variables in the model—since ObjectStore does not support persistent class variables—and using more instance variables to hold onto the information held by class variables took some effort. This is an area where ObjectStore could have made the migration process a little simpler by providing support for persistent class variables. On the other hand, changes in the design allowed each coverage to have a unique spatial indexing scheme. Before the integration, only one spatial indexing scheme was used for all features. This change promotes the possibility of using the spatial indexing scheme that is most optimal for a specific coverage, which should provide faster access and retrieval.

ObjectStore required use of cut-points to prevent pulling the graphic user interface into the internal database. From an application design standpoint, this improved the modularity of our code and helped us identify places where actual feature or primitive objects were sending messages directly to the map window objects. In our design, the map GUI object is allowed to talk to the features and primitives, but not vice versa.

With a spatial segment, the spatial indexing scheme as implemented in OVPF was migrated to the external database without any modification. This was possible since the spatial indexing scheme or quadtree is implemented as an independent class that contains feature-object pointers. This allows fast, direct lookup of geographic features in response to queries.

With the prototype, overall performance has improved in the areas of data import, display, and querying. There are two contributing factors to these improvements. First, ObjectStore uses the CacheManager to cache information retrieved from the internal database. Secondly, direct navigation to the object web is supported via clustering; therefore, resolution of spatial queries is fast and direct.

Furthermore, a sequential selection dependency for import no longer exists. Without ObjectStore, a database must be selected, then a library, then a coverage, followed by a selection of import type (e.g., point, line, area, or all feature types). If a user wants to display information from two different databases, one database has to be imported and displayed first before another database can be brought in. However, this is no longer true after the integration. All of the database can be selected down to the coverage level at once for an aggregate display on screen.

Aside from these improvements in the OVPF model, the pure advantage of having a database management system is a gain in itself. The concept of persistent objects allows accessing data without having to load the data into memory as in the model before the integration. Multi-user access and configuration control are provided to allow more use of the data without having to maintain a copy of data on every user's computer and subsequently having to be concerned about consolidating the changes.

For future work, we have to address fast retrieval for queries based on values of feature attributes. This is a common type of query, but unfortunately we have not indexed any of the attributes of features. The first level of support for this kind of query from the ODBMS is to use an effective clustering strategy, so perhaps features will be organized on disk on some order based on attribute values. This is not very flexible, though. A better approach will be to create and manage B-trees or hash tables for fast lookup of objects based on a given attribute. To facilitate this, it will probably be necessary to make real instance variables for each attribute to be indexed.

REFERENCES

[Arc+95c] D. K. Arctur, E. Anwar, J. F. Alexander, S. Chakravarthy, M. J. Chung, M. A. Cobb, K. B. Shaw: *Comparison and Benchmarks for Import of Vector Product Format (VPF) Geographic Data from Object-Oriented and Relational Database Files.* Proc. Fourth Symp. on Spatial Databases (pp. 368–384). New York: Springer-Verlag, 1995.

[Arc+95a] D. K. Arctur, J. F. Alexander, M. A. Cobb, M. J. Chung, K. B. Shaw: *OVPF Chapter: Evaluation of Illustra Hybrid Object-Relational DBMS.* Naval Research Laboratory, Stennis Space Center, MS, 1995.

[Arc+95b] D. K. Arctur, J. F. Alexander, M. A. Cobb, M. J. Chung, K. B. Shaw: *OVPF Report: Issues and Approaches for Spatial Topology in GIS.* NRL/MR/7441-96-7719, Naval Research Laboratory, Stennis Space Center, MS, 1995.

[Chu+95a] M. J. Chung, M. A. Cobb, K. B. Shaw, D. K. Arctur, J. F. Alexander: *OVPF Chapter: Network Investigation Results.* NRL/MR/7441-95-7713, Naval Research Laboratory, Stennis Space Center, MS, 1995.

[Chu+95b] M. J. Chung, M. A. Cobb, K. B. Shaw, D. K. Arctur: *An Object-Oriented Approach for Handling Topology in VPF Products.* Proc. GIS/LIS '95, Nashville, TN, Vol. 1, pp. 163–174, 1995.

[Cob+95] M. A. Cobb, M. J. Chung, K. B. Shaw, D. K. Arctur: *A Self-Adjusting Indexing Structure for Spatial Data.* Proc. GIS/LIS '95, Nashville, TN, Vol. 1, pp. 182–192, 1995.

[DMA92] Defense Mapping Agency: *Military Standard: Vector Product Format.* Draft Document No. MIL-STD-2407, Defense Mapping Agency, Fairfax, VA, 1992.

[NS87] R. C. Nelson, H. Samet: *A Population Analysis for Hierarchical Data Structures,* in Proceedings of the ACM SIGMOD Conference on Management of Data, San Francisco, CA, pp. 270–277, 1987.

[Sha+95] K. B. Shaw, M. J. Chung, M. A. Cobb, D. K. Arctur, J. F. Alexander, E. Anwar: *Object-Oriented Database Exploitation Within the GGIS Data*

Warehouse: Initial Chapter. NRL/FR/7441-95-9639, Naval Research Laboratory, Stennis Space Center, MS, April 1995.

[Sto+86] M. T. Stonebraker, T. Sellis, E. Hanson: *An Analysis of Rule Indexing Implementations in Data Base Systems*, in Proceedings of the First International Conference on Expert Database Systems, Charleston, SC, pp. 353–364, April 1986.

IV

Performance

INTRODUCTION

There are many papers that present object database performance benchmarks, but few that discuss experiences tuning applications on a specific product. Issues like bottleneck identification, workload characterization, etc. have not been widely reported. Fortunately, Chapter 16 by Gardner provides one example illustrating the many difficulties involved in tuning object database applications. The system described is one that must remain online on a 24 x 7 x 365 basis; there is no downtime tolerated. The product being used is GemStone, which uses automatic garbage collection. According to Gardner, explicit memory deallocation may be more efficient, since the garbage collection process caused performance problems in his environment. Gardner also provides some examples of application tuning by detailed code reviews. Other important discussions cover the relationship between product evolution and performance; a new product release may require re-coding some applications. The characteristics of the particular object database used can have significant implications for application design.

Similar to Gardner, Jaehne describes experiences using ObjectStore for Smalltalk (OSST) in Chapter 17. One of the problems with many object databases is the lack of suitable tools to perform database administration acitivities and to collect detailed information about database access patterns to support optimization of physical database design. ObjectStore provides both navigational and associative access. According to Jaehne, the latter is where better performance gains can be achieved. He describes how an in-house tool and ObjectStore Performance Expert (OPE) can be used to study database access patterns and provides some general guidelines for optimization. An important conclusion is that analysis and tuning can result in considerable performance improvements.

Chapter 18 by Wellner and Ikenn describes experiences building a federation-wide indexing facility for Objectivity/DB. The chapter also reports useful experiences about product development with Objectivity/DB and criteria that users may wish to consider when undertaking their own object database evaluations. An important recommendation (supporting the view expressed by Rudge and Moorley in Chapter 14) is the need to undertake prototyping. However, possibly the most useful and important contributions of this chapter are related to Objectivity/DB's deficiencies (e.g. lack of support for collections) and how these "holes" were filled.

16

Performance Tuning Considerations and Required Tools for an OODB Application

Charles Gardner, Texas Instruments

ABSTRACT

Distributed reporting (DR) is an application that is currently being deployed as a replacement for a mainframe reporting system. Since DR was replacing an existing mainframe reporting application that had well-defined performance requirements, the DR system made a good application to use as a performance benchmark for a Smalltalk OODB and UNIX-based application. Since the majority of the application code was resident in the OODB, the application was also isolated from network loading issues that may have clouded the issue of OODB performance. In this application, direct comparison was made of reports created on the mainframe and reports created on DR.

DESCRIPTION OF THE APPLICATION

DR can be broken into three main groups that can be tuned independently relative to their interface with the OODB and Smalltalk. Figure 16–1 shows the general outline of the application. The three groups are the batch and real-time updates (1, 2), the query and report engine performance (5), and external reporting interfaces (3, 4). The batch load is run infrequently, but when required to be run, it is usually during

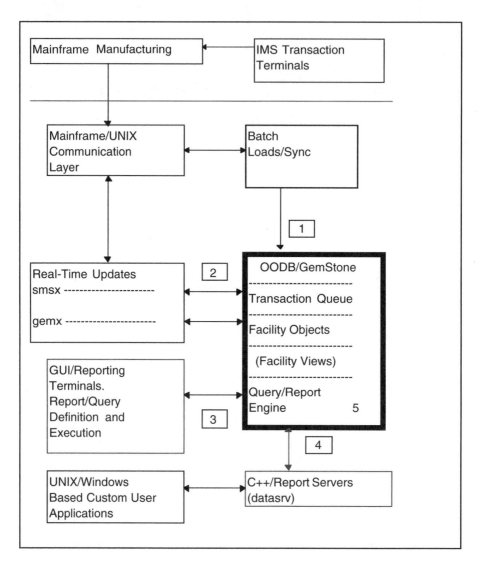

Figure 16–1   Distributed reporting application architecture.

a critical time such as after a hardware failure or other system failure. The online
updates programs (smsx and gemx), take messages from the mainframe (smsx), and
load the information into the facility objects (gemx). These two operations generate
the most new objects in the system. Updates are random to the collections. Once the
information is loaded, then it is available for reporting from either GUI interface (3)
or a report server (4). Either interface uses the Query/Report engine, which uses the
View system to access the information. The application is basically a single updater
with many readers.

This chapter will describe the steps taken to improve and stabilize the performance of the DR application. Initial test of the completed application indicated serious problems with report performance. An additional problem was that performance was unstable. In one report case, a report might run in 15–20 seconds for one user while the same report for another user might take 120–200 seconds. As the number of users increased, so did the problem of unstable performance. After system resource, hardware, and OS configuration problems were eliminated as causes, potential problems with the application and OODB were examined. Once performance within the application was dealt with, then performance based on OODB and application interaction was looked at. This part of the performance tuning involved such items as application commit rates and size and clustering frequency. The last major item to be examined during the testing phase of the application was specific tuning factors of the OODB.

Performance Criteria

The performance requirements for each of the parts of the application were determined based on legacy system performance. The main areas of concern for performance in this application are listed in Figure 16–2.

The updates to the OODB had to occur within a specified time frame based on the frequency of the data required. Queue counts on the mainframe side and on the OODB side could be measured as an indication of timeliness of the data. Queue buildups on either the mainframe side or on the OODB side indicate that the system is falling behind. The queues for this application include the IMS queue count for the feed from the mainframe (not discussed in this chapter), the queue count for placing messages directly on the OODB (smsx), and from the transaction queue to being loaded on the facility objects (gemx). Based on some initial loading, test numbers were determined for acceptable update performance. The transactions received from the mainframe also contained the time stamp of the event on the mainframe. The logs for the transactions contained the mainframe time along with the time it was processed by the smsx process. During normal loading, the updates would occur within 1–2 seconds of the actual event on the mainframe. Update frequency on the OODB under heavy loading from the mainframe would see commits of groups of ten transactions within 1–2 seconds.

> **Update from feeds.**
> **Report performance.**
> o   **Query performance.**
> o   **Report performance.**
> **Maintenance function.**

Figure 16–2 Performance areas.

The update performance requirements were determined by user requirements for data updates based on the expected usage. User requirements were that the updates be no more than 10 seconds behind the mainframe event. While the OODB application was capable of keeping up with this rate, other points of failure such as communication links could provide slowness at certain periods as well as over long distances. Those issues are not discussed in this chapter as they are issues of communication stability and speed between UNIX and mainframe systems over local and remote systems.

Query performance numbers from the mainframe were not available. Many of the reports run on the mainframe were done from preformed and presorted queries that consisted of indexes maintained by the IMS/DL1 system. Query performance or actual return of the result set for formatting to a report was measured and could be separately tuned for this application.

Report timings from the mainframe were determined by using scripts to automate and time the transactions. These data were also hand checked by manually running the transactions. Each mainframe transaction was timed for first screen return and all screens returned. These numbers were later applied to the OODB reports, which were created to measure acceptable performance. Since the report timings included query performance, the OODB application also reported a combination of query and report formatting times. The individual reports selected were determined by using programs to report the actual usage by individual sites. OODB reports were matched to the mainframe versions for selection fields and sorting and return fields. The frequency of these reports was also determined so that an expected unit of work could be set as one of the performance requirements. A unit of work was based on the current level of activity of reporting on the mainframe in a one-hour period. Graphs were developed that showed the OODB report times as a percent of the mainframe report times. This final report was used as the primary indication that the application was performing at acceptable levels.

Maintenance activities required to be run during normal production activities were also tested with regard to their effect on overall system performance. Maintenance activities include manual garbage collection (full OODB sweeps), epoch garbage collections (periodic small sweeps per session), backups, object audits, and any other activities required during normal operation of the OODB application.

APPLICATION SYSTEM TUNING

The DR application was tuned in a three-phase effort. The application code was first examined to make sure that all efforts were made to use the correct coding of methods and that the behavior for classes was in the correct place. After several passes on the application, the application was again tuned, but this time with respect to how it interacted with the target OODB. Aspects of code and method use, clustering, caches sizes, and other factors were examined and tested to see what settings would provide the best performance over the long term. Once those aspects were accounted for, the OODB environment was examined for best throughput. In some cases the application was revisited due to required changes in the other two areas. Each area is discussed below.

Application Tuning Factors

Application factors that affected performance were excessive object creation, method selection, and coding practices. Very little consideration was given to issues of object creation, loop optimizations, and data structures that gave the best performance during early development. Object creation and subsequent garbage creation is always a problem. However, selection of methods and classes to use based on speed of execution is somewhat of a moving target due to improved releases of the OODB and other system parts. The underlying object engines are evolving during the development of the application as well, which makes method selection more difficult. It was also assumed that like functionality from one class to subclass members would perform in a similar manner, which turned out not to be true.

Object Creation

Because object creation and cleanup is performed by the smalltalk environment automatically, the developers did not spend time actually thinking about memory allocation for objects and the necessity of object removal or freeing of memory. While automatic removal of dereferenced objects removes many of the possibilities for memory leaks and invalid memory references common in C/C++ programs, it can lead to excessive creation of objects that have to be cleaned up by the internal garbage collectors. Because internal garbage collectors must check the entire memory space for references to the object, this was a somewhat less efficient process than explicit memory deallocation. On small test and prototype code, the problem of object creation would not be apparent since often the tests were not run for long enough periods of time to create a problem, and the code was rarely profiled for new and garbage objects created during code testing.

To check for this type of problem in the OODB, several tools were available. To track object creation and garbage directly in the application, the ObjectInventory class provided the necessary behavior to query the types of objects found in any collection. To perform these object traces, a garbage collection was run prior to each test. The epoch garbage collection was turned off during each of the tests. Small blocks of code could be executed and then profiled in terms of execution time and number of objects created during that execution. Collecting the disconnected-Objects after each run will give an indication of what objects were generated and then thrown away during that execution.

An inventory of the objects was available to help identify the type of the objects being created. This would discover sections of code that the programmer would expect to have only one to two objects of a certain type created—the programmer might find ten to fifteen objects. While ten to fifteen objects is not much in the short term, after execution of the code 20K times each day, the garbage generated becomes significant and has serious effects on performance. It is critical that the application programmer take part in this evaluation since this person is the one more likely to see excessive numbers of objects. Object creation and execution time profiles should be included in any production level code reviews.

Using this method, we were able to determine that several objects were being created an excessive number of times during a single message processing from the mainframe. This included several instances of lot structure objects when only one should have been created. The code revealed that the initialize code would create an initial object that was replaced several methods later. Because not all mainframe messages contained one of the specific types of objects, it would not always be updated, but the full application (including the reporting part) would require that the object at least respond to appropriate message sends. The code had to be adjusted to look at the root object to see if an object already existed and just update that object rather than create a new one and test for nil objects when sending messages to sub-parts of the message object.

Initialize methods can also create problems when they are included in the **new** method for a particular class. If the developer was not aware of a custom **new** method and that it calls the initialize, the developer may also call the initialize method after the **new,** which automatically doubled the number of objects created.

Duplication of string objects was also common in the batch and online update code. The C++ code and Smalltalk code required modifications to check on existing values for simple objects such as string values, common float values, and DateTime values. The C++ code constructors were modified to not instantiate complex objects and to reference items contained in the preloaded symbol dictionary, if possible. Where possible, such objects as single characters were used rather than their String counter-parts. Objects that are special objects in the OODB should be selected when possible.

Figure 16–3 shows the results from a single one-hour execution of just one of the feed processes. The same process as was used for small code blocks was used to determine overall object creation on a process. For example, the online load process would be executed over the same one-hour set of transactions and then measure-

```
  2157  Float
  2561  DateTime
 14218  String
  3450  Other
 ----------------------------------
 22,386
```

Figure 16–3   Hour execution of a single feed process.

ments taken. The list shows objects created from information of object inventory. It was determined from this list that a significant reduction in object creation could be achieved if many of the string, float, and date/time objects were preallocated in the OODB and then referenced by the feed program as they came in from messages. Figure 16–4 shows the list of string object values and how many times they occurred within the one-hour run. Most of the string values were predictable based on the facility information and could be preloaded.

Strings such as "MLA" (facility names), single-letter status flags ("P," "N," etc.), four-digit number strings (logpoints), and transaction codes could be preloaded to save a large number of objects. From this one-hour run of data, 7,666 objects could be saved if only the obvious ones are loaded into the symbol table.

After reporting the actual date/time values, it was discovered that the values occurred in groups of three or multiples of three. The mainframe transaction sent several date/time fields in each message that represented different information but were very often the same date/time value (passed date/time values were only reported down to seconds to the application from the mainframe application). Code was modified in the C++ program to store each date/time for a transaction and not create a new one if that value had already been processed. Float values showed a similar pattern. Of 2,125 floats created during the run, 1,886 of them were zero value.

The batch load programs were modified to first scan all the incoming information and create a symbol table of common strings. Just removing the majority of duplicate string object creation reduced the overall object creation by two-thirds. The reduction in objects created by smsx also helped the performance and reduced the garbage generated by gemx. Gemx created garbage by replacing strings in current objects with new values received from smsx. Very often the same value string

String Objects			
Value	**Count**	**Value**	**Count**
0200	77	FTS	115
4800	107	0000	757
W06	240	0120	255
0300	111	8	108
0180	116	P	856
SI2	811	MLA	964
705	186	1000	723
N	596	0295	124
2120	176	2950	171
3150	95	W03	1082
W13	166	063700	101

Figure 16–4   Occurrences of string objects.

strings			
Value	**Count**	**Value**	**Count**
MLA	72	0012	74
P	270	0000	277
0010	37	SI2	202
W03	306	633	21
FTS	47	N	267
W13	86		

Figure 16–5   Common garbage values.

was being replaced (just a new object). Having common values pointed to by smsx and gemx, reduced the garbage on both processes. The common values that turned up as garbage in processing the same messages as listed in smsx data tables are shown in Figure 16–5. There were 451 date/time objects removed, of which at least 50 percent would be redundant. During this same run, 660 zero value floats were garbage.

Code

Code profiling for percent of execution time by methods allows the application to be analyzed in small groups to attempt to isolate method calls that seem to take more than their share of time. The two most common problems were loop optimizations and selection of nonoptimized methods within the OODB Smalltalk. Additional problems also revolved around the use of the **perform:** method. Extensive recoding of the query and reporting engine to generate blocks rather than use the performs was necessary. This may be a common practice in smalltalk programming [Pir96].

Loop optimizations occurred in the most simple form as well as optimizations over a series of message sends (Figure 16–6). The code in Figure 16–6 shows that it is very easy to simply make message sends that are effectively constants for that single execution within a loop structure. The **SMSSystem runDt** message retrieves the run DateTime stored when the report started. If one was not there, it created a new DateTime and returned that value. The same DateTime should appear on each message send. The lower block of code shows the corrected loop code. While the message send itself may be relatively cheap, it cannot be optimized out by the compiler in Smalltalk since the receiver is dynamically determined with each loop. The programmer would have to know if the receiver is always the same. An additional problem was discovered when a harmless message send from one class method results in the invocation of several message sends to other objects below as well as possible calculations. In this example, the **runDt** method would actually produce a different date on each execution and not only produce incorrect results but also pro-

```
|result|
result := Set new.
aSet do: [:each |
   (each startDate = SMSSystem runDt)
   ifTrue:[resultadd: each]
   ].
^result.

| runDt result|
result: = Set new.
runDt : = SMSSystem runDt.
1 to: aSet size
  do: [:count| | item |
        item := aSet at : count.
        (itemstartDate = runDt)
        ifTrue:[ resultadd: item]
      ].
^result.
```

Figure 16–6   Loop optimization code example.

duce hundreds and thousands of DateTime objects. Thus, a simple single message send can add many ms to the execution. The programmer must be aware of the depth of the execution when using either application methods or system methods. The problem can be compounded when the application may create several layers of methods.

Performance problems may be related to the selection of methods that are not optimized from the vendor. The looping construct shown in Figure 16–6 is one example. It turned out that the looping structure (**n to: m do:**), executes faster than the **<object> do:** construct. Within the OODB smalltalk, several methods were typically available to perform basically the same function. In some cases this involved methods that did not create new objects during their operation, but more often the performance differences were determined by the use of low level primitive calls rather than direct execution in the native language. Many of the math functions for conversion were determined to show this characteristic and in some cases, even a series of message sends involved primitives executed many times faster than a single method invocation executed in Smalltalk. Figure 16–7 shows some of the pairs of slow and fast methods as determined at the time of this application. The **asNumber** method was many times slower than using the combination message send of **asFloat asInteger**. The second set of methods is faster because it allows the program-

```
<aString> asNumber
<aString> asFloat asInteger

<aString> copyFrom:To:
<aString> copyFrom:To:into:startingAt:

<aString> + <string>
<aString> add: <string>
```

Figure 16–7   Some slow and fast methods.

mer to pass in his or her own string object and take advantage of the dynamically sizable String object in GemStone[1]. Many of these differences will be removed when the vendor supplies native code execution for the compiled Smalltalk.

The **perform:** method was found to very slow if used in any looping or iterative processing. This problem became clearer in the query and report formatting code when executed on nonindexed or otherwise nonoptimized fields. While the perform is useful for testing ideas and small code fragments, it cannot actually be used in production level code. The query and report formatting code was modified to generate direct message sends by creating code blocks for each of the major parts of the query or report format. The report formatting code can generate the code at report definition time, but the query code must be generated at run time due to the flexibility in the query engine. Even with the additional overhead of the compiler, the query times would go from 15–20 seconds over a 20K collection to 1–2 seconds for a result to be returned on a nonoptimized or nonindexed query. Individual view fields could also be optimized to provide faster access and calculations in some cases. Additional work on the view application may provide additional speed enhancements [KR95]. Specialized sort view fields were created to sort on what the end user considered a calculation field but was really using a static field. This minor change reduced that particular report by 15–20 seconds.

The general performance of collection classes relative to the type of use expected must be considered during development. As a general policy, **OrderedCollection** was used when dynamic collections were to be added to. Since GemStone supported a dynamically sized **Array** class, this was found to be better and faster for most uses where **OrderedCollection** was used. In this case it would have been better to look carefully at the capabilities of the classes being used. GemStone also supported a dynamically sized **String** class that significantly reduces the object cre-

---

[1]GemStone is a registered trademark of GemStone Systems, Inc.

ation during string building for formatting reports and other activities. This Gem-Stone feature allowed the reduction in object creation overhead as well as object garbage collection. Since the standard was to use "+" or "," to build strings in Smalltalk, most of the code using these methods had to be changed to take advantage of the dynamically sized string classes. Collection classes that permitted indexes to be built could also modify the schema of the application. If the designer was unaware of index availability in the OODB while building the application, there could be serious performance problems with individual implementations of indexing and collection class usage.

Monitoring of the new and total objects committed statistics allowed the progress of removing excessive objects to be measured without additional code added to the application code. Data produced by the statmonitor program provided by GemStone allowed the specific tracking of new objects committed and total objects committed to the database. Each successive modification to reduce the objects created was measured by gathering these statistics during test runs based on a standard set of transactions received from the mainframe. Figures 16–8 and 16–9 show the output of two very different parts of the feed program for the two statistics just mentioned. The statistics are useful for showing the numbers of objects produced during execution but do not help with identification of what the objects are or any other details about the objects. It would be useful for the statmonitor to produce some numbers about the class of objects being produced during debugging stages of code development.

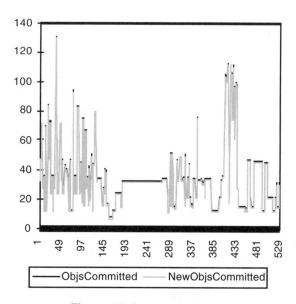

Figure 16–8   smsx Commits.

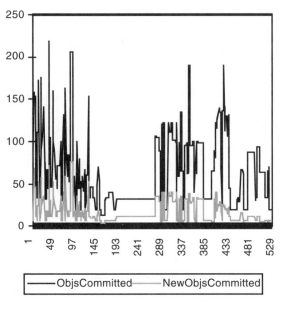

Figure 16–9   gemx Commits.

Application/OODB Tuning Factors

Application/OODB tuning factors are factors that are really OODB design specific that must be accounted for in the application design. While each OODB may have the same concepts of clustering, shared cache, and commit record sizes, each must be dealt with based on those OODB characteristics. The attention paid to these parameters is not trivial and can have profound effects on application performance.

Commit Rate and Size

The commit strategies for this application changed based on the version of GemStone they were run with. In original versions of the application, transactions were grouped into large commits to take advantage of the design of the OODB. Profiles were taken to establish an optimum commit size under that architecture. We had to later modify the application feed and batch loading programs to reduce the size of commits due to changes in the design of GemStone.

The size of commits is based on the number of objects either created or updated during a message processing event. We were able to reduce the size of commits by a reduction in the number of objects being created for the transaction loading program (smsx). The creation of the symbol table with preloaded values contributed significantly to this reduction. Based on hit rates for current running sites, the online feed processes have about an 85 to 90 percent hit rate for string ob-

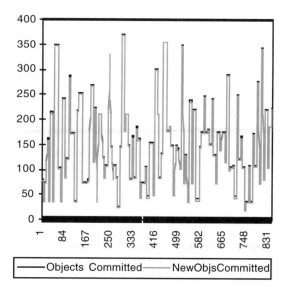

Figure 16–10   smsx Commit (old).

jects from the symbol table. Comparing the maximum objects committed on Figure 16–8 to those on Figure 16–10 shows the improvement made by the addition of the String object symbol table.

We also added parameters within the application that could be adjusted during execution to modify the commit sizes if the system was getting behind in processing. The batch load process had commits placed in various functional positions within the code. The commits could be adjusted based on objects processed. The commit changes resulted in a 50 percent decrease in the time to batch load the data. The online feeds also have adjustable commit rates, but the time requirements from the customer actually drive the commit frequency on these programs.

While the statmonitor provided by GemStone provides a good way to track information based on fixed intervals of time, a transaction/commit-based statistics monitor was necessary to obtain information about the behavior of each of the processes. This would allow the determination of the specific number of objects dealt with during any one single commit/transaction boundary. A user primitive was added to a relinked special executable that could be called from specified places in the code. While this did require application coding modifications, it could be easily removed for production code. The goal of this monitoring was to keep the number of objects added to the OODB on each commit relatively small. The difference in the maximum total objects committed shown in Figure 16–8 versus Figure 16–10 shows the relative success in reduction.

Clustering

Clustering of objects within the OODB is vital to the long-term performance of any application. It will reduce the number of pages required to hold the information that must be accessed by any user session. This can reduce the cache requirements for each session and reduce physical growth of the OODB if the clustering can be maintained. Clustering of information is broken down into several different areas, which are shown in Figure 16–11. Each of the categories was assigned a different cluster bucket on the OODB.

Static application objects are any application classes and methods, static collections of objects, and related objects that are basically loaded when the application logic is loaded. When the majority of the behavior is in the OODB, the application code and classes and any associated static data can be clustered and protected from movement on a production OODB. Each time a new release of the application was fanned out, all of the application classes and behavior were clustered as they were loaded. Static facility data such as the above mentioned string value symbol table were clustered along with the other data loaded at install time at each site.

The dynamic application data must be considered as a separate issue. The remaining four categories deal with application data that may be written while the application is in production. When application objects are modified or added to the OODB, they are written onto new pages in the OODB. This creates a special problem for the clustering of frequently updated data. Clustering of the dynamic data within the application did not follow class definitions. During the initial loading of the facility objects, the objects are clustered according to the expected access and update patterns for each item. The clustering scheme must also consider whether the object is a separate object or an object that may be shared by other objects in the same class. Additional special clustering can be done when information about the object header is known. Some objects are stored directly on the header of the object and as such do not require any clustering above that done for the parent object. Other instance variables on that object will be stored separately, regardless of the their size. Thus, the clustering mechanism was further modified to skip any objects that are always stored with the object header.

o **Static application objects.**
o **Frequently updated.**
o **Static information.**
o **Updated rarely but reported on frequently.**
o **Updated rarely and reported on rarely.**

Figure 16–11   Clustering categories.

Objects for the application were placed into each of the categories based on the following criteria. Objects that tended to be updated frequently (1–2 times/ minute) were only clustered on demand or when performance of the reporting application was affected. Static information is information that would be only loaded at object instantiation, and committed information was clustered at initial loading time and then was not included in the real-time clustering. Within each of these categories some objects were maintained as pointers into another collection that might be pointed to by other objects. For example, lot objects contain the pointers to device objects, which are clustered separately as a collection. As the lot is clustered, no attempt is made to cluster any device information with the lot data. Special clustering methods were added to each class to account for information that might be stored as pointers.

Clustering effectiveness was measured in several different ways. The effectiveness of clustering the static application objects was measured by tracking the number of pages required to read in or access the classes and methods. In this case, fewer pages for most of the methods was better. Using methods that are described in [Alm96] and using methods specifically designed to cluster class information, the application code was compacted on the OODB.

For the application data, simply counting the pages the objects occupied was not sufficient. The primary approach was to measure report times under different clustering schemes on initial loading in both cold and warm conditions of the OODB. This method provides an end user view of the results of clustering the data. For this test a complete set of reports that covered the known patterns of access for this data was required. This method of measuring clustering was also used when the data were being updated. This gives some measure of how fragmented the data are becoming on the OODB. During this evaluation, testing must be done on both cold and hot OODBs.

GemStone provides some additional statistics to measure clustering of data in terms of total space required. For each process, the pages read/written can be measured and used as a meter of how disperse the data have become. This is only good for measurement during "cache up" periods and cannot be used after some percentage of the data are contained in the shared cache. Another useful tool is the report of how many pages have some percentage of space available. This can be run during application execution and provide some indication of fragmentation of the data in the OODB.

There are two major problems with implementing clustering and keeping free space down in GemStone. Clustering in GemStone is done at the application request and may involve the movement of many additional objects. Its effect on the other applications running in the OODB can be dramatic if shared objects are being moved to other OODB pages during the clustering. Figure 16–12 shows the pattern of objects committed to the OODB during clustering of application objects. Compare that chart with Figure 16–9. The chart shows that while the normal commit of objects for the gemx process ranges between 100–200 objects per commit (Figure 16–9), after a clustering activity the number of objects committed ranged from 20K to 25K objects. This problem manifested itself as reduced report performance and expanded processing and commit time for the process doing the clustering.

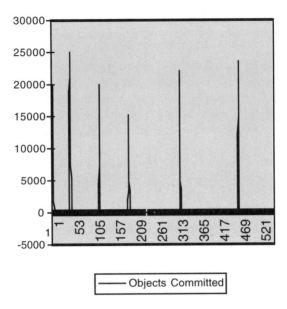

Figure 16–12   Objects committed during clustering of application objects.

The clustering of application objects would be better handled by an outside process that kept the objects constantly regrouped based on clusterBucket id or some other additional information about each object. However, the act of moving objects around on OODB pages and the act of actually updating the objects (gemx) cause commit conflicts between the two processes. The OODB handles the commit conflicts correctly as far as a generic solution to the problem, but in this case we require that the gemx process always win in any conflicts with the clustering process. The reason for this is that the gemx process has a narrow window of time to commit transactions received from the mainframe and the compression of objects on pages is really a background maintenance activity.

As a result of this problem, the clustering of individual objects within the OODB was revisited to reduce the number of objects clustered at any one time. The final result was to cluster only those objects that had been updated and to only cluster the relatively small amount of objects updated each time. This required some additional code for the feed application to track what objects it updated until they were processed by the cluster methods. Initially, we had tried to cluster parts of the root set of objects based on a transaction count, but even doing small percentages of the collection proved to be too much to take in terms of performance losses (Figure 16–12). In some cases, for some facilities, it was decided that no clustering would be done at all since the lifetime of the objects involved was only a few days. However, other facilities reported objects that lasted over longer periods of time with the potential to contribute to the fragmentation of the OODB and reduced reporting performance.

Cache Requirements

The two major C++ processes (smsx and datasrv—and GUI reporting) behaved in very different ways with respect to the OODB. The smsx process takes large numbers of relatively small messages from the mainframe and turns them into objects that are placed on a transaction queue. This transaction queue is processed by the gemx process, which is a Smalltalk-based process. Nearly all the objects created by smsx are committed to the OODB. The datasrv process is responsible for processing report requests from other processes and users. This process never actually commits to the OODB. It runs outside of a transaction during most of its processing. While it does not create very many new objects, it can create one very large object—the report output text string.

Both programs were monitored for their interaction with the OODB in terms of objects committed to the OODB (new and total objects). For any C/C++ process the **exportSetSize** must also be monitored and periodically dealt with by specifically flushing objects present in both memory spaces. The **exportSetSize** will cause OODB growth especially on long-running feed processes if not correctly taken care of. The **makeRoomInOldSpace** parameter can be used to adjust **tempObjCache** for each process. This statistic indicates the number of objects that were temporary objects but were moved to the OODB anyway. The **disconnectedObjects** statistic was important for the datasrv process. This statistic is mostly used to monitor large objects being moved from client space to OODB space due to an 8 K preset limit on object size. Objects larger than 8 K will automatically get moved to the OODB page.

The smsx process will commit large numbers of relatively small objects to the OODB relatively quickly. The **makeRoomInOldSpace** parameter for this process never showed any objects. Additional tests were run to determine the least amount of memory required for this process to run under a variety of loading conditions. This process also had a very small collection in the OODB to reference when it added messages to the transaction queue. This queue under normal conditions was never over five to ten messages. Additional efforts may be looked at to reuse IMS messages from a pool of IMS message objects. As necessary, these additional steps will be taken.

The C++ servers were modified to save the allocation of known objects, which would be common during the execution of the processes. Information that stayed the same during execution included such items as facility name, server names, and message type. These objects—which were considered constants or rarely changed—were assigned C++ memory and then not reinitialized on each message. This reduced the object count created on each pass and reduced the problems downstream for the epoch and full sweep garbage collectors.

The report windowing interface required the same level of monitoring but required a different level of cache for temporary objects due to the windows and supporting widgets for the interface. The datasrv and GUI reporting interfaces require access to large collections. Additional statistics on cache hits and misses were monitored to judge the effectiveness of both the shared cache and the local and private caches for these processes.

OODB Tuning Factors

Backups

Backup and maintenance of hot backup systems was implemented with as little impact to the production system as possible. The backup process was given as much private cache as possible. Backup files were maintained on a separate disk from either the OODB file or the transactions logs so that no I/O interference with the report or feed processes would happen. Improvements in the time for a backup to happen have made it easier to schedule them more frequently. The scheduled times are mostly dependent on site requirements for recovery time should a disk failure occur or some other disaster that would necessitate the use of a backup. After these minor adjustments, the backup was not typically a factor in any performance problems as long as it did not run during other heavy maintenance activities.

Garbage Collection

Two types of garbage collection mechanisms are available in GemStone. The epoch garbage collection is a process that runs all the time for each session. It scans local memory for objects created and then disconnected (or dead) within a specified time window. This provides a constant sweep of temporary objects or short-lived objects created by applications. The full sweep of the OODB is the other type of garbage collection. It is run as a separate process, usually in batch mode based on some schedule appropriate for the activity at the site.

Even with the two different schemas available for garbage collection, the most effective garbage collection in terms of performance is not to generate it in the first place. After every effort is made to reduce the waste generated by processes, then tuning the garbage collector must take place. The basic strategy is to even out performance to the end user. The performance of the two garbage collection processes has improved over several releases, but the actual performance hit for the application comes during the time when each process must "vote" on all the marked garbage. If this is a large amount, then these processes could become busy for several minutes and give the appearance of being dead or hung. The epoch garbage collector was tuned to be busy all the time in small increments. This provides a small amount of garbage to be voted on each time and provides the reclaim process with steady work. This may not provide the best performance possible, but it does provide predictable performance.

The full OODB sweep was configured to pull as much of the OODB into memory as possible. The primary monitoring here was of the system memory available so that the full sweep did not interfere with any other processes but took advantage of the available memory. The local cache size for this was set to about 0.25 of the shared memory allocated for the application.

Application/OODB Monitoring

Monitoring

A combination of statistics must be proactive on problems if they occur. Execution statistics were found to be valuable in monitoring the long-term system performance. Output from the epoch garbage collector and the mark for collection (full sweep) were kept and reported on to look for changes in number of objects collected. The epoch garbage collection statistics did require the creation of objects in the OODB and could produce some additional load on the system. Under normal conditions these statistics were not run for that reason. It would be better if the statistics were output to a logging file. Report logs from the application could be turned on with a flag and generate a file that can be reported for comparison report times. GemStone also provides an external statistics gathering that can be run over some sample period and provides information about each process. Special executables could also be put in place to provide transaction-based GemStone statistics and the debugging code is only activated when those executables containing special routines were present.

Maintenance

The two primary activities that are required to take place during normal operation are clustering of objects and defragmentation of objects (**scavengePageWithPercentFree**) on pages in the OODB. Both of these operations cause write conflicts with processes that may be updating objects that are involved in being moved. For these activities, the clustering and scavenge operation would be better executed similarly to the epoch garbage collector and run basically all the time based on some set of application parameters or supplied methods. Under the current environment this was impossible to do.

EXPERIENCES AND SUMMARY

The overall result of the tuning effort was that it brought the application within the specification of the user. Under most circumstances it out performed the mainframe application. Figure 16–13 shows the normalized comparisons of mainframe versus DR reports. Query performance was improved 3.5 times, and in all cases it was as fast as hand-coded queries. Queries that ran for 30–40 seconds were running in 4–7 seconds for standard accesses (message sends) to large collections (12–17K). Queries using indexing usually ran from under 1 second to around 2 seconds. Report performance (formatting and sorting) was improved to be as fast as hand-coding output. The report that was significantly slower than the mainframe (Rpt 3) was a report that took less than 1–2 seconds total time on the mainframe. While we usually displayed the same result in 1.5–2 seconds, it was still slower than the mainframe for a finished display. For longer reports, we also made some adjustments to

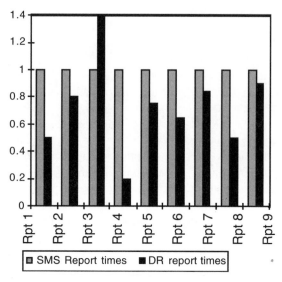

Figure 16–13   Normalized report times.

the display in X-windows so that the code would only display the first screen if requested. The rest of the report would then be formatted in the background while the user was viewing the first page or two.

To obtain this type of performance from the OODB, extensive recoding of certain areas was necessary. Once code was changed, then changes to the application to handle specific features of the OODB were made. Finally, changes in the OODB parameters that controlled the activities of the applications as well as the OODB activities were made.

With the cache adjustments, the processing time for such processes as the batch load, sync, and backups was improved significantly. Just adjusting the cache sizes would account for a 50 percent improvement in processing time for some of the processes. With correctly placed commits and increases in local and temp caches, the batch load was improved from an 8 hour run to 1.5 hours for the same facility information.

Currently the tools to help find problems such as mentioned above are very limited. These tools must be available to help the developer tune the overall application as well as parts of the application during the development phase rather than during the testing phases. Code profilers are useful for execution problems but often do not suggest the real problem, which may be excessive object creation. Object profilers would be a useful tool addition to the developers. Very large overall gains with regard to long-term performance were achieved when developers became aware of the type and value of many of the objects being generated. The developers could then take steps to eliminate objects that were being created in large numbers with the same values.

Maintenance activities as described above were very difficult if not impossible to execute on a 24 x 7 x 365 production system. Big improvements in the long-term performance will be gained when these activities can be performed by processes without interruption of the application code. In high update applications such as DR, OODB pages and objects are constantly being created and moved, which rapidly begins to show in performance measures.

The involvement of a project DBA/OODB person is very important to get optimum performance from the application. This person must be involved in every phase of the application to avoid massive rewrites of the code and should be able to suggest coding, class usage, and other methods that would make each part of the application more efficient. Developers must also be more knowledgeable on the internals of the OODB such as data structures to use under certain conditions and what methods are good and which are bad. Simple timing information for common operations on collection classes and mathematical operations on Numbers and DateTime objects could be supplied as part of the overall documentation about the OODB. The DBA should be in the role of providing this information to the developers. S/he should also be involved in performance testing various areas of the OODB for new optimum behavior. Developers are typically very knowledgeable about domain information and how it is accessed but require some tools to help suggest better use of the features of a particular OODB.

REFERENCES

[Alm96] J. Almarode: *Tuning Multi-user Smalltalk*. The Smalltalk Report, 5 (6), 18, 1996.

[KR95] A. Kuno, E. A. Rundensteiner: *The MultiView OODB View System: Design and Implementation*. Accepted by Special Issue of Theory and Practice of Object Systems (TAPOS) on Subjectivity in Object Oriented Systems, 1995.

[Pir96] K. Piraino: *A Performance Challenge*. The Smalltalk Report, 5 (6), 4, 1996.

17

Performance Evaluation and Optimization for a Financial OODB Application

Alexander Jaehne, Union Bank of Switzerland

ABSTRACT

The author is working as a database architect for the Union Bank of Switzerland in Zurich. The product under development is a backoffice system that is designed with Objectory, developed in Smalltalk, and has ObjectStore for Smalltalk, Version 2.0, as its object-oriented database system. ObjectStore for Smalltalk (OSST) was based on a wrapper of ObjectStore for C++ [DS96].

Essentially, our system gets Deals from the frontoffice and does typical bank backoffice processing such as booking, paying, and confirming Deals, matching incoming confirmations or enabling backoffice staff to validate and to change Deal contents. The goal of the project is to replace a suite of different backoffice systems with a customizable system that can be installed in many trading branches of the bank. Key issues are increasing automation and reducing maintenance cost. Volume is expected to read up to 12,000 Deals a day, each Deal being a complex data structure, consisting of many objects and references to other data in existing relational databases.

INTRODUCTION

The theoretical performance capabilities of object-oriented database systems are considerably higher than relational database systems for many application domain areas. Various reasons contribute to this. The most important one is that traversal between objects is faster than accessing via keys and having to perform joins between relations. However, many users have found out that this promise does not always hold true. What are the reasons for this? We experienced the lack of expertise with physical database design and performance evaluation and optimization as the main reasons. One has to understand the specifics of object-oriented database systems (ODDBs), such as different access types, limited querying capabilities, explicit extent maintenance, or the importance of object clustering to avoid performance drawbacks before OODBs can fulfill their performance promise.

Physical design of object databases and their integration with software development methodology are discussed elsewhere [Byu95, GF95, Cas+95]. A good series of articles on object-oriented database design issues based on experience with GemStone can be found in the Smalltalk Report [Alm95]. This chapter will concentrate on how we evaluated the performance of an object-oriented database with limited effort and give directions on how this data can be used for optimization purposes. Our goal is to present an approach for evaluating performance with respect to execution time. We do not, however, discuss OODB-specific and OODB release-specific issues such as client and server cache size or locking algorithms used.

Because of our background, many suggestions are particularly applicable to developers of general business type applications. We hope this chapter helps practitioners to move a step closer to the performance promised for object-oriented databases.

DATABASE ACCESS TYPES

Performance evaluation starts with monitoring database accesses. In object-oriented database systems there are two fundamentally different types of accesses: navigational access and associative access. *Navigational access* (i.e., performing pointer traversal) is the primary reason for performance gains of OODBs over relational database systems (RDBs). This is a physical address and no hash table lookup is necessary for following a reference in the database. *Associative access* means finding objects based on certain properties. This usually involves querying all instances of a certain class (the class extent). OODBs do not provide a common approach for associative access requirements. In fact, some OODBs provide little or no support at all. Clearly, OODBs that do not provide index functionality or support for large collections can only be used for a restricted range of applications. OSST provides nested queries and indexes based on B-trees or hash tables.

We are not developing a technical application where navigation access is central but a typical financial business-type application with frequent associative accesses.

GENERAL DIRECTIONS

Where to Optimize

Performance optimization should be done in parts of the code where optimization yields maximum overall performance gain. What is needed for this is an operational profile that describes how the system is used. We spent most of our optimization effort on the use cases (loosely speaking, the functions of the system) that are executed most often, as their performance determines the overall performance of our system.

What to Look For

Performance optimization should be concentrated on database accesses where high performance gains are likely. With OODBs, this is mostly with associative accesses. Navigational access is very fast, so only rewriting a large number of those accesses didn't make any performance differences. However, we found that there are a lot of areas where we were able to increase performance for associative accesses, such as for lists with many entries where certain access patterns execute multiple times for each entry.

LEVELS OF COLLECTING STATISTICAL DATA

Transaction Level

The atomic level for collecting statistical data is the transaction level. Sometimes it is quite difficult to map statistical data to appropriate parts in the code. To overcome this we found it very helpful to associate each transaction in the database with a unique name. This can be done by extending the transaction API with a parameter for the name.

An important issue for collecting statistical data for transactions is that while being in a transaction, the application is not necessarily working with the database all the time. In fact, the application might be busy with internal computations. Tools such as the ObjectStore Performance Expert can be used to measure how much time within a transaction is spent on database accesses. We will come back to this issue later.

Use Case Level

Transaction boundaries are not always clear. Therefore, there should be a coarser unit of measure which can be a use case, for example. Jacobson [Jac92] defines a use case as a description of a behaviorally related sequence of transactions (not necessarily database transactions) in a dialogue with the system. We found that for most use cases it made sense to collect statistical data such as overall transaction time, overall execution time, or number of pages read/written.

Choosing use cases as a unit to measure performance is only one possibility, of course, and is due to the fact that we modeled according to Jacobson and already had use cases defined that specify rather complex operations. We also do simple workflow processing and have numerous workflow process definitions. It was natural to monitor overall database access for workflow process instances during process execution as well.

Using use cases and workflow process definitions enables us to make test cases for database performance easily repeatable. We can specify, for example, that the use case "inception processing" for a Money Market Deal takes on average x seconds (y seconds of which within a transaction) and n pages are read and m pages are written. Creating transaction logs for our use cases and the workflow process definitions is an ideal basis for performance optimization.

PERFORMANCE ANALYSIS TOOLS

This section shows how we collect statistical information for performance analysis. We partially automated this process using two different tools. One is called Transaction Monitor and has been developed here in Zurich. The other is called Object-Store Performance Expert and is sold by ODI. We will concentrate on the tool's principles to make this section applicable for users of other OODBs, too.

UBS Transaction Monitor and Perl Scripts

The Transaction Monitor developed at UBS collects the following properties for a transaction:

- Duration in ms
- Type of transaction (R = Read, W = Write)
- A short unique description for each transaction intercepted

Optional information includes the id of the Smalltalk thread that started the transaction, the number of pages that were read/written for each transaction, and the number of retries due to deadlock.

The user can select a line and request to see the place in the code where the transaction is defined. He or she can manipulate and filter the transaction list, saving the list or a section of it. Furthermore, it is possible to define breakpoints so execution stops and the Smalltalk debugger is opened the next time the selected transaction is executed. This is useful, because the Smalltalk environment offers no breakpoint construct. The breakpoint functionality avoids inserting "self halts" into the code that would get logged by the code management tool unnecessarily.

Figure 17–1 illustrates the information displayed by the Transaction Monitor. New entries are added to the top so the user always see the latest transactions. Lines with no duration time but the word "event" in them indicate customizable events such as the beginning or the ending of a workflow process instance.

The Transaction Monitor's implementation is simple and basically consists of two parts. The first part is a wrapper for the OODB's Transaction API. We intercept each transaction call and collect all the data we need. The second part is the Transaction Monitor application itself, which displays the information to the user. Both parts communicate via the Smalltalk dependency mechanism to ensure loose coupling/minimal intrusion.

We intend to use the Transaction Monitor for distributed analysis, too. Therefore, the wrapper and the Transaction Monitor will communicate via a socket so that server processes can be debugged as well.

We use Perl Scripts to create lists of all transactions with min/max/average execution times and number of pages fetched. Those scripts are essential to condense the information collected over a longer period of time or to compare old traces with new traces of the same "performance test case," that is, a well-defined use case, to detect degradation in performance over time.

Monitoring overhead is acceptable (less than 30 ms per transaction in our case, including updating the list) unless the option " number of pages read/written" is selected.

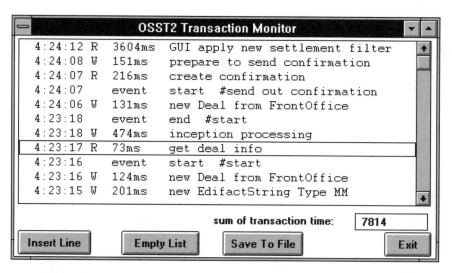

Figure 17–1   Typical performance analysis with the Transaction Monitor.

ObjectStore Performance Expert (OPE)

Performance Analysis with OPE starts with tracing your application. A special component called the OPE Receiver collects the required information during program execution and writes it into a trace file.

After this trace phase has been finished, the OPE Analyzer can be started using the formerly created trace file. Next, the database analyst will get a top level view of the application run in the OPE Analyzer window (Figure 17–2). In this timeline diagram, the user can navigate through the trace, seeing transaction boundaries and various database client metrics. Those metrics displayed in the top third of the window may include: pages fetched for read or write, pages refetched, pages flushed, deadlocks, timeouts, or cache hit rate. The goal is to identify parts that might have performance problems. Usually, this requires getting into further detail. Therefore, the user can select a single transaction and analyze it, for example, using the Elapsed Time Diagram (Figure 17–3), which displays in a pie chart what processing categories contribute to the total elapsed time of the transaction. Those categories include: fetching data, opening or closing a transaction, page evictions, or non-database related processing such as application algorithms.

Other interesting features of OPE include page state diagrams that show a trace based on different storage levels and information on paging and locking events. Last, but not least, it is possible to create transaction summary files with various metrics for each transaction traced.

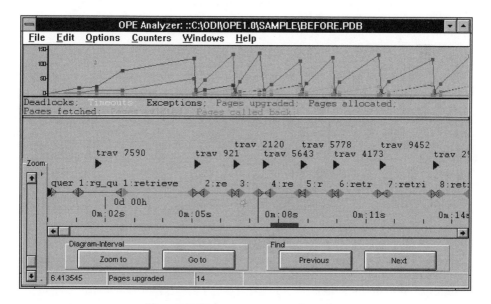

Figure 17–2   OPE Analyzer snapshot.

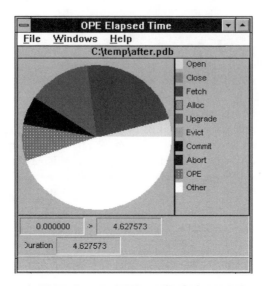

Figure 17–3   OPE Elapsed Time diagram.

OPTIMIZATION AREAS

In this section, we have listed areas where we did most of our performance optimization. Those can be considered representative for a typical OODB business application.

Use Object References, Not Foreign Keys

It is essential to understand that the performance potential of OODB is not reached if object links are implemented via foreign keys that require an index lookup or worse, a sequential scan. This is an important issue if a database design which was developed for a relational database is used as a starting point. Instead of foreign keys, object references should be used to take advantage of the navigational access capabilities of OODBs. This should dramatically increase performance and reduce the numbers of pages fetched.

Select Appropriate Transaction Boundaries

Choosing very-wide transaction boundaries usually has no negative effect in single-user systems. This has to be kept in mind when doing initial performance analysis in a single-user environment. However, concurrent applications are greatly affected by wide transaction boundaries because locks are held for long periods of time. This issue is even more important in OODBs such as ObjectStore, which use page locking as opposed to object locking for ensuring isolation and consistency of transactions. That is, not only single objects are locked, but all objects on the same page.

Concurrency problems are noticeable by high variances in response time and a general system slowdown whenever the number of OSST clients is increased. Detecting hot spots for concurrent access that cause lock contention is not easy. A possibility is to analyze transaction summaries created by Perl scripts or by ObjectStore Performance Expert (OPE) to find out which transactions have deadlocks or timeouts. When critical transactions are identified, OPE may be used to determine what are the hot spots in those transactions.

According to our experience, the following data structures are common hot spots:

- Metadata in the schema segment, for example, during object allocation and deallocation
- Extent collections
- Indexes

We use four strategies to reduce lock contention:

- Make sure hot spots are on separate pages so they never get locked together.
- Acquire locks as late as possible within each transaction.
- Use a special kind of accessing mode of ObjectStore, called multiversion concurrency control (MVCC), so read transactions are never blocked. However, the tradeoff is that the view of the database as seen by the transaction might not be up to date. This mode can be useful for certain background batch functions or time-consuming GUI support transactions.
- Use narrow transaction boundaries, potentially splitting transactions. This is especially attractive if many non-database related operations are done within the transaction boundaries. This strategy might slightly increase the amount of data transferred in the absence of concurrency.

While short transactions are generally desirable, we found that we had to take great care when narrowing transaction boundaries. This is because we use the atomicity property of the transaction to ensure that the database always goes from one consistent state to another. The following pattern can be useful when a write transaction takes too much time and creates concurrency problems: replace the write transaction by a read transaction where we copy the needed data into memory, followed by the time-consuming calculations, and a write transaction to write back the result. The overhead of this pattern is one more read transaction and additional data transfer.

Too many short transactions can also reduce performance, because of high transaction overheads. We did not experience this overhead anywhere as high as Goodman did with some apparently older version of ObjectStore [Goo95]. He was forced to commit periodically every 10 minutes to avoid high transaction overheads.

Reuse Instances to Avoid Frequent Object Creation and Deletion

Multiple users in our application get the same list of business Deals that need manual intervention. The users then take any Deal, open a detail window, and specify missing payment or booking instructions for it. Clearly, only one user should be allowed to work on the same Deal at any point in time. We therefore came up with an approach called "semantic locking" where we log business objects such as Deals, Confirmations, or Payments as being "owned" by a certain entity. This entity can be a user as well as the Workflow Engine that performs processing based on workflow process definitions. Although creating and deleting a semantic lock takes only a short period of time, performance analysis using Perl scripts showed that the total time per Deal processed was noticeable. In these transactions, we constantly created and deleted objects, which took time and increased fragmentation of our database. We tackled this problem by predefining empty slots for semantic locks, which we also reused. Instead of deleting old locks and creating new ones, we defined a semantic lock controller that marked them internally as scratched when they were no longer used and reused them later. The result of this optimization has been a reduction in execution time as well as in the number of objects created/deleted.

Indexes for Associative Accesses

Probably the biggest performance gains can be reached by analyzing the associative accesses within the database application. Adding indexes can provide performance benefits. However, does the increase in accessing speed offset the additional update costs? In the absence of a simple cost model, only performance analysis and comparison of the index's effect can give you an objective answer. Because the presence of an index is determined automatically by ObjectStore, no change in the queries is required when adding/removing indexes.

Extent Queries

ObjectStore, like many other OODBs, does not offer automatic management of class extensions. Instead, we had to define collections for extents and maintain them when their respective instances were created or deleted. Because queries in OSST2 can only use indexes for instance variables that are common to all instances in a collection, we had to define separate extents for each Business Deal type. On the other hand, most of our queries access only attributes that are common to all Deals, such as the numerical Deal id or the "value date." Those queries would have to be translated to multiple queries against each specialization of the Deal Class's extent. That is, one query would be translated into nine subqueries whose results had to be merged. This, of course, added additional overhead. We solved this by defining an additional class-hierarchy extent to support class-hierarchy queries for our most general Deal Class. This solution was only possible because our application is more access oriented than update oriented. That is, we access the Deal extent far more often than we update it or its indexes.

Reduce Data Transfer for the GUI

Our application has a lot of user interaction, and having a good approach to avoid unnecessary data transfer between the server and the clients is important for overall performance. We decided to make transient copies of objects in the database when we opened a detail and write back data when closing the window. OSST has synchronization functions between the transient memory space and its persistent counterpart. When synchronizing these two, we did not want to do a "deepcopy" of each object structure. Rather, we defined customized copying routines that only copied data we needed for each window. When writing back to the database, we use the object's version id to avoid unnecessary writes and write back only actual differences. This optimization resulted in a reduction of the execution time as well as in the number of pages accessed.

Object Clustering

The placement of objects in the database can have a huge impact on performance. If objects that are frequently accessed together reside on the same page, fewer pages need to be accessed during retrieval and lock contention is minimized. Furthermore, less memory is needed in the client cache, resulting in a higher overall hit rate for database accesses because more data can be cached. To come up with good object placement, one needs to understand the application's access patterns. Prioritization is essential, or the developer can get easily confused, trying to take into account too many, sometimes conflicting access patterns. We found the following three observations to be important for defining our clustering strategy:

- Our Blotters, which display large lists of Deals to the user, perform queries and then do a sequential scan on the result set. Our users often filter by Deal type. This led to the definition of separate segments for each Deal type.
- Various parts of a Deal are seldom accessed, some almost never. We placed those parts in separate segments from the information that is displayed in the Blotters lists and accessed most often. This required changes in the physical database design because of the following: clustering is only possible at object level in OSST, as it is based on the C++ ObjectStore database. C++ distinguishes between literals and objects, while in Smalltalk everything is an object. As an example, our Deal has an instance variable of type String, 500 bytes in size, which contains the original information our backoffice application received from the frontoffice application. This information is hardly ever accessed; still, it was not possible to place it into a separate segment on another cluster because it is a literal and not a first-class object for our database. We solved this by changing the object structure and came up with a Deal header and Deal body class, the latter containing the 500-byte string.
- Each extent is usually accessed as a whole. When we create them, we reserve a single contiguous area of memory space by presizing them.

EXPERIENCES AND SUMMARY

While the physical database design's purpose is to come up with an initial efficient data model, our estimate is that the last 10 to 30 percent of the performance possibilities can only be reached with analysis and tuning. This number, of course, depends on experience from previous projects and the amount of time spent on physical database design. We found that it is better to iterate between both phases in the same way because object-oriented software development is iterative in nature. In this case, performance monitoring can pinpoint areas to work on next and it is also useful to have numbers about the performance gains handy for each iteration. In addition, one also needs to compare the actual performance with the user-stated performance requirements in order to determine when the optimization phase should be finished. Furthermore, performance monitoring also helps to detect gradual degradation in performance over time, which is an important issue in maintenance. We found that while the value of performance evaluation is without doubt, its true value can only be reached in conjunction with a tool such as the Transaction Monitor or the ObjectStore Performance Expert which produces various metrics quickly and inexpensively.

REFERENCES

[Alm95] J. Almarode: *Getting Real: Queries in Smalltalk.* The Smalltalk Report, 4 (8), 1995.

[Byu95] S. L. Byung: *OODB Design with EER.* Journal of Object-Oriented Programming, 8 (3), 1995.

[Cas+95] T. Case, B. Henderson-Sellers, G. C. Low: *Extending the MOSES Object-Oriented Analysis and Design Methodology to Include Database Applications.* Journal of Object-Oriented Programming, 8 (9), 1995.

[DS96] K. Dick, A. Swett: *Product Review: ObjectStore C++.* Object Magazine, 5 (6), 1996.

[Goo95] N. Goodman: *An Object-Oriented DBMS War Story: Developing a Genome Mapping Database in C++.* Modern Database Systems: The Object Model, Interoperability, and Beyond, Addison-Wesley, 1995.

[GF95] A. Gorur, J. Fotino: *The Physical Design of Object Databases.* Object Magazine, 5 (4), 1995.

[Jac92] I. Jacobson: *Object-Oriented Software Engineering—A Use Case Driven Approach,* Addison-Wesley, 1992.

A Subjective View of Objectivity/DB

Richard Wellner, Object Environments
Amy Ikenn, Landis & Staefa

ABSTRACT

When undertaking a large software project, one gains a lot of useful knowledge from experience and hindsight. The following essays are based on the knowledge gained from developing a database to be used at the core of a large building controls system. The goal of this project was to create a database system that developers could use to build applications around. The first two sections describe how and why we accomplished some extensions to the Objectivity database to meet our own needs. The third section describes what we have learned about databases and how that information can be applied when doing a product evaluation.

FEDERATION-WIDE INDEXING IN OBJECTIVITY

Background

In our experience constructing a system to control the HVAC, security, and energy usage for a building or campus network of buildings, we were presented with opposing goals: performance and transparency of the network. Performance in this case implied that for data retrieval we needed to have fast access times, as loosely defined by users' perceptions. The user base consists almost exclusively of what can euphemistically be called the computer naive. This implies that they don't much care about the technical reason for a given system pause, they just want it to go away. Unfortunately, while a moderate database search time may come in around the usability threshold for the user, when combined with firmware and campus control network activity, the pauses would be too long. Transparency of the network implied that we needed to be able to present a view where physical boundaries (data on separate machines, possibly in separate buildings) were not apparent. In order to keep performance from indicating when data are going across the network instead of being obtained locally, we needed to be able to keep data on the machine that is most likely to access them.

The area where these goals started to conflict was in searching the entire database for a particular object type containing a "key." Because Objectivity/DB's index scheme is only applied at the container level, we would need to have all of the data that we wanted to search through in one container to use them. Without federation-wide indexing, it was necessary to scan every object of the search class to search for a specific object using a key. In a system that stores at least thousands of objects, that is unacceptable from a performance standpoint. The best solution to meeting both of our goals would be an index that spans the federation. Since Objectivity does not provide one, we were challenged to create our own.[1]

Approaches Considered

Clustering by Object Type

To take advantage of Objectivity/DB's container scoped indexing, we looked at the possibility of clustering our containers by class that would need to be searched. This might be acceptable in some systems, especially if there is no network involved. Our network configuration is such that for any type of data, there is a subset of objects of that type that are relevant to each machine. In order to gracefully accommodate our network requirements, we must place these objects into a database on the machine that they are pertinent to. Since a container cannot span databases, and a database is contained in one file on one machine, all objects of one type cannot be in one container.

The next logical step would be to have a container for each data type on each machine. This does not run into the problems discussed above, but does cause fatal locking problems and makes it harder to optimize for performance in other areas. Locking problems would occur because Objectivity/DB uses container level locking. Any time that you lock one object of a type, you would lock all of the other objects of that type on that machine. This choice of locking mechanism prevents course-grained storage of objects and therefore eliminates this scenario for all but single-user systems.

---

[1]We understand that as of this writing Objectivity is testing federation-wide indexing capabilities for a future release.

Mechanisms for Federation-wide Indexing

In the course of investigating our options we considered three options: a linked list, an AVL tree, and skip lists. We considered a linked list only briefly for reasons of retrieval speed. While insertion and removal are quite fast once the activity location is found, the average object search would require a hit on half the objects in the list. For this reason we quickly abandoned linked lists in favor of AVL trees. The existence of AVL code in another project first led us to believe that we could reuse some code for our own purposes. The AVL trees would provide consistent speed that was needed on searches in order to have reasonable response in all circumstances and we were willing to overlook the fact that the insertion times were approximately 50 percent slower. Unfortunately, it quickly became apparent that the code in question would require much rework due to its platform being an embedded system with an ancient compiler (i.e., pre cfront 2). Finally, we considered skip lists. Based on their potential for comparable overall performance (described below) and the fact that we felt they would be more simple to implement than the AVL trees, that was the route that we chose.

Skip List Algorithm

We chose to implement skip lists as described by William Pugh in the June 1990 issue of *Communications of the ACM* to create a federation-wide index. A skip list is a data structure that uses a pseudo-random number generator for balancing, rather than algorithms that rigorously enforce the balance. This is an advantage at insert and delete time over algorithmic balancing and the search times are less than 10 percent inferior on average as compared to more commonly used data structures like AVL trees.

The key for us was that the 10 percent degradation in search speed would be acceptable and we were quite enthused about the simplicity of the implementation. Generally, the algorithms rely on randomization of the data in order to produce a structure that is highly unlikely to yield poor retrieval times.

In Figure 18–1 we show what a small skip list might look like. Each element in the structure consists of the data being indexed and a set of forward pointers indicating how a search will traverse the list. It is the set of forward pointers that the randomness of the structure is built around. A key type is used that allows for the

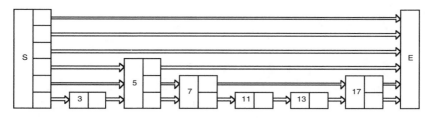

Figure 18–1   Example skip list.

list to compare the keys for sorting. Any data type that the "less than" operator can be applied to may be used as the key.

Each node has between 1 and MAX_HEIGHT forward pointers. The number of pointers in the node is referred to as the height of the node. The height of the list refers to the height of the tallest node in that list. The height of a node is randomly assigned when the node is added, creating a list of nodes where there is no pattern (or more precisely only the pattern generated by the pseudo-random number generator) to the heights. An "empty" list consists of a start node and an end node; both of these will be the maximum allowable height as defined by either a compile time constant or DBA intervention at construction time. In our example the first node is shown with a height of six while the next highest node is three.

Searching

The search begins at the start node and follows the top most pointer to another node. Then we determine if the key value of that node is greater than the key value being searched for. If the node's key value is too high, then we back up a node, drop down a level to the pointer below, follow that pointer to another node and test again. If the node's key value is lower than the search value, we move forward in the list to the next node at that level and execute the same test. Eventually, we will work down to where the desired node is or should be and can return. We know that we have found the location where a node should be if we are at the bottom level, and our comparison value is too high. In that case, there is no match in the list. In Figure 18–2 we show what a search for the value 13 would look like. If we reach the end node at the bottom level without finding a value that is higher than our search value, we know that there is no match in the list. The end node can be constructed a few different ways. For example, it could be considered to have a value higher than any in the list. It could be a special value, an implementation of NIL perhaps. The special value could also be a completely different implementation from the node class as long as comparisons can be done against it.

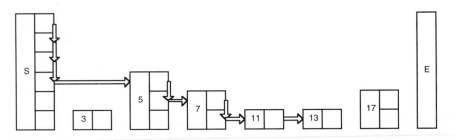

Figure 18–2   Example search for the value 13.

Insertion and Deletion

In order to add or remove items from the list, the search is enhanced to keep a vector of nodes traversed en route to the activity site, which, in the case of our example, would be S,S,S,5,7,11. This allows us to have available all the nodes that require modification for their node lists when we are ready to do the insertion. For insertion we can generate our new node of random height and insert it in the traversal path at any height without any overhead associated with going back through the list. For deletion we can remove the node, and reassign those who pointed to it in the same fashion.

Making It Generic

The original version that Pugh made available allowed for genericity only through the use of typedefs to a keyType and valueType. Since our implementation language was C++, we were able to expand on this through the use of templates. We created our list using two parameters, the key type and value type (modeled after Pugh's implementation). Objectivity/DB does allow the use of templates, although we found it difficult to discern how they are supported from the documentation. The downside of using templates here is that the types for the template must be known at ODL processing time (the DDL preprocessor implements this). While it is easy to understand why they have chosen this route, it does prevent application developers from instantiating new types without assistance from DBAs.

Benefits

Performance of database-wide searches is greatly increased because we don't need to open every object in order to consider it against the search criteria. While this statement alone has intuitive implications, its value is enhanced even further due to the page driven "dumb server" model of Objectivity/DB (as opposed to the "smart server" of Poet, for example). In the Objectivity/DB model we would expect to pass back a large amount of unwanted data in the form of objects that by coincidence reside on the same pages as the ones we are searching through. However, we might receive all these nodes in one request and not have to leave our machine to get more information. In an object server, each of these steps would require a database hit to get the object. Specifically, in our Figure 18–2 example, notice the single step hits across 5-7-11-13.

Costs

In order to make a cost determination for the implementation of skip lists, we looked at a variety of factors, including coding, training, maintenance, and execution times. Due to the speed of the algorithm, our cost considerations focused almost exclusively on the lifecycle costs for the skip list code. Our development costs from start to finish were about three weeks for one developer, with much of that time being spent in anomalies with Objectivity/DB's ODL processor and documentation as they pertain to templated persistent classes. In light of our requirement that federation-wide searching be available, this was a small cost compared with the other options outlined above.

ENCAPSULATION OF A DATABASE PRODUCT TO ACHIEVE VENDOR AND APPLICATION INDEPENDENCE

Two of the major goals of our database design were application and vendor independence. We define application independence as those issues that would expedite the production of our system by decoupling the application from the database. Vendor independence is based on a company policy of not single sourcing solutions.

Application Independence

The size of this project and the number of developers made it desirable to hide the specific details of the database from those developers who were working on applications. This meant that fewer people had to learn Objectivity/DB, allowing us to have lower training costs and fewer people tied up with a learning curve. We also had problems with the "multiple solution syndrome" that seems to affect many corporations. When a large project (ours is about 320,000 lines not including firmware and application code) is being undertaken, it can be difficult to sift through the available code and identify pieces that will be of profit for the programmer to reuse in his or her own application. We felt it prudent early in the project to identify areas that would be best to standardize immediately and allow application developers to use this library base as the foundation for their code. Fortunately, this seems to have worked well in the case of the object database layer, and we have been able to speed development time by offering services, either transparently or through extension of our own layer, that would have been extremely difficult had the layer not been put in place early.

It was also desired that application code should not be affected by changes in database design or implementation. This would be unlikely to happen if we allowed applications to speak directly to the database engine. If, for example, Objectivity were to come out with a new version that provided OQL support, our wish would be to have application developers use this new capability in order to gain the presumed speed increment over writing such code ourselves. With our layer in place we can easily pass through OQL to be processed and allow the native engine to do its thing. Alternatively, let's pretend Objectivity/DB was currently ODMG compliant. Even in this case the standard itself is changing, so while we would probably not have elected to put our layer in place under these circumstances; we may have put in a more application level layer in order to encapsulate the changes that are not under our direct control. Fundamentally, we made the decision that application code cannot call the database directly. Since the application developers need to be aware of the most basic database concepts and use the database, we elected to build an ODMG-style layer for the database that was available to the applications.

Vendor Independence

In an ideal world, once you have chosen a database, there is no need to ever consider another, but in the real world there are many possible factors. We are attempting to maintain vendor independence for two primary reasons: the evolution of products (ours and theirs) and a general approach to using vendors.

From a technical standpoint, the ongoing evolution of database products is a good reason to maintain vendor independence. As the products evolve, we may see that some of the features that are key to us are being implemented by vendors other than the one that we have chosen. We may also find, as our product evolves, that we need features that we didn't predict early on. If these features are available in other products but not the one we are using, we could evaluate a switch.

From a business standpoint, this can be compared to the hardware dilemma of second-sourcing. Landis & Staefa hace a policy not to design hardware that incorporates products that are only made by one source. This can result in severe back orders (not generally a software problem), or a company that goes out of business or abandons a package and leaves you without a product (or support for a product).

Ideally, all of the database products available would conform to the ODMG standard, allowing a database swap with minimal effort. Since this is not the case, we needed to encapsulate the database we were using in order to keep all of the code specific to that database localized for easy replacement without affecting the overall system.

Why Choose ODMG as the Model?

The ODMG committee is composed of GemStone Systems, IBEX Computing, O2 Technology, Object Design, Objectivity, Poet Software, and Versant Object Technology. These companies represent the majority of the database offerings that are currently available—that itself speaks for the forces behind the standard. The driving issue behind this motley crew of vendors is that the IS community demands standards for the stuff it uses as a daily part of its data generation rituals. The glue that binds the group together would appear not to be love of the user base, but pure financial motivation. After all, who would intentionally bet the corporate life on a database that is only marginally better, but completely nonstandard?

This in mind, we felt that the best course of action would be to jump on the bandwagon and create our layer using a model that lots of smart people had already worked to refine and make generic enough to be implementable on a variety of platforms and products. For clarity's sake, it seems necessary to state explicitly at this time that we supported only the ODMG collection mechanisms and smart pointer implementation, rather than ODL and other more cumbersome features.

One positive side effect is that, because the applications developers have been using the ODMG-like encapsulation, they will be better prepared to deal with a database that conforms to that standard in the future. This implies realization of soft dollar cost recuperation when the company later does other projects in an ODMG-compliant database, or needs to train a new employee in our system and can begin with one of the database training classes that is being performed in an ODMG-compliant database.

Costs

Any time a project is required to abstract a problem a step further than the application itself requires, there is cost involved. In our case, there were some fairly substantial costs due to our decision to encapsulate the d_Ref and d_Collection classes without any smart pointer or database container experience. As most with experience in the subject will attest, the issues involved with completely generic programming are not at the forefront of most programmers' experience. We learned through the metaphorical blood, sweat, and tears of building our layer that the experienced programmers had a point. The problems in our instance centered around efficiency versus genericity. We had, for example, several instances where we could greatly speed up queries and provide better type safety if we knew more about the objects we were handling. However, getting such information was difficult (most of our work was before the everyday availability of RTTI) and adding the information we needed automatically targeted us for either slower response or more resource requirements. In the skip list code, we realized that we could provide substantially faster queries with additional knowledge of the type of the object being referenced. We provided this capability by storing the type number of the object along with the key information in our list. This cost us a small amount of space and required us to rewrite Objectivity/DB's type identification system because it would work only when at least one of the objects being evaluated was in memory. While we certainly expect this work and resource decision to be of tremendous value to the end user in the form of queries that are on the order of 1000x faster for our large databases, it did have a price.

In addition, we incurred some costs due to rogue programmers using the Objectivity/DB iteration and containers in place of the ones we supplied. While this is a management issue more than anything else, it is worthwhile to recognize that the event occurred. Our encapsulation section makes the point that we wished to protect our developer clients from having to reinvent the wheel every time they wished to touch the database. Iterating through a container doesn't exactly strike us as being the kind of activity that will doom a project to failure, but we do feel that by coercing these developers to adhere to the rather minimal project standards that we did choose to put in place, we prevented a run down a slippery slope into the pits of developer anarchy. We now have tools that find such behavior automatically; however, it did cost us some rewrite time to repair the code that had been incorrectly coded.

Performance

Could Objectivity/DB implement this same kind of functionality with greater performance? Almost certainly. We cannot claim with basis that we are better implementers than the engineers in Mountain View. However, given the restrictions that we were working under, our implementations do exploit well the idiosyncrasies of the selected algorithms and work within the guidelines of Objectivity/DB's implementation of locking and distribution.

Creating a Model to Fit the Underlying Database Architecture

The Transaction Class

One portion of our support layer that bears close examination is the transaction class that we modeled after the ODMG and used to extend Objectivity/DB's support structure to include multithreaded application support. When we began the project, Objectivity/DB did not support multithreaded applications in any way. This was not a particularly good solution for several of our applications, especially our loader module that works to accomplish bulk data transfers between the firmware located throughout the buildings and our PC-based system. When the power comes back after a failure, the loader will be asked to receive updates from potentially dozens of firmware modules. Due to the nature of the work being done, it is an ideal scenario for exploiting the multithreaded capabilities in Windows/NT. The obvious failure of our vendor to support this operation was of great concern to us. Our transaction class allowed us to encapsulate the Objectivity/DB functionality that could not be allowed to collide and provide the needed services to our applications. With the current release, our vendor has chosen to begin supporting this mechanism and our layer is allowing us to easily migrate to the more robust capabilities intrinsic to the tool from a multithreaded standpoint including the eventual migration to concurrent transactions.

New and Delete

In order to maintain efficiency of access to objects in a database, vendors typically provide some kind of clustering mechanism to allow the application to provide hints concerning where to place an object. Our application has very definite access patterns that we wanted to exploit to provide quick access to needed objects. The problem was in educating our application developers as to how they could control the placement of the objects, yet not encumber themselves with database knowledge that wasn't relevant to their tasks. We chose to do this by creating static member functions for each of our classes. By using this idiom we were able to encapsulate the clustering of the objects into a fairly maintainable format, yet still provide a highly intuitive developer interface into the classes.

Invocation of the delete operators was easy, since the information required to properly clean up an object was contained in the object itself and in its implementation by way of the static make function. It would be fair to say that of the portions of Objectivity/DB that we encapsulated, the static make function and transaction encapsulation are among the most valuable.

CHOOSING A DATABASE—ACADEMIC COMPARISON
VERSUS REAL-LIFE USAGE

Evaluating a Product

In all choices, cost and performance are a factor. Beyond that, there are many things that make one object database different from another. To sort out which product is right for a project requires an evaluation of some sort. When we began ours, we were under a lot of time pressure and were not able to be as thorough as we would have liked. As it turned out, we were able to learn a lot from our evaluation process, and from the surprises that we encountered once we had chosen a vendor. This information will be incorporated the next time we have to evaluate a product and is used here to provide a guideline for others.

Before beginning any type of evaluation, it is necessary to understand what the requirements of the project are. It is also important to understand which of your goals are long-term and may not need immediate support. In our case, some of the evaluation criteria that were used to see if a vendor even qualified for our evaluation turned out to be the ones that we didn't use until near the end of the project (ODBC support, for example). By that time, other vendors had added those features. If we had been able to see that these were long-term goals, we might have been able to talk to the prospective vendors and add those that were planning these features to our list of those that qualified for evaluation.

Product literature provides a starting point to verify that a product has all of the basic features that you require, but it is important to verify the strength of the claims through a full hands-on appraisal in coordination with the academic one. It is our goal in this section to provide some ideas on how to approach the problem.

Academic Evaluation

We began our database selection process by choosing specific criteria that all potential candidates had to meet. We made the initial list of vendors by looking for an object database that:

1. Was working toward the ODMG-93 standard (in 1994 no vendor was compliant)
2. Was compatible with the Microsoft Visual C++ product and its tools (though, whenever possible, starting with this requirement is discouraged)
3. Had a distribution scheme that would allow transparent access to data on different computers
4. Had or was planning ODBC support
5. Was available in several countries

Once we had chosen several vendors that met our basic criteria, we evaluated them against the following items:

- *Architecture of the System:* Consideration should be given to the architecture that the product has adopted. There are at least several architectures in use, including the predominant themes of page-driven versus object-driven servers. The appropriate server for a project will be largely based on the application you are building. If the installation will have slow connections to the database and expect small result sets from standard queries, then a smart/object server will lead to improved response times as accompanying information will not traverse the data path with the objects you are actually interested in. Conversely, if fast connections are available and large result sets likely, then perhaps a page-driven scheme will result in better desktop speed for your application.

- *Method of Persistence:* How an object becomes persistent affects how you design the database. In an ODMG-compliant database all objects that are derived from a persistent class are persistent. This means that a lot of useful functions are provided via the inheritance (and the ODL processor) so the developer doesn't have to write as many basic routines. In a product like Object-Store, objects are made persistent on an individual basis. This allows for more flexibility in what type of data are stored, but means that more basic functions need to be explicitly written rather than automatically generated. Possibly more importantly this means that ObjectStore does not comply with the ODMG standard for gaining persistence, thus eliminating the possibility of easy transition were their market share to force them into early retirement.

- *Transactions:* Transactions should be minimally looked at based on the "ACID" rules: Atomicity, Consistency, Isolation, and Durability. Atomicity implies completeness of a transaction, either everything is written (commit) or nothing is written (abort). Consistency refers to the fact that the database will change from one consistent state to another. Isolation indicates that two transactions cannot affect each other (except via lock waiting). Durability implies that the results of a transaction are persistent.

- *Operating System Independence:* We needed a system that could be ported to other operating systems with little effort, and where we could share data heterogenously between two operating systems.

- *Operating System Support:* All the databases we evaluated were heterogeneous; however, it was obvious to us that some were more dedicated to supporting their "native" platform. We ultimately put this issue aside and selected Objectivity/DB for our Windows product, for reasons that had more to do with business issues than technical merit.

- *Network Independence:* We hoped to be able to isolate our product from network type, but Objectivity/DB does not work unless some form of TCP/IP is running.

- *Query Capability:* One of the issues that we gave a lot of weight was the ability to do an ODBC or SQL query on a database. This was important for us because a lot of our end customers would like to be able to pull our data into other applications.

- *Available Utilities:* By this point, most vendors should have some type of graphical browser for the database. In many cases it would also be helpful to be able to edit the database through a graphic utility. While Objectivity/DB does have a graphical browser, editing the database is still a command line utility.

- *Locking Granularity:* Granularity of locks will be very important in some systems. In the case of Objectivity/DB, all locking occurs at the container level. This implies that you should consider how you will incorporate your data into the physical layout of the system to see if you will be able to live with the locking granularity. This becomes important when considering Objectivity/DB because indexes can only be applied at the container level. If you have data that you want to use an index on, you must be prepared to lock all of the data that index is applied to at once. This is fine in applications where there is a low requirement for concurrency within a container, but if the application does not meet this criterion, an architecture like Poet or VERSANT that allows object locking might be a better choice.

- *Locking Transaction Types:* In Objectivity/DB, there are Read, Update, and MROW (Multiple Reader, One Writer) transactions. MROW transactions grant some flexibility to the locking scheme. Objects opened using a Read transaction may not be updated, but objects opened during an Update transaction are not locked for update until necessary. Objectivity/DB leaves a hole, and you can upgrade the lock on an MROW transaction, but it is not recommended by objectivity. This scheme implies that you must have an idea of the eventual intent of a transaction before you can open it, or you should always use an Update transaction (which will affect performance).

- *Locking Concurrency Control:* Each database system uses either an optimistic or pessimistic approach to concurrency control (the ODMG standard uses pessimistic as the default). The optimistic approach assumes that simultaneous access of the same object is rare and therefore only checks for conflicts during the commit. The pessimistic model checks for lock conflicts when the object is loaded. Conflicts can be set up to cause a "wait state" until the lock is freed.

- *Template Support:* To our knowledge, template support has not yet become universal. Certainly in the case of Objectivity/DB, it has not yet acquired a history of good support. If the project requires the genericity that templates provide then it would be best to identify where those needs lie early in the evaluation and verify the vendors' ability to provide for those specific requirements.

- *Triggers/Network Event Support:* While most vendors claim to be working with a CORBA vendor these days, pervasive support will probably be a long time coming. Some object databases already support event notification across the network and have for years, while others provide none. This is another point that would be valuable to model in the prototype as it is somewhat difficult to get a handle on the user perception of this feature without actually using it. More importantly, this is a key issue that should be considered when determining requirements.

- *Handling of Collections:* Objectivity/DB doesn't provide any real collection functionality beyond the creation of iterators, so we ended up creating our own class of iterators to follow the ODMG model. The section on database encapsulation deals more fully with the issues involved with providing for the lack of this feature. We wish to add that if you have an option of creating a layer to make up for a lack of capabilities in the database or creating one that extends the database, it will be easier to spend time on application specific programming if the vendor already provides you a solid base to build from.

- *Clustering/Storage Hierarchy:* Figuring out how you want your data clustered is generally a very complicated task. How locks and other functionality (e.g., indexes) are applied to the storage hierarchy will have a big impact in your design. It is important to understand the implications of the storage hierarchy as each vendor has implemented it. Objectivity/DB uses containers as both the granularity of their locks and the scope of their indexes. This needs to be taken into account when clustering data.

- *Multithreading:* Not all vendors support multithreading. This can be a major issue, as we mention above. It is also, as are most multithreading issues, quite difficult to do well. If multithreading cannot completely be eliminated from the design we recommend strongly that the purchase of the database use this criterion in a highly weighted fashion.

- *Schema Evolution:* For a project where there may be multiple releases being produced, schema evolution can be very important. In our situation it is not acceptable for a user to lose data when upgrading to a new version of our product. If we have made any schema changes since the old version, we will need to make use of schema evolution. Not all vendors provide this, and among those that do the performance varies substantially. Consideration as to the frequency of utilization of this feature should be the primary focus when evaluating this feature.

- *Handling of Security:* Some vendors supply a security scheme independent from that of the file system. If a project is going to require more security than the standard file system, this can be a feature to look for.

- *Availability of Data Dictionary:* If a project is going to require that any external utilities be written, the availability of the data dictionary may help simplify those tasks.

Hands-on Evaluation

The hands-on evaluation must consist of a fairly complex real-world example, preferably part of the system that you are planning to build. To make this a relevant prototype, you need to consider how applications will be calling the database interface. If the application code will be calling the database directly, a prototype needs to demonstrate how the functions that the database provides would be used. In our case, since we wanted to provide an ODMG-93 compliant interface, we knew that we would be placing a wrapper around those calls, and we should have tried to prototype parts of that wrapper. Because we did not do a complete prototype in our evaluation, we ran into issues that surprised us and made it difficult to put the wrapper in place.

In many cases, the evaluation process is not given enough time or funding to do a thorough prototype with each system. Minimally, an "evaluation" training class should be considered to find out some of the quirks and "gotchas" of a product. In our case we were able to use one such class to eliminate one possible vendor whose architecture would have been very difficult to use with our data. Our evaluation would have definitely been more complete if we could have attended similar classes for all of the vendors that we considered. While it can be difficult to convince manager types to fork over the cash for extensive training in a multitude of products, it can be advantageous to attend even two or three and ask plenty of questions about not only the database being used, but how it compares to others. Remember the class will be populated by folks that have done evaluations already and an instructor that presumably knows the industry.

Understanding Your Own Requirements

We began the process of evaluating databases before our own project requirements were complete, and long before our design was really well thought out. When possible, it would be helpful to have a first iteration of a design on paper before looking at the database vendors. That would allow a good example for the hands-on evaluation, as well as an understanding of what some of the issues will be.

Having a design implies a lot more than the class hierarchy. All of the object databases should handle basic object-oriented characteristics (inheritance, polymorphism, etc.). More important in the evaluation process are things like:

- How many users will want to access a single object at a time (locking)?
- Will an application need to be notified about changes to data (triggers)?
- Will I need collection functionality?
- Will I need indexes, and across what scope of data?
- Will I make use of schema evolution?
- Is file level security sufficient?
- Will access to the data dictionary give me any benefits when writing tools for this database?
- Is multithreading an issue?

There is a good chance that no one vendor will be able to provide all of the features that will be best for a given project. Priorities must be given to each feature, and those should be based on the level of difficulty in duplicating the features if they are not there. Since you are buying a tool to help you create another product, you should pick the one that allows you to do the least work to support it.

EXPERIENCES AND SUMMARY

Based on our experience, it is clear that Objectivity/DB did not cover all of the features that we ended up requiring. Since it is a rare case when there is a vendor who meets all of a projects requirements, this is not surprising. However, we did end up extending Objectivity/DB in some fairly major areas, as described in earlier. It would have been preferable to have started with a database that provided enough features that the extensions we spent our effort on were more application related. What we did get out of the project was a system that meets our immediate needs and a lot of experience to take with us for next time.

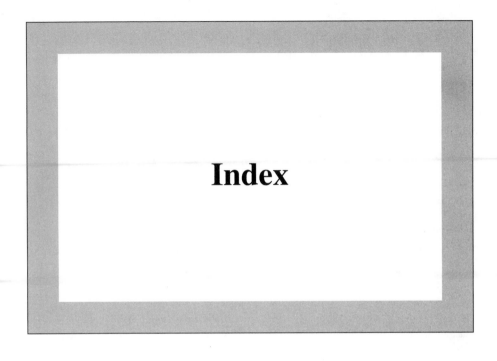

Index